Narrative Subversion in
Medieval Literature

ALSO BY E. L. RISDEN AND
FROM MCFARLAND

Tolkien's Intellectual Landscape (2015)

Shakespeare and the Problem Play: Complex Forms, Crossed Genres and Moral Quandaries (2012)

Heroes, Gods and the Role of Epiphany in English Epic Poetry (2008)

EDITED BY E. L. RISDEN

Sir Gawain *and the Classical Tradition: Essays on the Ancient Antecedents* (2006)

Narrative Subversion in Medieval Literature

E. L. Risden

McFarland & Company, Inc., Publishers
Jefferson, North Carolina

LIBRARY OF CONGRESS CATALOGUING-IN-PUBLICATION DATA

Names: Risden, Edward L., 1957– author.
Title: Narrative subversion in medieval literature / E.L. Risden.
Description: Jefferson, North Carolina : McFarland & Company, Inc., Publishers, 2016. | Includes bibliographical references and index.
Identifiers: LCCN 2016027982 | ISBN 9780786477784 (softcover : acid free paper) ∞
Subjects: LCSH: Literature, Medieval—History and criticism. | Narration (Rhetoric).
Classification: LCC PN671 .R57 2016 | DDC 809/.02—dc23
LC record available at https://lccn.loc.gov/2016027982

BRITISH LIBRARY CATALOGUING DATA ARE AVAILABLE

ISBN (print) 978-0-7864-7778-4
ISBN (ebook) 978-1-4766-2586-7

© 2016 E.L. Risden. All rights reserved

No part of this book may be reproduced or transmitted in any form or by any means, electronic or mechanical, including photocopying or recording, or by any information storage and retrieval system, without permission in writing from the publisher.

Front cover image © 2016 PhotoDisc

Printed in the United States of America

*McFarland & Company, Inc., Publishers
Box 611, Jefferson, North Carolina 28640
www.mcfarlandpub.com*

Contents

Acknowledgments	vi
Preface—Narrative Subversion: A Step Toward a Simple Theory of Narrative	1
1—Lost in the Not-So-Funhouse: Subversive Threads in the Medieval Narrative Labyrinth	15
2—Narrative Subversion and the Solutionless Problem	38
3—An Aesthetics of Subversion in *Beowulf*ian Narrative	49
4—Subverting Authority: Dryht, Allegory and Old English Exile Poems	62
5—Subverting Ends: Death and the Dead—or Not—in *Völuspá* and Some Sagas	76
6—Grail Quest Romances: Subverting a Happy Ending	88
7—Plowing, Bowing, Burning, Journeying: Penance and Subverting Penance in Medieval Literature	103
8—Malory's *Morte*: Subverting the World's Greatest Knight	113
9—*Troilus and Cressida* and Subverting Genre	124
Postscript—*Meta-*, *Para-*, *Neo-*, *Socio-*phrase: Gavin Douglas's Sub-versive *Eneados*	157
Chapter Notes	167
Bibliography	177
Index	183

Acknowledgments

Thanks to Mary Paplham for considerable help preparing the manuscript and to Stefan Hall for expert help with the bibliography for Chapter 5. Parts of the manuscript have appeared in the following publications: earlier versions of Chapters 1, 7, and 8 appeared in *Enarratio* (the journal of the Medieval Association of the Midwest, in numbers 13, 16, and 7, respectively); part of Chapter 3 appeared in the appendix to *Beowulf: A Translation for Students* (Witan Publishing); part of Chapter 9 is from *Shakespeare and the Problem Play* © 2012 E.L. Risden by permission of McFarland.

Preface—Narrative Subversion
A Step Toward a Simple Theory of Narrative

In recent years narratology has gained impetus as a growing subset of literary studies. It has attracted considerable interest among scholars and critics of various theoretical persuasions, has even generated a journal of its own, and has in the breadth of its applications acquired nearly a life of its own. Scholars and "creative" writers have much more yet to say about it, perhaps the main tool in the literary box. For this study I'd like to suggest that for a narrative to *work*—that is, for it to generate pleasure and continuing interest—it must use at least one and probably many *subversions*. Subversion is perhaps the single most powerful and persistent narrative technique.

A narrative subversion creates a sub-version, or at least one potential sub-version, of a story. A teller or writer can create any number of subversions within a narrative, allowing for infinitely many potential story lines. Once an implied trajectory of narrative undergoes a subversion, the new direction of the narrative becomes, at least for a time, the main version, even a super-version—the narrative overtop other potential sub-versions—until the author or narrator decides to subvert the course of the narrative again, once again turning it under, moving it from what it had suggested to something new, something veiled, *chiaroscuro*, until a "main" narrative emerges as full and followable. In *Tristram Shandy* Laurence Sterne famously used humorous subversions, a long series of them, never getting to any sort of full story of the eponymous character. The act of subversion had become the purpose, the result, the impetus of a narrative going nowhere but more deeply into the cavern of itself with no drive or intention to come out again: the voice, the thoughts, the humor, not the plot, became the goal.

The kind of subversion and where it leads tells us something, then, about the story. A mystery may sub-vert as a detective follows various leads and suspects, clues, red herrings, illuminations, until a solution appears—or it may subvert its genre entirely by reaching no solution. It may find the solution and nullify it, as in Umberto Eco's *The Name of the Rose*, with the unearthing of a manuscript only to have it then destroyed by fire.[1] A Romance may come to a seemingly happy ending, such as in *Sir Orfeo*, only to have one of the principals die soon after: a sad ending to follow a happy ending to remind to us to feel wary even of happy endings. A sub-version is subversive: it implies something beyond a single, dependable, stable narrative. A subversion *folds* a narrative, and any one fold implies the potential for many potential folds: it creates what Deleuze calls Baroque narrative: stories "enclosed one in the other," with a "variation of the relation of narrator-and-narration" (61)—and one may add of reader as well. The reader folds old and unfolds new interpretations as he or she goes, just as the author folded away possible directions and unfolded a new one at each plot turn. Children often expect a storyteller to repeat the story exactly the same way each time. Sometimes adults enjoy the same process: we may repeatedly re-read favorite books or watch again favorite movies with no expectation that they will turn or end differently. But we all move on to new stories with new enfoldings and new unfoldings: adding *subversions* that add new *versions*, versions that point to or diverge from super-versions. Even notions of time undergo various kinds of folding, unfolding, and enfolding in the Middle Ages.[2]

Subversion works a little but not exactly like Mieke Bal's "text interference," but it implies not only a disjunction between actor and narrator (52); it is a little like Friedrich Schlegel's idea of irony as "permanent parabasis" as discussed by J. Hillis Miller, a "continuous suspension, all along the narrative line, of any single identifiable rational meaning" (37), but it applies not only to meaning and implies the lack of a single, unified narrative line; it is a little like Susanna Onega and Josè Landa's ideas of narrative intrusiveness and defamiliarization (2), but it does not foreground technique—it simply uses technique to foreground an unexpected movement in plot. It is simpler than those ideas and more fundamental. In "The Law of Genre" Jacques Derrida begins satirically with the blank and bland assertion, "Genres are not to be mixed.... I will not mix genres" (202), but he turns instead to the real law of genre as "precisely a principle of contamination, a law of impurity, a parasitical economy" (206). He calls such inclusive textual miscegenation a phenomenon of "edge, borderlines, boundary" that can "not arise without a fold" and the process of "enfoldment" (216). *Fold* is a good term for narrative subversion, as it implies something necessary, homey, even comfortable to the reader: any interesting plot must have it, just as a blanket, to keep one warm, must have folds. The strategy may have comfort even when the narrative event brings suspense or terror.

Plots may take many forms: linear, cyclical, episodic, chronological-historical-sagic, recapitulative or spiral, eschatological, monomythic, biographical/autobiographical (with personal reflection rather than narrative as focus), allegorical, framed, epistolary—just to name a few. Narrative implies *pattern*, so we are necessarily considering a structuralist poetics, in this case not imposing a structure on a text, but looking at structures in texts, searching for an Elementary Particle, the basic building-block element or move that a story structure must have to work. I'm not considering a list of instructions for the assembly of a safe and sturdy office chair, though the idea may apply to a grocery list. Subverting assembly instructions may lead to the failure of the chair and so perhaps even an injury. The grocery list may plot my way through the store where I shop: peaches, bell peppers, red lettuce, organic milk, eggs, yogurt, butter, fish, bagels, frozen peas, coffee ice cream, black beans, olive oil, mustard, peanut butter, paper towels, light bulbs, bath soap, and some lactose-free milk for the cat—then to the cashier. But any number of problems, preferences, or events may subvert my course. But subversions interrupt my quick shopping trip. The peaches are old and soft, so I will get pears in the next aisle instead. I hadn't realized I was thinking of yellow bell peppers, and they have only green and red—the red look better. Only one gallon left of organic skim: they must be selling lots of it now. They're out of my favorite yogurt: try a new brand, get the one my wife doesn't like, or skip it for the next trip? The only fish that looks good is the salmon—we had that yesterday, but I'll get it anyway since it was (and is) fresh and very good. Blueberry bagels: maybe too sweet.... The guy at the meat counter stops me to talk about Sunday's football game. We're both optimistic. Better skip the ice cream, as I would do well to lose a couple pounds—though as I look at it, it seems to me almost irresistible. I resist on principle. They're out of Extra Crunchy peanut butter—a different brand will do. Oops: forgot to put cereal on the list, but better get it anyway: bran flakes and fruit-and-grain medley. Only large packages of bath soap—no problem, since we have room to store the extra. Cashier asks if I found everything I needed—did I forget anything (batteries, bread, broccoli—no, have all that at home). A series of events with brief and largely inconsequential subversions: typical shopping adventure.... The end came out almost as I expected. Not a very interesting plot, but still a series of events—largely predictable: predictability can be all right sometimes.

In some genres we want typical narrative movement with minimal surprises: the rows of romances and police procedurals in the bookstore illustrate that desire. In some ways medieval literature works much as they do: the plots use multiple (and predictable) levels of allegory to get to pretty consistent problems and themes: life is transitory, so we must not cling; sin is deadly, so we must pray and try to avoid it; evil is active in the world, so we must stay wary; adventures take us across harrowing boundaries, so we must show courage, composure, and piety.

In *The Nature of Narrative* Scholes, Phelan, and Kellogg explore many aspects of story from tradition and oral heritage to meaning, character, plot, and point of view. They define plot most basically as "the articulation of the skeleton of narrative" (12); *skeleton* makes a good image because of the accompanying images of articulated bones and attached layers of muscle, organs, blood, and skin—we layer narratives and can break them down to their sinews and corpuscles as we wish. There really is no "linear simplicity of primitive epic" (209), but all good plots do depend on "dynamic, sequential" events (207),

Narrative Subversion

which we may call either *fabula* (the chronological sequence) or *sjuzhet* (the order in which the author relates events) (288)—either must still have it subversions, and sjuzhet provides the means to subvert fabula, turning simple chronology into complex story.

Allegory is a kind of sub-version, and the story to which an allegory points is its super-version: the idea to which the story calls our attention. The medieval play *Everyman* makes plain its antecedent, as early as its title: it tells the story of every human being, that we must march our course through life on our way to death—we have no recourse outside that narrative as living humans, only as God's grace draws us to Him beyond this life. Perhaps the greatest of all allegories comes in Spenser's *The Faerie Queene*: at least it may be the most Baroque, the most complicated and enfolded. Though it is of course a Renaissance rather than medieval text, Spenser intentionally harkened to medieval models, especially in his use of allegory, to antique his work and so give it a weightiness of something from the authoritative past rather than the unstable present. He was doing medievalism based on models of medieval Romance and aiming to create thereby a Renaissance epic of the search for virtue. Spenser's "real" story, at least when he began, is that allegorical meaning, the search for virtue that a young person must follow to become a good adult. The sub-version, because it is individual and not collective, is the story we find in the text, one example of that search that may serve as a guide, but that more probably comprises simply an example—fortunately a complex example with many foldings and unfoldings to maintain tension, interest, and the urge to join and interpret the narrative. The Redcrosse Knight doesn't yet fully embody Holiness: he represents it and strives to achieve it, succeeding at last sufficiently to defeat the dragon and free Una's parents—he must still, then, return to the court of the Faerie Queene to serve her for his promised time. And as the whole of *The Faerie Queene* grew, the literal story gained momentum—who knows if, had Spenser completed it, it may have overtaken the allegory at last.

The narrative of Book 1 does not go smoothly: even in its relative allegorical simplicity it has many subversions, many enfoldings. As Redcrosse and Una ride along, a sudden downpour drives them into a nearby wood, where they meet their first adventure together, the den of Foule Errour, where with the lady's encouragement the knight must defeat a distorted representation of papistry. A series of similar subversions occurs: the wiles of Archimago that drive apart the lady and her knight; Una's encounters with the lion and Sansloy and her rescue by Satyrane; Redcrosse's diversion from his course by Duessa; Redcrosse's imprisonment by Lucifera and his release by Arthur, through Una's help; their confrontation with Despair, Redcrosse's convalescence, and the climbing of the Mount of Heavenly Contemplation; finally the achievement of the quest by the freeing of Una's parents through Redcrosse's three-day battle with the dragon (which includes two more symbolic deaths and resurrections). Redcrosse suffers many falls, and accomplishes, with help, many returns; the subversions prepare him for the main event, the dragon-fight. Even on the achievement of his quest, the story subverts again, as his married life with Una must wait until he has returned to the Fairie Queene's court and served his commitment as her knight. The traditional allegorical levels, moral, social-historical, and anagogical, remain palpable throughout, as perhaps super-versions to the subversion of this literal story that embodies them.

While Book 1 has its many referents and plot turns, the subsequent books begin to sway more and more from the continuous allegory of Book 1, interweaving more and more plots and characters. In Book 2 Archimago tries to subvert both knights' quests by lying to Guyon that Redcrosse has raped a young woman. In the second Canto Guyon's horse oddly disappears, and the chivalric knight must proceed on foot. In Canto 6 Guyon leaves behind his companion, the Palmer. In Canto 7 Mammon literally takes Guyon underground and nearly kills him, but in Canto 8 the Palmer and Prince Arthur save him. Inn Canto 12 Guyon passes the temptations of the mermaids and the Bower of Bliss and arrests Acrasia, who represents not only Guyon's opposite, intemperance, but also the idea of moral and rational failure in general. Each episode serves as a sub-version of the movement of the Book as a whole. By Book 3 the nominal hero Britomart fades in and out of the story as the plot threads more varied and complicated subversions. The Book begins with Redcrosse and

Narrative Subversion

Guyon but soon introduces Britomart, and it includes even a defense of women as knights (Canto 2). Canto 3 includes flash forwards and flashbacks as well as the beginning of Britomart's quest to find Artegall. Canto 5 strays into the stories or Marinell and Florimell and Timias and Belphoebe, and Britomart doesn't return as the center of the narrative until Canto 9. The conclusion of Canto 12 has variant versions, the first of 1590 and the final: in the earlier version Britomart succeeds not only in releasing Amoret from Busirane, but also returning her to Scudamore, but in the later version when the two women depart the magician's lair, Scudamore has gone. The knights of the first books appear now and then but not consistently as *The Fairie Queene* moves into its final books, the narrative becoming more Baroque and even pre–Rococo in its twists and complexities, the ultimate in Renaissance narrative subversion antiqued in language and plot to resemble medieval Romance-epic.

While Book 1 sticks to the story of Redcrosse and Una, Book 2, nominally about Sir Guyon, the Knight of Temperance, swerves already into even more diverse digressions. Jonathan Goldberg notes that "Spenser's text offers continuous disequilibrium, frequent disruptions in narration, and characters who exist to disappear" (xi). In *Endlesse Work* (a particularly apt title for the interpretation of Spenser) Goldberg aims "at describing the narrative principles that induce frustration, that deny closure, but that also produce the disturbed and disturbing narrative procedures of Spenser's text" (vii), a "fractured—and fracturing—text" (xiv). He finds "deliberate cancellation of an ending" (1)—of many endings, as well as the necessary ending to a book barely past half finished, Spenser's untimely death. Goldberg observes that the 1596 edition with its revised ending of Book III "refuses us even the partial and displaced satisfaction of the first ending and draws all the characters, and the reader too, into a situation of general frustration that appears to be necessary to generate further narration.... For one thing, the 'new' ending makes demands upon the reader to reevaluate notions of narrative satisfaction to defer or even to deny the pleasures of conclusion" (2).

Goldberg continues, "the final installment of *The Faerie Queene* does not include the pleasures of resolution that characterize the opening books," yet "those failed pleasures *are* the pleasures of the text" (3): the lack of resolution comes from repeated subversions that draw the story further and further from simple allegory into complex Romance. For example, in Book 3 "Britomart has been repeatedly replaced by surrogates," and "the disappearance of the heroine, her failure to be present at the center of the book, her insubstantial victory, her repeated wounds" characterize the book (4)—yet she remains, as the "Knight of Britain," as successful and heroic as any of the knights, in fact, probably the most successful of all of them. Later "the erosions of narration highlighted by the new ending of book III have become the central features of narration in book IV" (5): the subversions of one book's narrative become the substance of the narrative in subsequent threads of the evolving story, more at this point a spiral narrative than anything resembling linearity or circularity. Yet the goals remain the same: the location and acquisition of virtues. We find repeated examples of "[a]bsorption into other voices, subservience to other texts: this is the problem encountered in Spenserian narration" (31)—both its problem and its accomplishment, its method and its end—because finding the virtue is much easier than acquiring and keeping it.

Frank Kermode in *The Genesis of Secrecy* argues that we read/interpret to find closure, yet we often find that search frustrated: narratives may even come from frustration of such desire—we tell stories to make up for our lack of closure, to deal with it psychologically. The act of interpretation creates a new story, Kermode suggests, a point also made by Reader Response critics. In *The Sense of an Ending* Kermode, considering St. John's Apocalypse, suggests that the cultural context has become a personal context: the imminent end has become immanent (25)—the sense of narrative ending, personal or cultural, becomes ambivalent, humanized and individual, destabilizing the relationship of story to its own end. We tend to subvert endings as well as events on the way to that ending, suggesting our doubts about the truth (or our understanding of the truth) of either. Among the "codes" that Roland Barthes explores in *S/Z*, the "hermeneutic code" creates delays and interruptions, enigmas and suspensions, that maintain suspense in the narrative—that is another way of phrasing how

Narrative Subversion

we employ narrative subversion. Ronald Arthur Horton, in *The Unity of the Faerie Queene*, shows interpretive means of connecting the narrative around its subversions: "The poem has been generally regarded as ... combining unsuccessfully two or more conflicting structures, and remaining an awkward composite of at least two distinct stages of revision" (5), and other critics have found "a psychological drama of maturing consciousness" rather than any sort of "unified narrative" (7), but a balance occurs in the how Spenser's individual books distinguish their ideas of virtue: "The odd-numbered books reveal the splendor of their virtues by theophany; the even-numbered by apotheosis" (178). "Avatars of character and situation associate the later cantos of Books I and VI and strengthen the impression of Books I through VI as a rounded unit," with a general "movement from private to public virtue" (179), Horton adds; the movement of the component books generally shows a receding importance of allegory, which lends to the subversion/complication of simple plot in lieu of the virtue of individual complex ones.

Jonathan Culler, reading Barthes in *Structuralist Poetics*, argues that the reader "must be able to imagine 'counter-texts,' possible aberrations of the text, whatever would be scandalous in narration" (223–24)—of course the subversion may but need not produce scandal; it need only turn the plot in an interesting and, ideally, unexpected direction. The logic of story and the logic of discourse meet, clash, and meld. Culler notes R.N. Veselovsky's "rudimentary structural analysis" that a plot comprises a series or collection of motifs (207)—not such a bad idea for a rudimentary one. He refers also to Vladimir Propp's deeper view into the structure of plots, where he found thirty-one "functions ... whose presence or absence in particular tales may serve as the basis of a classification of plots" (208), and to Claude Bremond's additions to Propp that "every function should open a set of alternative consequences" (208) and that all plots turn on "moments of choice or bifurcation" (211). That idea is essentially what I mean by subversion, though I find the matter more complicated than bifurcation: we get rather continual branching, something not quite fractal, but repeatedly subversive. Levi-Strauss's *mythemes* and Dorfman's *narremes* particularize Veselovsky's idea and generalize Propp's: recognizable pieces that one adds to construct story. Susan Stanford Friedman added the idea that plot has a vertical as well as horizontal movement, spatializing notions of plot further. Every text has intratextual and intertextual tensions, instabilities, and plots may rise and fall (subverted from a "traditional" narrative or super-verted back to it).

Perhaps the most subversive of medieval texts, Chaucer's *Canterbury Tales* also includes an array of subversions and sub-versions. The book applies the method of frame narrative, much as did its most closely related predecessors, Boccaccio's *Decameron* and Gower's *Confessio Amantis*, but unlike them and like *The Faerie Queene* it suffered a subversion in the author's death well before he had got near to completing his plan for the work. C. David Benson finds that "unlike the Italian work [*The Decameron*], whose careful symmetry demands that each of the ten characters tell a tale on an assigned topic on each of the ten days, the English narrative [*The Canterbury Tales*] permits violent and unexpected changes in direction" (128)—I would add that such changes quickly become expected. Barry Windeatt notes Chaucer's general trouble with endings, the "challenge and strain" he met "in inventing an appropriate close to the structures he had created in his poems" (214)—an ending can still create a subversion (or even multiple sub-versions by challenging the notion of an ending). Helen Cooper observes stories linked to highlight related themes and to establish multiple perspectives in a "cobweb effect" of joining one narrative point to many others (69). Any given printing of *The Canterbury Tales* represents a sub-version, since we don't know the "correct" order of the tales—other than certain groupings, we don't know what order Chaucer would have chosen. What George Lyman Kittredge identified as the "Marriage Group" comprises a sub-version into a sub-version of the whole, dedicated to concerns over sovereignty and what makes for a happy and successful marriage: subversions come from the desire for control rather than mutuality. In *The Canterbury Tales* not only doubts about the order of the tales but also the "absence of end-links" for some of the stories "makes for a sense of fragmentariness ... as we jerk from one story to another" (Ellis 5), even if one does the believe the book complete in the form in which we have it.[3]

Narrative Subversion

Harry Bailly begins the sequence by asking the Knight to tell a tale, and he apparently intended to go in order of social class, asking the Monk to speak next. But the Miller interrupts and insists on telling his tale immediately. That subversion changes the possible ordering of the tales immeasurably, since the Host then has the impossible task of getting back on any kind of track beyond what the natural interaction of the characters will produce—the Reeve insists on following the Miller's tale to tell one that insults a miller. As Derek Pearsall put it, "From the beginning, almost, nature rules" (38). Even the "General Prologue" provides a kind of sub-version of the whole, collecting the characters largely by social-class order and giving hints in the portraits of the kinds of tales they will likely tell. Chaucer subverts many of the characters even in their portraits: the Knight and the Parson, the bookend storytellers, are positive characters with little if anything negative said of them. The Monk lives more like the overly free son of a nobleman, devoting his time to *venerye* (hunting, but probably with a hint of sexual exploits as well). The Prioress, like the Monk, would probably have preferred court life, but she lives rather well instead in her convent, daintily enjoying good food, pets, and probably fantasies of romance (her brooch reads *Amor*—not *caritas*—*vincit omnia*). Even the Franklin, who tells such a lovely tale, is "Epicurus owene sone." The Reeve is perhaps an embezzler and murderer, and the Wife of Bath a serial killer.

The tales, too, have their fascinating subversions (often self-subversions). The Wife of Bath, who argues for the sovereignty of the woman in relationships, entirely forgets about the young woman raped by the knight, who ends up happy at last. The Knight's tale requires a subversion, the sudden, accidental death of Arcite, to allow the happy ending for Palamon and the fulfillment of Emelye's *secondary* prayer: since she may not remain a virgin devotee of Diana, she would at least have the man who loves her more. The Miller's tale leaves the poor carpenter broken and bruised—he suffers not for being a bad man, but for having chosen his bride frivolously, a young beautiful girl for a thoroughly average if rather well-off *gnof*. The Franklin's tale ends not with the clear statement of a moral, but with a question for its audience: which character was the most generous?

Preface

The question can lead to many interpretations, and thus many subversions, of the tale.

The Prioress's tale, for the modern audience not just a pious saint's life but also a horrifying instance of anti-semitism, offers for her time a saint's brief life, terrible death, and miraculous lingering, the story of the lovely child she would never have—potentially alienating its audience with a tale that undermines itself as holy narrative. The Pardoner does similarly: he tells a neat, tightly constructed allegorical story of the deadliness of greed, and then immediately exhibits his own greed by asking his audience to buy what he has already identified as false relics. The host interrupts Chaucer's "Tale of Sir Thopas" and so subverts it, and, similarly, the Franklin interrupts the Squire's tale—no one has ever wished the first any longer, and the second has enough youthful asides and redirections that the Squire may not have been able to finish it anyway. The Cook's tale, probably headed for a fabliaux even less tasteful than the Reeve's, simply trails off into silence, and the Clerk subverts his own tale by undercutting its apparent moral in his Envoy.

The many fascinating and often subtle subversions move the tales beyond simple allegory, morality tales, or fabliaux into territory that invites speculation, interpretation, laughter, and prayer—subversions that together *bricolate* the elaborate if unfinished monument of the *Tales*. Subversion makes the perfect tool for humor, as in the Merchant's tale, or to create adventures serially, as in the Man of Law's Romance of Custance, or to mix a moral/horror story as in the Physician's tale, or to collect short tales (each a sub-version of the other) to elaborate a theme, as in the Monk's collection of mini-tragedies.

The simple but flexible theoretical notion of narrative subversion gives us a means to see where those and other authors adjust or redirect plots and to what effect. It works in the same fashion as Victor Raskin's script-based semantic theory of humor, suggesting the overlay of plots with trajectories varied in this case not just to create laughter and comedy, but any sort of result for which the author aims, from suspense or surprise to satisfaction and resolution. It applies regardless of the type of narrative, with anything from traditional oral narrative (which re-creates itself with each performance) to fan fiction to hypertexts. The subsequent chapters of this study will consider narrative subversions in various medieval texts, examining what they do and how they do it, as well as what effects result (and what *affects*). This simple, essential, nearly ubiquitous plotting tool determines the success of any narrative beyond the simplest; it creates play, horror, or anything in between, and it invites, even demands, interpretive engagement. Subversions create multiple perspectives on characters, alternative endings, even resistance to endings—as *Piers Plowman* shows, endings may not even be possible before this life comes to its close.

The following chapters are truly essays: attempts. They aim to show how various medieval texts subvert narratives, what they subvert when they do so, and what happens as a result of the subversions. They take a serious tone when the texts require them to do so and a playful one when the texts allow it. Criticism, Derrida suggested, is necessarily playful: it uses the interpretable play of inexactness and variation; it also may, I hope, as literary texts do, aim to please. I have chosen the subjects for the chapters as they struck me, not with any notion of covering the subject fully: that would take many lifetimes. Here I aim to show that good plots do more than *twist*: they *subvert*.

1

Lost in the Not-So-Funhouse
Subversive Threads in the Medieval Narrative Labyrinth

In a famous Zen koan a student asks a master, "What is happiness?" The master replies, "Grandfather dies, father dies, son dies." Surprised, the student asks how such a scenario can comprise happiness, when everyone is dying. The master responds that the best we can ever hope is that events follow a natural, orderly pattern: if father dies before grandfather or son before father, that's tragedy; death, inevitable, looms, so we can only hope that it takes us in proper order and at an appropriate time.

With the succinctness of a proper koan, that story suggests that we intuit a natural sense of fabular or narrative order and that we depend on that order to understand our world and tolerate the vagaries of life. Koans, products of Buddhist meditative practice and often of ascetic discipline, act as a lens that enlarges an exactness of perception. But for most Western stories, at least for scholars and students, we prefer elaboration and entanglement, an intricate, even knotty weave that we can *un*tangle, learning and enjoying as we go. Separating the threads opens the complexities of character and experience; examining warp and weft confirms or unravels our assumptions or expectations of our place in the universe or, as science fiction fans may say, multiverse. Postmodern stories, fully unbraided, even suffering the cool incisions of the surgical critical eye, seldom *confirm*; instead, they scald, freeze-dry, deconstruct, lay bare, or complicate every hint or suggestion to unsettle our perspective and bejangle our lethargies.

Not always so: past ages have often lived if not breathed stories that recapitulate limited but publicly accepted notions of the right and true—in our time we tend to think of thematic directness or didacticism as "facile." Historically narratives have taken forms fitting their time, just as they've exploited themes central to their time. But stories share at least one trait: they have always subverted. By ripped-bodice passion, face-slapping satire, or even occasionally hoist with their own petar, and despite Wimsattian and Beardsleyan argument, stories trope their way to some Horatian purpose. Even if that purpose lies in our contemporary obsessively psychoanalytic unraveling of every conceivable pleasure or pain, turning viewers into little Saurons who seek and exploit the weaknesses of others characters, our fictions still have *reasons*: they thrash, trash, confess, upbraid, warn, eviscerate, repair, titillate, lampoon, but largely by unstitching rather than suturing. We prefer the broken, the unhealably subverted.

Consider please the notion of a story that doesn't *subvert*, that never turns under or aside, that encourages no alternative versions or interpretations. Even allegory subverts: it turns the literal story beneath the implied one, the meaning taking greater importance because it forms the interpretive goal of the former. Consider rather a story that presses ahead like a perpetual motion machine through perfect episodes to a perfect end.

Let's try one. A child is born to middle-class but hard working, god-fearing, kind and appreciative parents; she shows many talents, excelling in school, sports, and church choir, but without becoming arrogant or dweebish; she earns PhDs in physics and philosophy, wins teaching awards at an Ivy League university, publishes a Pulitzer Prize–winning book, invents a means to pulverize deadly asteroids, marries a handsome, witty, and successful physician, has two lovely children whom she accepts as they are and nurtures to their own successes; she retires to become a philanthropist and ambassador to a politically and economically troubled country, advises them as they set themselves in order, retires again to write what P.G. Wodehouse would call "improving books" for children and to tend her aging friends; at age 102 she passes away in her sleep leaving a large, loving family, thousands of friends and admirers, and a body of work that rivals Shakespeare's for its beauty and understanding of the human condition. Ta-dah. What would we do with a story like that? Would we like or admire it? Would we read it at all?

Our sample story, lacking subversion, also lacks any real human interest. Many of us may want to live such a story, but it hardly draws us *as a story*. Even koans imply a subversive element: they rip the rug from underneath, throw open the trap door that holds us up, or pull the curtains from the window, exposing how in our common darkness we cling to absurdities that themselves subvert our ability to see clearly.

Subversion makes a story. Unlacing and re-lacing the threads make the reading experience meaningful and bring the pleasure. As Walt Whitman wrote, don't we just feel so good when we understand a difficult poem? Many of us love mystery novels; mysteries hinge on subversions, each twist and clue subverting the narrative from one likely solution toward another. Each possible solution dictates a sub-version of the real story until the clues build to the true conclusion. Subversion creates the pleasure of finding a solution. In a joke, sub-version creates the incongruity that allows for the punch line. Solving a mystery creates a pleasure akin to discovering a punch line: it ties the incongruities into well-knitted and acceptable whole, raising the actual solution to public view while letting the sub-versions sink away—except perhaps in a really good mystery, where their implications remain to haunt the apparently true solution.

This chapter will address a few more theoretical issues before we consider the tapestry of medieval narrative in the chapters to come—we will subvert that discussion to thread a theoretical web to catch what falls through the trap door of subversion into the fantastic world of interpretation. Contemporary narratology allows consideration of any art forms that recount or express a series of events. Aristotle separated narrated events, as in epic, from an imitation of events, as in drama; he used the term $\mu\nu\theta o\varsigma$ to mean simply the arrangement of incidents. If we extend our notion of *story*—narratologists often prefer the term *fabula* to express "a series of logically and chronologically related events" (Bal 5) or a "semiotic representation of a series of events meaningfully connected in temporal and causal ways" (Onega and Landa 3)—to any art form that creates, recounts, displays, or implies a series of steps that comprise an integrated and recognizable sequence, we may reasonably bring drama, film, music, and even visual art into consideration. But even such a simple notion of "sequence of events" can create problems, not only with postmodern theory and fiction, but more especially with medieval narrative. Allegory, more complex than a single layer of obvious reference, uses events not for their own sake, but because of personal or historical other events they parallel; tropological reading subsumes events beneath moral import; anagogical reading begins as intertextuality, but subsumes literary text beneath apocalyptic or eschatological *interpretation* of biblical text. Medieval "fictions" aren't merely metafictions; they're fables recalling attention to a fixed notion of an interpreted higher reality. Medieval *realistic* stories self-deconstruct before the ultimate *aporia*, the chasm of *transitory life*. They leave us fragments, sub-narratives, *narremes*, free of the need to make Gérard Genette's distinction between homodiegetic and heterodiegetic narrative: the narrator always participates in the narrative, as do the audience, because of the inescapably didactic and eternally present nature of both their moral purpose and their referent texts. Allegory is, in a sense, always with us, not just in medievalia. J. Hillis Miller calls the constant displacement from one sign to the next *allegory*: "Narrative is the allegorizing along a temporal line of this perpetual displacement from immediacy.... [It] expresses the impossibility of expressing unequivocally, and so dominating, what is meant by writing" (292). But the medieval world, while finding the process of storymaking allegorical, believed in the *supernarrative* that it created, in its real presence, and only the narrative thread need be present to invoke the whole in its wholeness and permanence. Medieval notions of allegory extended necessarily to all genres that allowed representation of incidents. For us now *narrative* has the same or even greater expansiveness.

    Shortly ahead we'll look at *Beowulf*, *The Quest of the Holy Grail*, the Wife of Bath's prologue and tale, *Sir Gawain and the Green Knight*, and *Piers Plowman* as examples, but before we do, I'd like to consider first some ideas on the usefulness and prevalence of subversion. It appears not just in literature, but in a composer's use of symphonic themes, in movie sequences, even in paintings that suggest motion: in anything that uses some sort of narrative *bytes*, incident motifs that begin the building process for constructible or deconstructable stories. We'll also pause to examine briefly some significantly subverted narratives from different literary periods; while I've chosen medieval narratives for this book, one could chose them from any time and anywhere. The kinds of subversions we find in narratives and the themes to which they lead us reflect and express the peculiarities of perception or the reigning thematic concerns of the ages from which they come. But subversion as a strategy appears ubiquitously. Subversions turn simple figures into tapestries, still shots into scenes, arias plus recitatives into operas, *pas de deux* into ballets—though sometimes phantasmagoric ones. Subversions may lead us to harrowing places in our intellectual and spiritual lives. Medieval narrative subversions tend to focus, not surprisingly, on the instability of human virtue and the necessity for vigilance in the face of both physical and spiritual corruption. Like John Barth's character Ambrose in his kaleidoscopic short story "Lost in the Funhouse," readers, as well as characters in the stories, may well find the fantastic world of the subverted narrative a "place of fear and confusion" (69). Medieval tales, while not Barthian metafiction, may exhibit in their layering an awareness of fiction as fiction and yet the sense that the fiction points to the solidest realities we can comprehend. Medieval narratives may express no less than more moderns ones a desire to challenge simple single interpretations and to vary perceptions.

Visual artists of the twentieth century exploited narrative subversions no less than have storytellers. For readers interested in art history, I suspect Pablo Picasso's *Guernica* (1937) will come quickly to mind. It displays the most violent of subversions, the fragmentation of explosion: what Frank Russell calls "the world's first experiment in full-scale saturation bombing" (2), the annihilation of the "sacred town" of the Basques by the Spanish Republic in 1937. The bombing subverted an agreement whereby the Republic had granted Basque independence. Combining elements of cubism, surrealism, and primitivism, the painting depicts fragmentation with a shocking immediacy: a subversion of ideas of order, center, anatomy, the living creature, humanity. While the painting visually narrates the story of the bombing, it tears narrative to fragments, barely readable narremes of light, body parts, and screams.

Marcel Duchamp's *Nude Descending a Staircase, No. 2* (1912) implies and interrupts narrative, stretching a single figure into what would normally be a series of panels rather than one painting. Also joining cubism and surrealism, this painting takes the expectation of a realistic, perhaps even titillating figure caught in mid-step as it descends toward the viewer and turns it instead into an artistic metaphor of a Riemann sum. Yet the increments of movement displayed syntagmatically are undercut by their own metallic quality: the painting displays mechanical, not organic movement—one can almost hear it clank. The artist subverts the idea of the nude moving, perhaps toward a sexual encounter, by focusing not on the nude as such, but on the idea of movement as comprising discrete yet sequential steps. The idea of increment replaces the narrative of descent and subverts speculation about what may follow the descent. The metallic qualities of the visual add implied sound and even smell to the elongation of the image.

We need not attribute this kind of process to modern art alone. Jan van Eyck's *Chancellor Rolin Madonna* (ca. 1435) subverts two narratives simultaneously by means of its diachronic halves: the Chancellor, the sort of person our time would describe as a "control freak," anachronistically meets the Madonna, who has been miraculously translated to Nicolas Rolin's palace. However, the painting also subverts its own interpretation: urged to see the Chancellor as worthy of audience with the Virgin Mary, and of a benediction from the blond Christ-child himself, we see him also as sufficiently arrogant to want himself placed in her presence. He doesn't even look astonished to see her; rather, he gazes intently, almost critically—Anita Albus calls it "a touch of impatience" (15)—as a diminished angel begins to crown her. "Rolin wanted to present an immaculate image of his own sanctity to an ungrateful world" (24), Albus explains: his presence subverts any likely Madonna narrative, and his visage undermines the self-created narrative he wished the painter to display.

In another example famous for its narrative collage, *Landscape with the Fall of Icarus* (ca. 1558) by Pieter Breughel the Elder subverts the story of Icarus' death by showing everyone else going about his business and paying the event no notice—W. H. Auden's famous poem "Musee des Beaux Arts" elaborates the emotional impact of this or any such a scene. Those persons in the vicinity of the event don't allow this unbelievable—in fact mythic—occurrence to subvert their purposes—a casual glance might not even turn up the Icarus figure. A seminal mythic figure thus becomes a relatively insignificant subversion of the mutually human experience of death, which the plowman, shepherd, fisherman, and sailors would rather simply ignore: they don't want their day subverted by iconic images of imminent demise and *memento mori*.

Piero della Francesca's marvelous *The Flagellation of Christ* (ca. 1469) foregrounds characters who go about their own casual conversation without apparently even noticing the horrible act that is taking place just behind them. Perhaps for them such torture occurs every day, and so this event is only a sub-version of the natural course of life and no subversion of their day's activities—even Jesus' common pose reinforces that reading. Yet backgrounded though we find it, we know the event's greater significance. In Christian terms the Crucifixion to follow will cast all other events into the realm of mere types of sub-versions of cosmological crises. Curiously, too, the man who attends the flagellation appears as either Pilate or the Byzantine emperor or both; the men in the foreground may have associations with the defense of Byzantium or with Urbino politics, or the middle figure may represent an angel moderating conflict between East and West (Deimling 270, 273)—such identifications lead down different narrative and interpretive paths. And of course the whole painting creates time disjunction or anachronism: the characters in front don't belong with those in back, the costumes don't match the time, and the lighting in the right and left sides of the scene suggest different times of day. The whole painting has invited varying interpretations or sub-readings, and its composition, with powerful irony, subverts the idea of a scene of cosmic significance to one of quotidian obliviousness.

The Gosforth Cross (ca. 930–50) in Cumbria, England, subverts the story of Ragnarök that the sculptor has told in its four panels with its allegorical reference to the sacrifice of Christ and the Christian Apocalypse. The events of the first three panels show the release and attack of the monsters upon the gods. The boxed figure near the bottom of the fourth panel serves narratively as Oðin, but a Christian audience recognizes it better as the crucified Christ, subverting the "pagan" in favor of the Christian reading, undercutting by refiguring all that the previous panels have shown of a story from Norse myth. Once the "reader" has observed the transformation of Oðin to Christ, he or she may read the panels "backward," symbolically: Viðar, son of Oðin, at the top of the east panel metaphorizes Christ, and the other *götterdämmerung* images suggest those of the parallel story of the Christian Apocalypse, which for a christianizing audience interpretively replaces its pagan cousin. The panels on the cross actually enumerate steps in a narrative, unlike the other art works I have considered here. Yet they, too, while nominally static, open doorways to semiotic series—that is, their "meaning" makes sense only as they constitute pauses in narratives. They aren't still lives (no more than are the Gosforth panels), what the French call *nature mort*, since in them the world is active, not dead. Visual art may in series depict static moments in a narrative, but even an individual scene may imply movement and continuity, a fore-story and after-story, of which the individual instant creates a sub-version.

One could choose hundreds of such artworks from any number of times and places. Musical examples abound as well. For instance, Franz Liszt's *A Faust Symphony* (1857) first establishes a character motif—if a dubious one of intense but conflicting emotions—for Faust. It climbs cautiously, plunges, then climbs again, then finally creeps upward, hinting at Faust's desires and fears—and also his relative powerlessness. The second creates a gentler, more loving, but tepid theme for Gretchen; it suggests support for but ultimately a different direction for Faust—one he doesn't take. The third theme embodies Mephistopheles, the center of whose theme perverts Faust's. Its quick, sawing violin strokes suggest the devil's goal to subvert or pervert Faust's course. It takes the nervous, eminently subvertable Faust theme and rushes it, almost humorously, towards an impish end. A variation and combination reasserts Faust in the third movement, but with a new musical line: something grand and victorious—clearly Goethe's Faust rather than Marlowe's—as again the pitch climbs slowly, but with greater power and resolve. Mephistopheles subverts the lives of both Faust and Gretchen, but the striving for grandeur in Faust's character emerges as the dominant musical and intellectual theme of the symphony. Thus Faust, in this (Romantic) case triumphant rather than damned, ultimately subverts the subverting devil.

More film critics than literary critics have noted the importance of subversion and subversiveness in the history of their art. The moving, visual medium provides the perfect opportunity for striking subversions that may last from an instant to a large portion of the film. In the musical, *Singin' in the Rain* (1952), Gene Kelly's "Broadway Melody" or "Gotta Dance" sequence follows a young man with a talent and desire to pursue it who finds success, rises professionally into Broadway highbrow, then falls for an exotic woman who prefers a rich gangster, leading him to self-doubt and disillusionment. When a second young man enters, renewing the "Gotta Dance" theme, the main character realizes what truly mattered to him, that he has in fact subverted himself, and he follows the "character double," his subversion, back to his roots as a performer and back to his true self. He regains the "true" narrative and thereby the adoring fans and colleagues that his misapprehensions had subverted. It is a pop-culture example, but it represents the point perfectly and shows the pervasiveness of subversion.

In the fascinating Alfred Hitchcock film *Spellbound* (1945), John Ballantine, Gregory Peck's character, having lost his memory and identity, lives for a time a life not his own. Only the devoted ministrations of his psychiatrist, Dr. Constance Peterson, played by Ingrid Bergman, lead him to confront the surrealistic dream-visions that return him to the trauma that subverted his identity and his life. Psychoanalysis returns him to his course through the sub-versions of his story that dream uncovers. The dream-images, designed by Salvador Dalí, provide sub-versions of the amnesiac's experience that help lead him and the doctor to the true but buried experiences of his past.

Narrative Subversion in Medieval Literature

The two characters together must read the symbols that unravel the web of his amnesia, extricating him from the sub-version of his life that he is currently living.

In the film *Sliding Doors* (1998), with Gwyneth Paltrow, a young woman's future depends on whether or not she catches a train home after she's been fired from her job. If she gets home in time, she finds her boyfriend in bed with another woman; if she misses the train, she doesn't. The film then follows both versions of her future, and its crux lies in the fact that we don't know which course will lead to greater happiness in the long run—sometimes the course of events that we assume will work better won't in the long run. Film criticism shows a good deal of interest in subversions of many sorts: cinematic, narrative, cultural, political. George Lucas famously used Joseph Campbell's monomyth from *The Hero with a Thousand Faces* as a sub-text for his narrative in the first three *Star Wars* films; we have in recent years seen many cinematic versions of Jane Austen's novels, each becoming a companionable sub-version to the original. A thoroughly public, deeply technological, and more visual than verbal medium, cinema provides an ideal milieu for exploring the opportunities that subversion permits.

Traditional stories, myth, folktale, religious text, also allow ample latitude for studying narrative inflections of all sorts. The assembly of the Bible presents one of the more interesting problems of narrative subversion. The canonical gospels recapitulate some elements and complement one another with respect to others—one can hardly call any one a sub-version of another, though the work as a whole has its socially subversive qualities. The problems lie not only in how we deal with narratives constructed after the fact, but also in what we term apocryphal or pseudepigraphal: there we find texts, not included in the canon but extant, that, if we take them as serious challengers to received tradition, sometimes incrementally add to or even subvert elements of Jesus' "story."

To return to my more general point above, narratives have always subverted traditional patterns or have even self-subverted, often, with the exception of some kinds of genre fiction, both at once and vigorously. While examples of narrative subversion, as we have seen, don't confine themselves to literature, literary examples abound in all historical periods. Can we begin anywhere but with that most obvious and hilarious of subverted narratives, Laurence Sterne's *Tristram Shandy*, which purports to be about the life and opinions of the title character, but which moves from digression to digression upon the digression to digression upon that digression. Sterne never did get around to concluding it: he eventually dropped the project, after nine volumes, to take up another, *A Sentimental Journey Through France and Italy*, and then he died—the ultimate subversion—before he could get back to the earlier book, if he ever intended to finish it anyway. The novel, which critic Gerald Weales suggests is largely a satire about jackasses who intend to go on being jackasses (535), finally peters out after more than 500 pages by suggesting that the whole story is about "a cock and a bull"—but at least "one of the best of its kind that I ever heard," at once subverting and promoting the author and his work. Not properly *a narrative* at all, *Tristram Shandy* comprises an enormous series of brief proto-narratives, each subverting the next, some occasionally rewound amidst the madly stitched tapestry where subversion rules.

Toni Morrison's *Song of Solomon* takes its protagonist, Macon "Milkman" Dead, out of his realistic world in search of a hidden treasure and more importantly the myth behind a haunting verse that purports to explain something of his family history. His story ends with that character taking a leap of faith off a cliff and into the chasm of myth. Stream-of-consciousness novels such as Virginia Woolf's *Mrs. Dalloway* background narrative to internal dialogue: the minimal story serves mostly to allow the mind to stray into the widest available range of imagination and experience and to explore where they meet and mix indistinguishably. In a sense, the narrative subverts the free play of meandering consciousness. The point of view moves mostly between Clarissa Dalloway and Septimus Warren Smith, a shell-shocked war hero; his sub-version of her perceptions casts a pall of madness and suffering on everyone's experience—horror lies just an unlikely and horrible turn of history away. Marlowe's *Doctor Faustus* and Goethe's *Faust* create a subversive pair: Marlowe's Mephistophilis subverts Faustus' quest for knowledge and some worthy pursuit, sub-

Narrative Subversion in Medieval Literature

verts his soul all the way to hell. Goethe subverts Marlowe's moral message with a Romantic philosophical notion that Faust's striving for something of value saves him not just from the devil, but also from himself, because striving for something worth accomplishing represents the highest of human endeavors. Coleridge's *Rime of the Ancient Mariner* despite its relative brevity involves two plot subversions: the guest on his way to the wedding, held up by the storytelling Mariner, and the Mariner's subversion of his own life to penitential storytelling for his having needlessly killed the albatross. Among the most-traveled of narrative subversions, Shakespeare's *Hamlet* famously suspends the progress of the ostensible plot—Hamlet's vengeance upon Claudius—with an insoluble philosophical problem: according to Germanic law, Hamlet must avenge his father; according to Christian law, he may not. All that happens between the appearance of the ghost and Claudius death in the final scene comprises subversion, in this case, Hamlet's waiting for the situation to take a course where he may act, which doesn't occur until Claudius and Laertes engage their plot to kill him. *King Lear* begins with a different kind of subversion: against the law of Divine Right—and its corollary Divine Demand. Lear, chosen we may assume by God to rule, abdicates, divides his kingdom, and exiles the one daughter who loves him, subverting the natural order, breaking the Great Chain of Being, and allowing chaos entry into what had been a peaceable nation. And *Lear* of course has its narrative sub-version: the Gloucester subplot parallels and comments on the main plot of the King and his daughters. Readers will immediately recall of any number of favorite narrative subversions: literature teems with them, and any piece worth reading will probably subvert itself repeatedly.

Our medieval narrative examples exhibit a range of what produces and results from subversion. A funhouse of sorts, as in Barth's image, a labyrinth of tightly woven passages, medieval narrative transports us into a frightful world where monsters and Death with his sickle emerge out of dark corners, where spirits and demiurges and Otherworlds of all sorts lurk a mis-step away. *Beowulf*, which will ahead receive a chapter of its own, moves from the heroes successes to the subversion that results in his death: even Beowulf can't survive

1—Lost in the Not-So-Funhouse

the dragon battle. Such a simple plot may seem otherwise to defy subversion: fight with the monster, fight with the monster's mother, fight with the dragon. But from its beginning and interspersed amidst the course of its major plot elements, the poem engages in a number of commentary digressions that, while they don't advance plot, reflect on what we need to know about the world of the story, its ideas and ideals, and they together comprise a large portion of the poem. Of course we don't know what title its author, authors, redactors, or recorders intended for it, but we may say with little fuss that the poem deals most importantly with the hero Beowulf. Given that fairly obvious assertion, we must find interesting if not problematic that the poem doesn't mention that character until nearly line 200, and he doesn't give his name until line 343. If we know the common name or purpose of the poem before we begin reading or listening to it, it *begins* with a digression of sixty-three lines: the story of Scyld Scefing, his funeral and descendants. With the kingship of Hroðgar and the arrival of Grendel at Heorot, the nominal plot begins its course, but several significant mini-narratives intervene through the rest of the poem: Beowulf's contest with Breca; the "Lay of Finn," perhaps better called the story of Hildeburh; Hroðgar's "homily" on Heremod; the fable of Þryð or Modðryþo, the evil queen; Beowulf's long recounting of his Danish adventures to his king, Hygelac; the "Lay of the Last Survivor," which appears in a damaged section of the manuscript that may or may not originally have included the origins of the dragon; the account of Hygelac's death, which doesn't forward the nominal plot because it appears as a flashback after the poem has telescoped from Beowulf's return to Geatland and the waking of the dragon; an account of the source of the Geats' feuds with the Franks and Swedes. We end up, then, with an episodic or periodic "plot," certainly a digressive one, rather than a simple, linear one.

But what do the digressions accomplish? They provide useful background that helps us understand the world in which Beowulf's story occurs, and they teach morals for the poem's original audience: how to be a good king and not a bad one; how to be a good queen and not a bad one. But those morals also demonstrate that the digressions serve as sub-versions of the main plot, as re-enforcers of the main plot's themes. If we see Beowulf's world as foregrounding important or heroic figures on their way to sovereignty, and we see Beowulf himself, like it or not, as fated to that same course, we must ask of him as we do of the others, does he make a good king? We study such points from the main plot, too: Hroðgar shows us all the traits of a good king, enumerated in the opening Scyld story, except the ability to retain the strength to defend his kingdom—though we don't know how Scyld might have done against monsters. Hygelac, a strong king, rules well, until he blunders by over-stepping his strength and harrying against too powerful a foe: that last point comes clear in a digression rather than in the main plot. Beowulf's story of his youthful exploits against Breca shows his physical capacities, but also hints at a tendency toward recklessness; most significantly, though, it helps him win his flyting against Hunferð and so gain entrance to Hroðgar's court. He will do what he must to accomplish his goals, as a hero—and sometimes a king—must. The episode shows the young hero battling monsters of the sea, a sub-version of his adult adventures. The Heremod and Modðryþo stories show the greed and vanity of bad rulers, providing sub-versive interpretations of Hygelac's and Beowulf's ends. The Hildeburh story shows that even good intentions won't often bring feuds to an easy end: that point Wiglaf clarifies at the end of the poem in his description of what lies ahead for the Geats. Unlike Hygelac, Beowulf sought peace, but attacks come (from without or within) unsought, bringing destruction with them—in this digression the Finn-battle signifies the rise of greed, pride, and enmity embodied later in the dragon. Beowulf's account of his Danish adventures serves as a sub-version of the actual adventures, adding his observations and commentary. He mentions, for instance, that Hroðgar's giving his daughter to Ingeld to end a blood feud between Danes and Heathobards won't weave the peace he hopes—the same theme as the Hildeburh/Finn story—so we know that Beowulf understands the problem. The "Last Survivor" story shows the powerful pain of loss when a people has met destruction through feuding; it may also have shown how extreme greed may turn a man into a monster: both of those points reflect Beowulf's battle with the dragon, symbolically a battle against greed and pride, one that he wins only at the cost of

1—Lost in the Not-So-Funhouse

his life. And unlike the "good king" models, Beowulf has not left an heir of his own bloodline, one sufficient to resist that old feuds that will arise anew in his absence, as the final digression explains. Each of those set pieces figures an element of the "good king" story against which we measure Beowulf's accomplishments. That's not a new idea in the discussion of the poem's themes, but we may see how the sub-versions structurally girding the digressions enforce the main plot and its well-rehearsed ideas. The problem is that such a theme leaves us, poor audience, in a frightening place: if even Beowulf, greatest and least power-hungry of monster-fighters, can't make much headway against human failings, how can we? For the Christian members of *Beowulf*'s original audience, that question must have had an easier answer than for the pagan—that notion may uncover, rather than merely a thumping good tale of our pagan forebears, the poem's real purpose.

The *Quest of the Holy Grail*, both in its French incarnation in the *Prose Lancelot* and later as the centerpiece of Malory's *Morte D'Arthur*, uses, oddly enough, a method of subversion akin to *Beowulf*'s. First, the whole quest subverts the remainder of the narrative in which it appears, a broad, sweeping tale of great but worldly knights and their adventures. Despite their frequent masses and confessions to holy hermits, the knights of those Arthurian tales pursue worldly if sometimes laudable ideals of human conduct. Notions of the Grail don't disturb activity at the court before the quest begins, nor do memories of it impede martial or amorous pursuits thereafter. Yet because it represents the pinnacle of achievement for the Christian knight, it undermines all other adventures: they serve as merely sub-versions of its ideal, and it subverts them as soon as they stray from holy concerns. We should not feel surprised that one of Galahad's first adventures removes a demon from a churchyard grave: "Christ-as-knight," Galahad subverts the subverter, turns further under what has undermined the sacrament of Christian burial. Born as a sub-version of Lancelot, Galahad becomes a super-version, subverting his father's place as World's Greatest Knight. All other knights and all other quests become, with the rise of Galahad, secondary versions, worldly alternatives to the ideal that dwarfs them in significance. Gawain, the most worldly of knights, becomes the first to follow Galahad on the quest, but he also fails first and worst. By taking up a quest not his own, he initiates the fall of Arthur's court that the Grail quest precipitates. Lancelot, too, is but a subversion of his sub-version son in seeking the Grail: greatest of earthly knights, flailing at vain hopes, he pledges repentance, to forgo his love for Guenevere, but he immediately takes up with her again upon his return to court, and end of Arthur's reign draws near—Lancelot subverts all that Galahad had done. Even the other successful Grail knights, Perceval and Bors, are merely subversions of Galahad: their spiritual success can't match his, despite their relative purity, and it doesn't. Nor can Bors, returning, do anything to subvert—turn under or even aside—the failure of Arthur's kingdom. The greatest of quests hasn't helped the court as a whole at all.

Now to a quite different problem: *Sir Gawain and the Green Knight* incorporates a major subversion that constitutes arguably the most important element of its plot, one that itself parallels and subverts the "Descent into Hell" story so popular in both Christian story and Classical epic. The knight must seek out the axe-stroke that must nominally end his life. I imagine most of Arthur's court would forgive him for not pursuing the Green Knight at all, but to fail to *attempt* would subvert his understanding of honor or *trawþe*: pledging and keeping one's word to the extent body and soul can manage. He sets out on his quest to find the Green Knight having no notion of where to find the Green Chapel and its denizen, and he has many adventures on the way to which the poet alludes with the utmost brevity—they don't matter, so at that stage they shall not subvert his purpose. But the *real* adventure of the story *does* subvert Gawain's purpose. He prays to God and Mary for help and harbor, and in a blink the Castle of Bercilak appears before him—a dubious answer to his prayer indeed, in that it provides not respite, but the sternest of tests, one far greater than the actual axe-blow of the Green Knight. The castle sequence subverts the Romance narrative from its course, from Gawain's quest for the Green Chapel. His hostess offers sexual temptations, which he resists handily; she offers a ring, which he resists easily; she offers a green sash, which he fails to resist: the argument that its magic can keep him from harm subverts his faith in himself and more importantly in God, in his belief that God will lead him aright if he remains true. By keeping the sash rather than giving it to Bercilak, and by trusting it rather than his faith, Gawain fails not the nominal quest, to reach the Green Chapel and receive the axe blow, but the actual quest, to maintain his trawþe both to his host and to God.

The whole castle episode is a "turning under" into a world of temptation and physicality. The poet vividly, tactilely describes Bercilak's hunting deer, boar, and fox and the Lady's hunting Gawain's virtue—the whole poems shimmers with vibrant detail, almost proto-Baroque in its love of decorative detail. While she can't catch him sexually, she can catch him in his weaker spot, spiritually. She subverts his honor by putting him in a position where he must fail: according the agreement he has made with Bercilak, Gawain must give him the sash; according to the agreement he has made with the Lady, he must not tell anyone of the sash. When the lord of the castle returns with his game and receives in exchange the kisses—the physical gifts—the moment passes in which Gawain may make a choice about whether to keep or remit the sash. By his silence he has strayed from the spiritual path, both accepting and keeping the sash without, as far as we know, questioning its validity or his choice. At that point in the story, failure is inevitable: it has already happened, and the Green Chapel episode functions merely as a formality to show Gawain his failure. The quest has subverted his sense of himself and any idea he may have harbored of attaining spiritual perfection in this life—perhaps it has fortunately subverted any prideful belief that he *could* achieve perfection.

Though the poet describes the scene of the Green Chapel as hideous and devilish, in a green and lush sort of way, not there does Gawain undergo his descent; he finds there instead confession and truth if not perfection and honor. He learns what he must learn. Gawain's "hell" appears instead in the castle, that place of warmth and beauty and pleasure: there temptation brings about his fall. Readers may apply the same implied pun as Chaucer makes explicit with his Monk, who enjoys "venery"—ostensibly hunting, but also things Venereal. As the *Beowulf* poet shows us that his hero is Christ-like but not Christ, Gawain too falls short of perfection; his rescue comes from mercy, the Green Knight's and God's, not because of his own abilities. He is among the harrowed rather than the harrower, and he returns to Arthur the sadder and the wiser—though as we know from the traditional end of the story, it won't do him or Arthur much good in the long run, since Camelot will fall anyway. We will see a bit more of Sir Gawain in the next chapter.

Chaucer's Wife of Bath provides an interesting—I daresay frightening—subversive model for women in the form of a murder mystery worthy of treatment by Umberto Eco without our having to stretch to locate any hidden codes. She asserts that she'll speak of the "wo that is in marriage," and she does, but largely of her husbands' woes rather than her own. Her long prologue, full of learned, ecclesiastical citations largely (and I think we may guess intentionally) misused, argues for a woman's remarrying as many times as she wishes; while it entertains and continues to win converts, especially young feminists, in the classroom, it fails as a display of logic, subverting her purpose. Her story argues ostensibly that sovereignty in marriage should reside with the woman, but it suggests that result can apply only when the man grants it so. The wife as narrator—and someone who should know better—seems to have forgotten that the enchanted woman saves not a laudable knight, but a rapist, and even she seeks no redress for the victim. The perpetrator gets not only amnesty, but all he could ever hope for: his story ends "happily ever after," though he has done nothing to deserve it. He has capitulated, I think, largely out of weariness and confusion rather than because he has learned something of value. Thus the wife subverts her own purpose: neither men nor women do better when women have sovereignty, nor has anyone a greater likelihood of justice.

As for her own marriages, "welcome the sixte whan that evere he shal," she says, and we have no reason to believe she will end at six—she mentions "octogamye" in line thirty-three of her prologue. We do well to consider what has happened to the first five. The first three, she explains, were "good" husbands: old and rich. She got from them their estates. How did they die? She wore them out in bed, pitilessly, she explains, and not because she loved them: she committed murder by sex. What of the fourth? He died young and was apparently a "bad" husband: she loved him physically, but he had no money for her to inherit. How did he die? She doesn't explain, but we do learn that his death didn't bother her overmuch: she had her eye on husband number five at his funeral. Number five she certainly loved physically, though at one point they fought brutally. Once he gave up the sovereignty, he must have declined and died, since she is now welcoming her sixth, perhaps with an eye on the poor Clerk of Oxenford. Another scenario appears as possible if not explicit. Did two strong, healthy young men pine and die because their wife took over the household, or having pressed the starch out of them, did she kill them as well? What did she learn from her pilgrimage to the Holy Land? Holiness? Or did she perhaps learn the chemical arts, better known in the Middle East than in England, of disposing of unwanted company? That possibility turns a proto-feminist into a serial killer who by sex or poison thoroughly subverts any validity to her claim or her tale.

The most interesting and persistent medieval narrative subversions of all occur in *Piers Plowman*, where they help to enliven an obvious though complicated and never static allegory almost Blakean in its permutations. Most significantly, the greatest nominal subversion, the subordination of any realistic plot to the allegory, creates not an actual subversion, but a superversion—that is, the allegory dwarfs the plot to the point that it becomes not just the *raison d'etre* but also the main *fable* of the work. The dreamer/narrator seeks Piers—Peter, Christ, the good, better, or best life—finds him, almost becomes him, learns what he has to teach, then must begin the search again: finders may not keep, but must begin the search again, though with greater knowledge and better experience than before. There the allegory turns both realistic and surrealistic. Even when we learn, the process of life and change doesn't end, because we continue to learn and struggle and forget, to relearn and re-experience what we've learned before—that's realistic. The poem subverts the idea that we can lastingly reach or achieve anything in this live. The dream reaches a higher level of reality than deluded, quotidian life, because, affixing us to materialistic ends, it allows access to perceptions of a higher reality than do passing, limited physical senses. We tend normally to think of dream as a subversion from the narrative of waking life, but in *Piers Plowman* the truth of dream surpasses our waking limitations, *superverts* our story to the greatest events of life: the crucifixion of Christ and the harrowing of hell, the moments of spiritual involvement and attainment, the turns of life that in the long run have meaning and lasting importance.

The narrative subverts also in the political sense. For instance, a king must rule by Conscience and Reason, should ideally return the society to a better agrarian age, though we know, as Langland did, though no such turn would be enough, and urbanism had begun an inevitable rise, at least until the next Apocalypse. Further, the Church, fallen under the sway of worldly wealth and power, by simony and the corruption of confession and penance, had turned itself into a labyrinth of hierarchy and privilege. While the poem seeks to dismantle neither kingship nor Church, it does suggest that neither succeeds fully even at its best, that the individual must still pursue goodness and holiness, and that ruling institutions which should guide us have instead been subverted by sin and the ill choices of our forebears.

Further (here I'm working from the C-text, though the principle applies to all three versions), the story as narrative continually subverts itself. The narrator does not tell us who or what he is, but says he set out dressed in the shroud of a shepherd, as though he were an unholy hermit, hoping to hear of wonders. Then on a May morning he tired from walking, as though from magic, and he lay down beside a stream and fell asleep and dreamed. He is neither shepherd nor hermit, and why is he so tired in the morning rather than the evening? Guilty of spiritual sloth, he finds himself in perhaps a Dantean wilderness, from which he sees a tower, a dungeon, and between them a "fair feld of folk," laborers, tradesmen, the vain, the penitent, minstrels, beggars, pilgrims, preaching Friars and a Pardoner, and priests who begged better lives from their Bishop. "Then I perceived," he says, "the power that Peter had to keep, to bind and unbind," and he comments on the presumption of Cardinals in appointing a Pope. Then follow a king and the secular powers, then a rout of rats and

1—Lost in the Not-So-Funhouse

mice, who keep their own counsel, with one arguing convincingly that they'd better not offend the cat. By now of course we've moved to thoroughgoing allegory and satire: the worldly folk who fear the powerful may not like them, but must, at least for the present, avoid offending them. Having subverted the account of the folk for allegory, we quickly subvert even the allegory for commentary on its meaning.

The remainder of the plot involves a series of subversions and sub-versions that would have impressed even Laurence Sterne. In Passus I Holy Church explains for the dreamer his vision, but with insufficient clarity or completeness for the dreamer to understand. He then enters into the ways of the world and has a vision of Lady Meed, hardly a gift, but rather the corrupting influence of money. The dreamer confesses, as do the Seven Deadly Sins, which leads the people to long for Truth, but with no clear way to seek it until Piers appears and offers to lead them if they will help him complete his plowing first. Less than entirely forgiving of their occasional sloth, Piers calls hunger to drive them, but Truth appears to pardon those who do help, offering a partial but insufficient explanation of how to live a good life. Piers disappears, and the dreamer, wondering what all that means, begins a search for Dowel. The poem then begins anew at Passus X, and the dreamer, bewildered, searches, gradually gaining partial answers. Eventually Piers, Christ, and the Good Samaritan, representing Charity, merge into one, followed by the Crucifixion and the Harrowing of Hell: spiritual sacrifice replaces the secular "meed" and logical truths of the first part. Even after this revelation, the dreamer must still pursue Truth, and the poem concludes with the Church besieged by sin and the dreamer renewing his search for the true Christian life. Note that each subsequent stage of the narrative subverts the previous: while they all episodically represent the pursuit of truth, no stage exhibits sufficiency. The first "half" of the poem, up to Passus X, represents a sub-version of the second half, which gets the dreamer to the apocalyptic vision he needs to see, but the conclusion subverts that finding, because it isn't enough: one must not only know and believe, but also live on and continue to pursue goodness—God grants redemption, but requires our labors to accompany our faith. *Piers Plowman* subverts the notion of ends or truths: they all represent only temporary and imperfect understandings, which is why the plot shift occurs at Passus X: the number ten represents in medieval numerology the crossing of a liminal boundary from one order of existence to another, as from life to death, or in this case from partial to fuller—but still incomplete—vision. Unpierced, we must search anew, and anew, and anew. The lonely process of seeking redemption subverts, by super-verting, the equally lonesome but destructive self-seeking that the early part of the poem satirizes. Even the manuscript tradition of *Piers* involves its subversion: which of the three does one study, and does one prefer the clearest and most finished version or the most poetically (and perhaps therefore spiritually) moving?

Curiously all of these stories hint at the loneliness of the moral act and also of the person who either commits or must fix the immoral one. We get no mention in the great Anglo-Saxon epic that Beowulf has any family or friends—he mentions Hygelac as his only kin and at his death turns over his kingdom to someone we have just met. Only Wiglaf stands with him against the dragon. He fights alone, and he rules alone, without peer or confidant. Galahad never seems to pine at being the sole perfect knight; he joys briefly in the companions with whom he completes the quest, but they long for his company more than he does for theirs. He seeks only the presence of God. So great a loneliness drives him once he has looked into the Grail that nothing can impede his desire toward a full vision of God in the death that follows. Gawain in *Sir Gawain and the Green Knight* meets his greatest loneliness only after he has returned alive, and therefore pretty successfully, from his quest, but no one at court understands what he's gone through, and they laugh off his failure rather than sharing its import. The Wife of Bath is lonely enough that after five husbands she still wants to marry again. And after all that Pier has said and done, at the end of *Piers Plowman* Conscience vows to begin the search for Piers anew to quell pride, and the dreamer wakes presumably to the same state in which he fell asleep: a fallen world in which the quest for goodness and holiness must remain constant and vigilant—no time for friends and family and the gentle pleasures of daily life. Literature, nearly all of it, subverts the escape and relaxation it purports to offer, enjoining us more fervently in the quest than we were before we read.

Equally good examples abound from traditions outside the English: I've explicated those above simply because I know them best. In Spain, for instance, *El Libro de Buen Amor* abounds in subversions of all sorts: Juan Ruiz, the *Archpriest*, attempts to seduce all sorts of women—acts we hardly expect of him, but that remain entertaining in their bungling incongruity. Don Quixote embroils us in a subversion of one personality (Quixano) who then subverts another (Sancho), then both suffer a sad return to less comical but somehow lesser superversions. The picaresque mode subverts a whole tradition of Epic and Romance in the adventures of some cunning wastrel rather than a noble hero—but such examples must await another paper and a better scholar.

Finally, medieval narrative subversions do, as John Barth explores, pinpoint the problems of human loneliness, and they do show, as Barth thematizes with his funhouse metaphor, "to get through expeditiously was not the point" (89). Similarly, Barth's attention to "self-contempt" (89) appears throughout the Middle Ages, but for a different purpose: not dime-store psychoanalysis, but the typical medieval Boethian distrust of this transient life. Subversions and sub-versions often show the audience that self-obsession and self-aggrandizement lead to pain or horror, and Nature and human weakness will betray us not at last, but first and last. Yet they may also show that, despite our failings, the world has a place for us, and that place may allow us to do something worth doing, even if its effects are minimal and fleeting. Beyond subversion, the quest matters, whether it aims for spirituality, understanding, human connection, love, or even, sometimes, worldly glory—as Shakespeare's Benedick would say, "man is a giddy thing, and this is my conclusion."

2
Narrative Subversion and the Solutionless Problem

The presence of *narrative* implies both some sense of order and a subversion of order. Narrative requires a structuring of events[1]; the ordering principle may vary, but an author or a narrator—or a tradition—has selected an order, or at least a principle of order, suitable to a medium of presentation. To retain any interest for an audience, however, that contingent order must imply something beyond the trivial. Children will ask to have favorite stories read to them again and again, and even adults will return to favorite narratives knowing every step of the plot—in such a case we read not primarily for the plot, but for the language, the characters, the "world of the text," in Ricoeur's phrase: an artistic facet of sufficient aesthetic pleasure that it stimulates our re-reading.[2] To reward re-reading, an author aims to construct an artful plot, one that may serve as foundation for character building or philosophical exploration or to create a catharsis—something that stimulates for a reader both intellect and emotion. A plot should have sufficient twists and turns that a single reading will not unravel it: subsequent readings bring into relief details that add pleasure and understanding to our first experience of the story. Any sufficiently complex story relies on actual or implied *subversion*s: sub-versions that recapitulate main or important subplots in useful or compelling ways, or subversive tropes that turn a light plot into an intriguing darkness, or darkling event-matrices that clarify, terrify, or even finally reify the light, or simple ambiguities inherent in language and character.[3] One subversion may do for a short tale, though a long one may need many to keep a reader's interest. One interesting question with which to begin is, where does a subversion lead? Then, does it take the story toward something that we should know about mutual human experience?

2—Narrative Subversion and the Solutionless Problem

In literature we still seek what Horace told us we should: when it works best, we find there something sweetly useful—we may apply what we have got there, and the getting has proven pleasant or pleasing. English renderings have often recast Horace suggestion as "to teach and delight." Both notions constitute addictions, intellectual or emotional highs, as when we solve mysteries, come suddenly to understand a difficult poem, or resolve a complex math problem. They return us, depending on our tastes, physiological or fetishistic, to similar shapes of narrative with slight variants or to vastly different shapes with similar centers but subversive surfaces. Any reading subsequent to the first—or the illuminating one that unveils the "meaning"—becomes a new sub-version, unless and until it becomes our new super-version, when a new ideal replaces an archetype, casting us from a new center, decentering or retiring old, overfished readings. Then new plots reconfigure the shoals of reading, creating currents of pleasing new subversions. The literary archeologist, philologist biographer, textual critic, or fisherman of old waters (or philandering reader) may seek an Ur-version (or the "pleasure reader's") diversion. But the subversive act remains common to all stories and all adult readings, part of the process of catching or unearthing, of making familiar or of flirting with the text for a temporary withdrawal from the known, the mundane.[4]

Among the most profound of subversions arises when a text turns us to some insoluble, unsolvable problem, something as squirmingly moving but more deeply convoluted than our youthful biology, as when our bodies tell us we *must* act while our parents tell us we *must not*. Received readings, from hierarchs or heresiarchs or simply from tradition, urge us that we must believe, while our intellects tell us we cannot believe, at least not the simple version of truth they have supplied. I mean something more situationally inherent than when friend Mary comes to us and says, "You can't be both my friend and Larry's," and Larry says, "You can't be both my friend and Mary's"—a junior high-ish sort problem that often continues annoyingly into adulthood. Occasionally we must all confront the deep-down problem that admits no solution from our own action; when literature finds that problem, it finds its immortality, but one fraught with immitigable pain and truth, with human experience naked, horrifying, alive, moribund, bleeding.

Oedipus Tyrannus establishes the model for the perfect, even archetypal narrative subversion.[5] Oedipus, when he learns the foretelling that fate will lead him to kill his father and marry his mother, must do all he can to avoid that fate despite the overwhelming Greek cultural imperative that fate rules our ends regardless of our choices. Who among us wouldn't do everything he or she can to avoid Oedipus' suffering? A pre-modern (or even Postmodern) *monster* might actually seek it, but the rest of us, even given a world that believes unstintingly in fate or Freud, would wrack our brains in attempts to find an escape. In *Casablanca*, when Louis speculates about what brought Rick to North Africa, Rick explains that he came for the waters. But Casablanca, Louis exclaims, is in the desert. "I was misinformed," Rick laconically and enigmatically replies. In *Oedipus* the protagonist's foster parents fail to identify their actual relationship, and Oedipus leaves them, figuring thereby to avoid or subvert the unavoidable. But he is misinformed. Laius, Oedipus' true father, has long ago acted in startling parallel, casting his son into the wilderness to die, hoping to subvert his foretold end. That plot impressed and troubled even Aristotle, who explained that tragedy hinges on a *hamartia* (a great error) often resulting in *hubris* (not pride, but *violence*), which causes the protagonist's fall, which produces his recognition of his own error and thus the suffering that accompanies culpability. Aristotle identified *Oedipus* as the most fitting of Greek tragedies; Oedipus drives himself on to the truth despite the fact that he has reached that most difficult, because impossible to solve, of human conundrums, the subversion of his will to act: he must *both* accept and yet try to avert his fate. The foretelling perhaps merely changed the means of the tragedy, not its occurrence.

The first actual subversion, then, is a self-subversion. Learning that *miasma* or blood-pollution has caused the plague that punishes Thebes, Oedipus declares the banishment of the person whom he will find to have caused it. He, of course, has caused it, killing his father and marrying his mother, the worst and most compounded of

2—Narrative Subversion and the Solutionless Problem

sins, since it offends *xenia*, Zeus' single commandment, and incorporates incest, patricide, and regicide. Oedipus' failure to yield the road to the king does not stem from, but results in *hubris*: again, to the Greeks the word meant not *pride*, but *violence*, dangerous and disruptive violence at that in the killing of such an important person. But the incident happens in the dark, and Oedipus sees himself as a prince; he therefore need not yield, and even the Thebans haven't added two and two to work out who has killed whom and why. So Oedipus ironically banishes himself before he understands himself the cause of the plague: the irony comes in the fact that the banishment matters not a jot. Such crimes as his should accrue far worse punishment. They do: he tears out his own eyes, and his children will make a mess of their lives without him. But as the Athenian audience knew, Oedipus finds not only redemption, but apotheosis later at Colonus: the oracle had never specified that Oedipus must *die* for killing his father and marrying his mother, only that he would commit those acts. The second subversion, then, comes as a sub-version to part one of the trilogy, the second play, where Oedipus transcends his fate; a further subversion comes in part three, where Antigone in her attempt to do right becomes a true sub-version of her father, where Eteocles and Polyneices, Oedipus's sons, have already, as wrong-headed sub-versions of their father, brought about their own destruction and the further suffering of their city. The *subversion* or turning under of the plot of *Oedipus Tyrannus* from light to dark, to tragedy—and thus the movement of the entire trilogy—comes before anything Oedipus actually does, in Oedipus' finding himself fixed in a problem that has no solution: he both must and cannot escape his fate. He moves toward it not only in time, but directionally in space.[6] That point represents, I think, a great human fear: that someone or something binds us, regardless of any choice we hope or wish we may have, to actions even worse than death, to an unhappy or even evil course that we bring about by or despite our own actions, with no one to blame for our misfortunes. When evil befalls us, we must respond rationally and keep going: circumstance may subvert itself again, we hope—pointlessly, the Greeks believed.

The most famous Renaissance incarnation of the "solutionless problem" appears in *Hamlet*. Again, that problem defies popular wisdom. Lawrence Olivier begins his film version of the play by identifying Hamlet as a character who can't make up his mind: a compelling but inexact diagnosis. The problem, actually, is even worse than that: he *may* not make up his mind. Olivier (and many academic critics) suggests that Hamlet is weighing whether or not to kill Claudius, but simply fails to decide, implying an indecisive character. However, situation and law forbid Hamlet from making any choice available to him, the reason he actually waits.

The Ghost, identifying himself as Hamlet's father, declares himself murdered by Claudius. "Oh, my prophetic soul," sighs Hamlet: *prophecy* means, of course, not foretelling the future, but diagnosing problems past or present, and Hamlet, with his piercing intelligence but hesitant judgment, has already guessed what happened. But Hamlet does not act on that information for several reasons. First, Hamlet is a Christian, and "'Vengeance is mine, says the Lord'": the faithful Christian has no right to take it. Second, why should he trust the Ghost? If the Ghost were fully good, he should dwell in Heaven, or at least in the "bosom of Abraham," and not walk the earth looking for trouble. If the Ghost comes from Purgatory, he suffers to purge himself from the sins of the world and would do well not to commit more. He will not free himself, and will damn Hamlet, by insisting his son seek revenge. That must mean that the ghost (who probably isn't even Hamlet, Sr.) comes from hell, in which case, though he may be telling the truth, Hamlet can't trust him: responding to truth or lie leads equally to damnation. Third, Hamlet can't trust his own judgment, because Claudius has come between him and his hopes, the throne of Denmark following his father's death. He knows himself biased, wanting to believe Claudius guilty, and so must acquire more information before passing final judgment on his case. Regicide without proof would make him as bad a criminal as Claudius appears to him. Fourth, if Hamlet seeks revenge, and Claudius knows he seeks it, the king will probably kill both him and Ophelia, whom Hamlet loves (he tells us so passionately in Act V, and I see no reason to disbelieve him). Hamlet's intimacy with Ophelia may have resulted or may result in his telling Ophelia his suspicions, making her nearly as

2—Narrative Subversion and the Solutionless Problem

dangerous to Claudius: she can make public his sin, condemning him, though she can't herself seek vengeance for it, perhaps making her a more credible source and thus a greater problem.

So Hamlet must not kill Claudius. But he *must* kill Claudius. One must take vengeance on his father's killer, and a strong and heroic part of Hamlet's will drives him to it as well—many of us today, rightly or wrongly, would yet see that as a just and righteous act. Further, the medieval Danes had not so fully committed to the Roman Christian worldview that they had forgotten the old Germanic law of blood-vengeance. Hamlet must take vengeance, or at least receive *weregild*, man-payment, for his father's murder. And murder we must call it: one could kill another man in a fair fight as long as he announced it publicly and paid proper recompense. We know from Act III, scene 3, that Claudius killed Hamlet, Sr., but we don't really know how, despite the Ghost's claims—the "Mousetrap" remains problematic, because in it nephew kills uncle, not brother, and so Claudius could have confused its message. The facts we have at hand, that Claudius killed his brother and didn't announce it publicly, make him subject to vengeance. But the situation gets more complicated: kin-slaying, brother-slaying in particular, represented for the northern Germanic folk the worst and most problematic of crimes, because one couldn't properly avenge it: blood-vengeance can't cleanse one of a crime *within the family*.[7] So the crime brings only unending sorrow and embarrassment. Even as he must, Hamlet once again must *not* kill Claudius. So we find Hamlet in a position that parallels that of Oedipus: he both must act and may not act. Unlike Oedipus he *can* do something effectual, but he can't and may not act without being wrong according to one or another essential component of his cultural tradition.

The subversion in *Hamlet* then comes in the natural course of the narrative—I use the term *narrative* according to contemporary narratology, which extends the study of fabula to any medium that exploits sequential events, to drama as well as ballad as well as novel or epic. The narrative subverts into variant streams of self-examination and twists and turns of plot, as well as the parallel subplot of Laertes seeking revenge against Hamlet for his slaying Polonius—as Hamlet ponders possible actions in the midst of a problem that has no solution.[8] The largest part of the play deals with that situation, as Claudius tries to kill Hamlet, and Hamlet tries to avoid being killed and put himself in a position where his vengeance can happen without his having to take responsibility for it, or until circumstance relieves him of responsibility. He waits, in fact, until such a position presents itself, and it does: Laertes' challenge. Hamlet expects, I think, that Laertes will kill him, eliminating his responsibility without placing Laertes in a bad position. Hamlet shows a great deal of kindness in the play, even at his most violent: he casts off Ophelia, for instance, not to make her suffer, but to distance her from Claudius' murderous fears. With a sword in his hand Hamlet may die at Laertes' hand, or he may find himself in a position to ensconce it in Claudius' heart—he can't know ahead of time, but he can place himself within the most tolerable and manipulatable circumstance. Now we can accuse Hamlet of committing suicide at Laertes' expense, but we may also see him making a choice that from his own similar position appears just (or, alternatively, horribly unjust): he allows Laertes to make the same choice he, Hamlet, has been trying to make.

Hamlet gets vengeance for his father's murder, and he gets it lawfully: he kills Claudius not because the king has killed Hamlet, Sr., but because he has poisoned both Gertrude and Hamlet himself in front of the entire court. But having killed Polonius, Hamlet must in turn suffer Laertes' revenge. Much as in *Oedipus* the play teaches patient waiting, however much that waiting may annoy the court or the audience. It also teaches the need for constant vigilance, attention to opportunities to act and awareness of continuing dangers. Claudius subverts Hamlet's kingship before the play begins, but by repeated errors he allows the results of Hamlet's desire for revenge without the prince's having to step outside the law to get it. That ending in a sense subverts Classical notions of tragedy: Hamlet does the best he can with the minimal choices he has to make.

Now to a medieval example: it falls neatly outside of its parallel Classical and Renaissance texts in its humor and kindly resolution, and yet it also exploits the unsolvable problem motif. In *Sir Gawain and the Green Knight*, that most artful of medieval Romances, the

2—Narrative Subversion and the Solutionless Problem

hero Gawain also finds himself in the midst of a subverted narrative and a difficulty for which neither he nor anyone could find an appropriate resolution. The narrative subversion sets up the problem, and that problem becomes the thematic heart of the poem. Once Gawain has struck the head of the Green Knight from his shoulders, he must in a year seek the knight's Green Chapel and receive a return blow. He does as he must, but the subversion occurs when Gawain, praying for lodging and some relief from deprivation and weather, sees emerge before him the castle of Lord Bercilak and his lady. There Gawain, with three days to wait before he must attend to his bargain at the Green Chapel, accepts the lord's offer of a game: while his host spends each day hunting, Gawain will remain at the castle resting, and at each day's end, they will exchange what they got for the day—a pact seemingly harmless enough, especially by comparison with the earlier pact that involves the loss of one's head to an axe stroke. The lord successfully and successively hunts stag, boar, and fox: symbolically speed and evasiveness, tenacity and power, cunning. Gawain in the meanwhile repels the sexual advances of the lady, receiving in succession one kiss, two kisses, three kisses—and also on the third day a green sash that the lady presses into his hand, asserting it has the magical power to save its wearer from harm. It thus nominally provides the potential to save Gawain's life from the return stroke of the deadly weapon. He accepts the sash, pondering the possibility that it may extract him from the peril ahead, and that acceptance places him in the position of the solutionless problem: the lady says he must tell no one that she has given it to him. She subverts Gawain's word and his quest.

The scene has odd elements in which Gawain self-subverts: when the lady offers him a ring—a dangerous gift for what it symbolizes—"I wil no giftez, for Gode," he says, and he "swere swyfte by his sothe þat he hit sese nolde" (Stanza 51), but she offers him the green and gold sash—colors that one might suspect would warn him, given the appearance of the Green Knight—as she draws it from under her mantle. The *kyrtle* thus retains, if less than the ring, a sexual suggestion. For the man who wears it, she asserts, "no haþel vnder heuen tohewe hym þat myȝt," and Gawain immediately perceives "Hit were a juel for þe jopardé þat hym iugged were: / When he acheued to þe chapel his chek for to fech,/ My3t he haf slypped to be vnslayn, þe sle3t were noble." He even has her speak more of it and finally "grants" her request that he take the gift: he reneges on his promise to accept a gift, takes not a ring but a jewel, and accepts it with full recognizance, both heart and thought: "He þonkked hir oft ful swyþe,/ Ful þro with hert and þo3t."

According to the pact with the lord, Gawain must that evening turn over whatever he has got for the day. In return for the fox pelt, Gawain allots Lord Bercilak the three kisses, but he keeps the sash. In doing so, he preserves the lady's honor. He has never admitted where he got the kisses—not a necessary part of the pact—and he has kept her from any dishonor that may befall her as a result of her giving him so precious a gift as the sash. He fails even to mention the sash because the lady says he must not do so. Also, presumably, he doesn't want to give it up if it may save him. Gawain's error, the Green Knight—Bercilak under Morgan's enchantment—explains, comes from his desire to preserve his life, a forgivable sin, particularly given the confusing, magical aspects of his situation—but a sin nonetheless. Gawain, of course, suffers enormous shame at what he has done: he ungenerously blames women's faithlessness (perhaps because of the only slightly veiled sexual aspects of the gifts she offered) as well as his own cowardice and covetousness for his failure. But the Green Knight—and the poet as well—argues that Gawain has done as well as any human could: he shows himself only imperfect, not a bad knight or a bad man, a lesson everyone must learn. But Gawain might have learned another important lesson as well.

The real problem for Gawain is that once he accepts the sash, he can't succeed: he both must remit the sash and must keep it and keep silent. He has helped the Lady and Morgan subvert his word and thus his honor. The agreements with the lord and lady contradict each other. Since one of the main themes of the poem, as the poet clarifies it, is loyalty, or more specifically *trawþe*, keeping one's troth, which implies one's word, code, ethics, faith, Gawain has allowed himself through a seemingly trivial incident to fail in what he holds most dear. That failure not only strikes his pride, but also cuts at the

2—Narrative Subversion and the Solutionless Problem

heart of the order of knighthood, since the author tells us that Gawain represents that order, its courtesy and accomplishments, better than any other knight.[9] The narrative subversion has set up the breaking of the bond, throwing the thematic weight of the poem upon a culmination that results from that rupture; the narrative and thematic climax occur within the subversion, and the rest of the poem turns not, as in *Hamlet*, to silence, or as in *Oedipus*, to apotheosis, but to explication, public confession, and metaphorical hints of a cultural immolation that lies ahead (the references to the fall of Troy at the beginning and end of the poem parallel the fall of Arthur's court). Ironically the poet cast the entire adventure in the unassuming form of pleasant Christmas games.[10] Here one must not wait, but confess, repent, and try to learn to live humbly and lovingly.

In each of the works I've considered here, narrative subversion, in forms particular to the individual texts, leads us to the same essentially and disturbingly human theme: we may well find ourselves in circumstances that, possibly through no fault of our own, or at least not by our own choice, offer no possibility of an acceptable solution. Any choice, including choosing not to choose, leads to suffering, ours and others'.[11] Particularly in a time when we actually believe we can and should take charge of our own lives, that idea creates an especially frightening specter, nonetheless true for the trouble it unveils. Sometimes our circumstances simply don't allow us a solution; we have no way available to solve our problem; sometimes, whether we fight or wait, we must simply endure and wait for events to take us where we can't take ourselves. The ancient Greek world had a partial answer to that problem: avoid violence, *hubris*, which may provoke *miasma*, infecting everyone around, not the ill-fated person alone. The ancient Germanic world had a response as well, the theory of courage, the idea that we can't change our fate, only the state of mind in which we meet it. Contemporary optimism as well as Christian theological traditions and even much existentialist thought reject the idea of fate, but one need not believe in fate as the cause to understand the truth of the unsolvable problem: the Christian faces it with patience, faith, and prayer. Our narrative subversions lead us to such solutions as we can find as part of a necessary realization of the true and troubling depths of human nature and of the potential pain of self-awareness. Even when we know the plot, we learn also its radical potential for subversion. That subversion may take us directly to our cultures' most treasured sources of strength, or it may lead us inevitably from them.

3
An Aesthetics of Subversion in *Beowulf*ian Narrative

> "The most ancient and best established concept in this [Augustine's understanding of the Classical] aesthetic was that of 'congruence' (*congruentia*), of proportion or number, a concept whose lineage went back to pre-Socratic times. It expressed an essentially quantitative conception of beauty."
>
> —Umberto Eco, *Art and Beauty in the Middle Ages* (28)

Beowulf subverts its central narrative repeatedly through digressions, as we have seen in an earlier chapter. It ties its sense of interpretation and structural beauty to those digressions, also to number and proportion, which it also then subverts. Digressions suggest interpretive strategies, though some readers may consider them interruptive. Numerology was alive for the medieval audience in a way to which modern readers are largely oblivious; numbers provide a way both to link plot elements and to separate them, to continue narrative or to break it. Similarly, narrative asides furnish additional data to fill out the world of the fable, and they add to the beauty of ornament—a hint of the pre-baroque in a Northern Romanesque world. The poet's method of apportioning the narrative—we may see it as three parts comprising increasingly difficult adventures or as two part linked by a recapitulative and incrementally additive suspension of the action—also implies either three-part symmetry or a comparison of narrative asymmetry with affective and thematic symmetry. *Beowulf* gives us quite a number of ways to consider an aesthetics of narrative structure: why should narrative—and narrative subversion—not contribute to the *beauty* as well as the *meaning* of a narrative? This chapter will re-fold part of Chapter 1 to look especially at the aesthetic implications of a digressive plot.

In *Art and Beauty in the Middle Ages*, Umberto Eco observes, "intelligible beauty was in medieval experience a moral and psychological reality; if it is not treated in this light we fail to do justice to their culture" (5). Aesthetic appeal draws us to many of the texts we study, but because we may have a hard time determining what that beauty meant to them, we seldom look analytically at notions of beauty in specific texts or across time and cultures. The conjunction of physical and moral attributes and their affective power drove medieval artists in their approach to beauty, Eco suggests, and to understand them we must at least attempt to contemplate them as beautiful objects within their cultural contexts. We can also see them plainly as subverted and subversive objects.

I'd like to suggest that a medieval audience could and a modern audience can experience in *Beowulf* beauty as an artistic as well as a moral and psychological reality; I think that we can dig out beautiful elements analytically from its poetics, but also from its use of and undercutting of movement and proportion (the purpose of this chapter). That is, we can break down "digressive" parts of the poem into elements we may reasonably call *thematic* or *beautiful* and that particularly shape the progress of the narrative. *Beowulf*, as Eco would suggest, exhibits a greater sensitivity to type than to individual; it certainly presents a moral and ethical immediacy: like the characters in the poem, the audience must strive for steadfast courage in the face of a dangerous world—that is the chief theme of the poem. Brief digressions subvert us from the "main" plot, but neither they, individually or collectively, nor the poem as a whole has enough length that they detract from its progress—"lack of steady advance" does more good than harm to *Beowulf* as a work of literary art because of what the digressions add to the experience of the poem.

We need look no further than Wulfstan's *Sermo Lupi ad Anglos*, delivered at about the same time as the copying of the *Beowulf* manuscript, for contemporary confirmation of at least the same thematic expression of moral concerns. But by using Eco's guides for determining the beautiful, I believe we clearly identify in the epic poetic

3—An Aesthetics of Subversion in Beowulfian Narrative

notions of physical sensibility, verbal proportion, and organic unity amidst dynamic variability nearly throughout *Beowulf*. The poet aimed, I think, not just at a didactic and manly tale for manly men, but at a work of art brimming with details bubbling up out of a cultural fund of artistic sensitivities. The movement of the hero from *kolbítr* to young hero to dragon-slayer gradually increases the sense of physical weightiness, and the metaphorical movement of the poem from opening funeral (Scyld's) to closing funeral (Beowulf's) gives it imagistic bookend closure. The poem deals with rising physical strength, composure, and confidence rounded with reminders of mortality. The steady balance of the alliterative poetic line and the movement of an obviously progressive plot mixed with reflective allusions give the poem balance, consistency, and completeness. The incrementally increasing difficulty in the monster fights moves Beowulf toward what Tolkien considered the perfect end: he must die, so how would we want him to die other than in the activity he does best against the greatest of possible foes?

The notion of type/typology applies also to the narrative and how it moves, not just to individual experiences of beauty. We can see Scyld and Beowulf as types for each other or as mutual Christ-types, or we can see the other heroes and kings as types leading to the fulfillment of the anti-type in Beowulf. Together the sample heroes build a culture notion of *hero*—what to do (Beowulf's defense of his people and the Danes)—and what not to do (Hunferð's brother-slaying). Together the various kings build a notion of kingship: Hroðgar exemplifies the generous king, but fails as heroic king; Eormenric, perhaps brave in battle, was also greedy, sexually violent, unfaithful to his friends, and perhaps at last suicidal; Beowulf, the generous and heroic king, fails to leave an heir of his blood to govern in the next generation. No one quite fulfills kingly perfection—nor may we expect one mortal to do so. The beauty comes from the construction—and self-deconstruction—of the poem and its characters as well as from its ideas and themes.

If we look at them as beautiful and instructive, we can also find method rather than madness in the so-called "digressions" of the narrative, which have to some readers seemed more like unnecessary strayings from the plot. As subversions from the simple plot—Grendel fight, Grendel's Mother fight, dragon fight—they add a great deal to our understanding of the world of the text. They reflect on one another, on the major plot episodes, and on themes: they add, clarify, inflect. While they provide poetic decoration, they also introduce essential *terrapoiesis*.

In his introduction Klaeber provides a complete list of even the briefest digressions, while Wrenn and Bolton elaborate especially on the longer ones. Adrien Bonjour in *The Digressions in Beowulf* makes a complete and detailed case for the validity and artfulness of the digressions, and I would add that the digressive nature of the narrative employs an especially powerful narrative *pattern*. I wouldn't consider an allusion a digression; the poet's mention of the future destruction of Heorot doesn't interrupt the story with another story, but it does add fullness and *feel* to the world by telescoping to a significant event, a loss that colors the textual present with sadness. On the other hand, Beowulf's recounting of his athletic contest with Breca (either a swimming or rowing match), part of his brief *flyting* with Hunferð, does introduce a new story with some narrative movement not a part of Beowulf's adventure among the Danes. It serves to tell us about Beowulf as an athlete and competitor, about his physical and heroic prowess, and it shows that in battle, even a symbolic one such as a flyting, he will win or die trying. He will cut through preliminaries and get down to serious battle, so while he would not dishonor a friend or even a competitor, he will allow no quarter in a battle once it has begun.

What Giuseppe Mazzota calls *cosmopoiesis* Tolkien had called *mythopoiesis*; for Mazzota "[t]he age of prose contemplates the poetry of the Italian Renaissance epic ... as if it were a distant dream of Edenic wholeness.... [T]his dream of the Italian Renaissance is the dream of the world: of world-making, actual worlds, golden worlds, brazen worlds, the creation of the world, and the metaphysics of infinite worlds" (97). World-building adds aesthetic quality to the text by filling out the reader's (or auditor's) experience. I've always found Paul Ricoeur's phrase "the world of the text" both apt and productive: as much as any other technical aspect, Middle-earth, the world of the text, beyond providing a place for adventures, makes Tolkien's fiction work affectively, gives its greatest source of power. Aside from

3—An Aesthetics of Subversion in Beowulfian Narrative

the monster fights, which take up relatively little of the text, *Beowulf* also works because it draws us into a compelling fictional world buttressed by common-knowledge historical allusions, a world fully physically sensual with an elegiac exactness of language and a dynamic unity based on the limits of the heroic ethos and what characters can do in it. And, as Mazzota adds (referring to Angelo Poliziano's *La fabula di Orfeo*), though that world be "fable" and a consequence of "language construction," it may succeed particularly when we find "no rift between the 'real' world and the 'fictional' world" (23). *Beowulf* blends historical characters and events with fictional if epic constructions: Beowulf and Wiglaf as figures of the imagination enter a world otherwise attested and understood by the poet's sources and audience, yet they add immeasurably to that world in the embodiment of its greatest virtues: courage, loyalty, and verbal and heroic dignity. The sense of dignity, part of what Tolkien identifies as the elegiac tone and quality of the poem, creates a context, medium, and example of an Anglo-Saxon ideal of beauty, a dignity of style as well as substance (58, 61). It has beauty because it addresses fine ideals in fine language, because it exhibits both magnitude and control. Tolkien discusses also unity of theme and style (62), the overwhelming power of the sense of *doom* (both *glory* and *judgment*), its "high seriousness" (63), the value of "unyielding will" in a hopeless world (70–71), the *pietas* of our memory of the "struggles in the dark past" (74), and the celebration of merited praise (91) as contributing to the beauty of the poem. But we can say more yet about its particulars.

Walter Pater in his study of Renaissance art (1873) describes the reception or experience of beauty in terms of "pulses":

> Not the fruit of experience, but experience itself, is the end. A counted number of pulses only is given to us of a variegated, dramatic life. How many we see in them all that is to be seen in them by the finest senses. How shall we pass most swiftly from point to point, and be present always at the focus where the greatest number of vital forces unite in their purest energy?
>
> To burn always with this hard, gemlike flame, to maintain this ecstasy is success in life... [249–50].

Or, one may say more punctiliously, our most trustworthy evidence of the beautiful comes from the pulses of pleasure and dramatic depth that an artwork evokes in us. Pertinently, John Hill describes the narrative movement of *Beowulf* as "pulses." Unlike Klaeber and Tolkien, Hill sees *Beowulf*—and so do I—as strongly narrative, not "lacking steady advance," but exhibiting a repetitive pattern of clearly punctuated narrative sequences (3–4), in fact a "dramatic, socially complex, and highly changeable pulse of variously characterized arrivals and departures" (96—Tolkien calls this idea "an opposition of ends and beginnings," 81). Those pulses, I'd like to propose, work much in the way Pater suggests artistic components should generally; they provide focal points for the kind of pleasure that narrative can provide: joy in action, the courage of esteemed heroes, suspense, and combative results, yet they also recognize our sad and common fate of mortality—as Tolkien wrote, the tragic motif of the human "at war with the hostile world, and his inevitable overthrow in Time" (67). They also provide parallel patterns, rhythms, and decorative, incremental variation.

The world of *Beowulf* builds around both narrative and poetic pulses, balladic leaping and lingering adventure with spare but energetic recitatives of lyrical intensity, carried ahead on balanced, ritualistic, drum-beat lines. Scholars have posed a number of different metaphors for its structure. Nist referred to it as cyclic, and Leyerle calls it interlace (a favorite pattern for Anglo-Saxon decorative visual art). The digressions actually expand the world, provide interpretive clues, and initiate individual passages that, on their own, bear the weight of close-reading. The larger narrative leaps from the Danish episode to the dragon episode; it lingers at length on each of those two narratives, but in the meantime in leaps—for either brief or more substantial lingering—on allusions or brief inserts that on their own deserve complete stories, stories that in most instances the audience of Beowulf probably knew. The emotional complex for the original audience would have been far greater: for the stories they knew the affect would resonated far longer and with greater force than it does for us, since we get hints rather than additional complete heroic tales.

A couple of lengthier examples will show imagistic, structural, and thematic integrity of their own while clarifying their value to the poem as a whole. Scyld's funeral floods the poem with both nostalgia and tangible respect for the great hero-kings:

3—An Aesthetics of Subversion in Beowulfian Narrative

Him ðā Scyld gewāt tō gescæp hwīle
Fela-hrōr, fēran on Frēan wǣre.
Hī hyne þā ætbǣron tō brimes faroðe,
swǣse gesīþas, swā hē selfa bæd,
þenden wordum wēold wine Scyldinga,
lēof land-fruma lange āhte.
Þǣr æ hyðe stōd hringed-stefna,
īsig ond ūt-fūs, æþelinges fær;
ālēdon þā lēofne þēoden,
bēaga bryttan on bearm scipes,
mǣrne be mǣste; þǣr wæs mādma fela
of feor-wegum, frætwa, gelǣded.
Ne hyrde ic cymlīcor cēol gegyrwan
hilde-wǣpnum ond heaðo-wǣdum,
billum ond byrnum; him on bearme læg
mādma mænigo, þā him mid scoldon
on flōdes ǣht feor gewītan.
Nalǣs hī hine lǣssan lācum tēodan,
þēod-gestrēonum, þon þā dydon,
þe hine æt frumsceafte forð onsendon
ǣnne ofer yðe umbor-wesende.
Þā gyt hīe him āssetton segen gyldenne
Hēah ofer hēafod, lēton holm beran,
Gēafon on gār-secg....

    (Scyld then left them at the set time,
still strong, to seek the lord's succor.
They then carried him, dear companions,
to the sea's current, just as he'd asked,
when he still wielded words, friend of the Scyldings,
the beloved land-leader who had ruled so long.
There at the dock stood the ring-prowed ship,
icy and eager, the prince's vessel.
Then they laid down their beloved lord
and giver of rings in the ship's bosom
by the mast in mourning. There was much treasure
from far lands and war-gear laden.
I have not heard of a seemlier ship
adorned with weapons of war and battle-cloths,
with blades and byrnies; on his breast lay
many treasures that must fare with him
into the flood's grasp far away.
Not at all was he less provisioned with gifts,
heirlooms of his people, than they once did
who sent him at birth far over the sea
alone on the waves as an infant.
For him they placed a golden standard
high over his head, let the sea bear him,
gave him onto the wind's-edge...) [lines 26–49, my translation].

Narrative Subversion in Medieval Literature

This passage offers the standard Old English tropes while providing especially good examples of physicality, verbal balance, and narremic variability amidst narrative unity. While Aristotle pointed out the great value of metaphor in making poetry both effective and pleasurable, Old English poetry uses it sparingly, preferring direct, tangible imagery rather than comparisons, embodied in a particular taste for kennings, litotes, phrases expressing praise, and understatement. We find here a fair concentration of all those poetic elements; they only briefly suspend narrative progress, and they add to the depth of the world, to the power of the sub-versions of stories. Though he was *fela-hror*, still very strong, Scyld's *hringed-stefna*, ring-prowed ship, *Isig on ut-fus*, icy and eager to go, loaded with *hilde-wæpnum, heaðowædum*, and *þeod-gestreonum*, war-weapons, battle-weeds, and folk-treasures or heirlooms, departs, given out onto the what is probably *gars-ecg*, the wind's edge—the final image depicts the sea either as the edge that the sharp wind strikes or as spear-sword: the water itself as weapon of destruction. The scene—rich, sad, dark, cold, shar, and liminal—oozes dignity, but also tactile and aural sensuality. The story of Scyld suspends that of Beowulf, but it presages and remains as an echo for its narremic sibling, Beowulf's death and funeral at the poem's close. Five times in eight lines we recall the close relationship between Scyld and his folk in words of love, friendship, or gift-giving, and the poet devoted thirteen lines to the abundance and quality of the gifts the people bestow on him at his departure: nor have I heard of a seemlier ship, notes the narrator, nor was it less well-stocked than the ship that brought him. They lay him in the ship's heart, on its breast, and place their treasures upon his breast. Yet Scyld has never decayed or fallen: he merely departs, still strong, though silent now, into the element that had borne him to the Danes years before—his *lof* and *dom* remain, the truest indicators of his beauty to his culture, remain.

In terms of verbal proportion, this sample observes standard the practices of Old English poetry best described, I think, by David Hoover in *A New Theory of Old English Meter*. The lines don't follow Southern European notions of metrical feet, either by beats or by duration, but instead present the Northern European standard of three

3—An Aesthetics of Subversion in Beowulfian Narrative

or four "lifts," their relationships enhanced by caesuras, per line: alliterated syllables highlighting the important words with a good deal of useful variability in rhythm permitted by the available combinations of naturally stressed or unstressed syllables. Tolkien notes of Old English verse that it has

> no single rhytmic pattern progressing from the beginning of a line to the end, and repeated with variation in other lines. The lines ... are founded on a balance, and opposition between two halves of roughly equivalent phonetic weight, and significant content.... They are more like masonry than music [83].

Wrenn/Bolton note that variable-syllable-number problems tend to resolve when we sing poetic lines, "for music is stress-timed" (57); *Beowulf* would have been chanted rather than sung, but the same observation applies, allowing for flexibility in delivery and thus variability of emotion within a controlled verse system. The building of sound, content, and broader rhythm grows into an unbroken artifact—a locale of ritual, history, invention—and a repository of values and cultural imperatives stored in a memorable, economical, culturally valorized verse form.

A second example, which scholars have called "The Lay of the Last Survivor," provides both an incremental addition and a counterexample to the rise and death of Scyld. Of the person at the center of the narrative we know little, only that he was a member of a once glorious troop who have passed from the earth. His Classical *ubi sunt* laments recall Scyld and foreshadow Beowulf's death. A damaged section of manuscript just before this passage complicates this part of the poem. As this passage lacks contextual completeness, so we don't know exactly what it was supposed to accomplish as a whole; however, what does remain fits perfectly with the poem's reflection on mortality as part of the heroic process, the source of the melancholy that matches the poem's joy in battle and achievement. The passage as a whole includes line 2233 to 2275, concluding with the appearance of the dragon, who takes over the lost treasure hoard of the dead people. Here is part of passage, which pours forth the old survivor's sorrow:

> ... gumena nāt-hwylc,
> eorman-lāfeæþelan cynnes,
> þanc-hycgendeþær gehydde,

> dēore māðmas.Ealle hīe dēað fornam
> ærran mælum,ond se ān ða gēn
> lēode duguðe,sē ðær longest hwearf,
> weard wine-gèomer,wēnde þæs ylcan
> þæt hē lytel fæclong-gestrēona
> brūcan mōste
> ... fēa worda cwæð:
> "Heald þū nū, hrūse,nū hæleð ne mōstan,
> eorla æhte!Hwæt hyt ær on ðē
> gōde begēaton.Gūð-dēað fornam,
> feorh-bealo frēcne,fyra gewhylcne
> lēode mīnra,þāra ðe þis [lyf] ofgeaf,
> gesāwon sele-drēam;nāh, hwā sweord wege
> oððe feormiefæted wæge.
> ... [D]uguð ellor scōc
> ... feormynd swefað.
> ... Næs hearpan wyn,
> gomen glēo-bēamas,nē gōd hafoc
> geond sæl swingeð,nē se swifta mearh
> burh-stede bēateð.Bealo-cwealm hafað
> fela feorh-cynnaforð onsended!"

(I know not which of men, a prince of the people, pensive-minded one, hid there a vast legacy of precious treasures. Death took all of them in earlier times, and the one then yet, veteran of the nation, who longest dwelt there, a guardian mourning for his friends, expected the same, that he might enjoy there a little time the long-kept treasure ... and spoke a few words: "Hold now, you earth, the possessions of men—indeed, it was bravely got from you before. War-death, deadly life-bale, took each of the men of my nation, those who gave up this life, saw hall-joys. I have no one who might carry the sword or polish the plate cup.... The veterans have gone elsewhere.... The polishers sleep.... Nor will the joy of the harp, play of the song-beam, nor the good hawk swing through the fall, nor the swift mare stamp in the fortress-yard. Baleful death has sent forth a multitude of [my] life-kin.")

The sense of loss combines with an unhealthy attachment to the treasure: we can do no good by clinging either to treasure or to life, as both sift through our hands.

The selection mixes unmitigated sorrow with the desire to cling to what the speaker knows he can't keep. Death is bale-ful because it takes first companions and loved-ones and later all that they left behind them. The hoard remains only for the dragon to keep: the worm won't share it, as humans should (but don't always), nor will it even enjoy or appreciate what it has got—only keep it from serving any sort of joyful purpose. Whether the speaker laments more at the

3—An Aesthetics of Subversion in Beowulfian Narrative

loss of comrades or of wealth—as some of the Venetians cruelly ask of Shylock in *The Merchant of Venice*—we don't know: therein lies part of the effectiveness of the passage. Even as we know better, we still cling to possessions obsessively, as Gollum does with the One Ring. Our sorrow comes from our clinging, and yet we cling to our sorrow—a point and a beautiful expression of poignant yet pointless grief. In many ways that's the nature of nostalgia.

With respect to organic unity, theories of Beowulf as a collection of lays passed away with the nineteenth century, but discussions about the value and impact of the digressions have continued. The digressions serve pretty clearly, I think, to fill out the world of the text and comment on the "main" narrative; they are not so much subversions of steady narrative as informative sub-versions of narrative. The story of Beowulf the hero has either two parts or three, depending on whether we divide by the number of significant adventures of the number of monster fights. But it also exploits quite a number of instructive asides that provide background, interpretive clues, and narrative metaphors moving for their own sake and as they contribute to the emotional range of the poem. The fall of Hygelac, as Wrenn/Bolton notes, "prepare[s] the darkening atmosphere for the dragon fight" (69), and Queen Hygd's proper trust in Beowulf contrasts with Wealhþeow's misplaced trust in Hroþulf (69). The Hildeburh/Finn episode shows the sorrow of failed peace-weaving, at which the poet hints again in the Ingeld/Freawaru match. It also foregrounds the human propensity for needless and deadly violence: the poet does not entirely condemn revenge, but does highlight the kind of violence that does no on good and destroys families. It also places center stage the plight of the woman in a society of violent men—a point one may apply as well to Wealhþeow, Freawaru, Hygd, and even Grendel's Mother. Þryð or Modþyðo causes her own troubles—needless violence that results from her arrogance—until Offa turns her to kinder and better behavior towards their followers. The Lay of the Last Survivor not only offers the *ubi sunt* lament, but also foreshadows the loss to the Geats of the dragon treasure that Beowulf wins them. The Death of Hygelac shows the dubious value of harrying, but also provides a chance to show Beowulf's ethics and lack of desire for power: he shows his mettle in another deadly battle and afterwards supports Hygelac's sons rather than taking the kingship for himself. The allusion to the future fall of Heorot mutes the joy of the moment and recalls the persistent interlace of prophetic/apocalyptic elements throughout the poem: beware of and prepare for the destructive element, the poet continually hints. Each of these stories comments on the "main" narrative, as both *contempus mundi* reminders and encouragements to defend the homeland and the faith. Each one helps clarify good behaviors and bad, and each urges honor, tenacity, respect for precedence, and composure.

The main narrative has an artful simplicity perfect for fairy tale, but not moral and psychological gravity sufficient for epic. Monster battles make great, hair-raising tales, but by themselves one could hardly hope them to rise to something "doctrinal and exemplary to a nation." If we see the fable as occurring in three parts, the progression is powerful, but predictable: Beowulf goes from a great challenge, to one slightly greater yet, to one much greater, in fact one that must prove unwinnable. Each of the three fights requires its own descriptions and its own account of conflict, along with accompanying issues of character construction and world-building.

If we see the fable as occurring in two parts, the verbal weight favors the first section, the battles with Grendel and Grendel's Mother. One may argue, though, that the greater affective and thematic weight appear in the second section, the dragon battle and its aftermath, set up by the hero's successes in the first part. Part one creates a Beowulf capable of facing and overcoming whatever challenges a human being can handle alone; part two shows that hero mortal at last—no less great, but subject like every human to aging, mortality, and the failure, in a pinch, of one's followers, however good a leader one has been to them.

Stephen Murray argues with respect to our appreciation of Gothic cathedral structure for a "need to move beyond the attempt to construct a unified, teleological, style-based master narrative, toward spatial, synchronic, modes of thought that will allow us to recognize, control, and correlate characteristic patterns in multiple stories over an extended period of time" (55): that idea may apply as well to how we read medieval literary narratives, as phenomena, not merely exemplars, and phenomena of extraordinary structure. *Beowulf* envelopes many stories in a master narrative of its own. Its interpretation varies with time and audience, but it continues to urge interpretation. It draws us back for repeated readings not by plot alone, but for its additive complexity, the attractions of its patterns, world, and language. We tend to neglect its beauties and its peculiar narrative turns in favor of its heroic actions and both physical and metaphysical themes. We may reasonably conclude, I believe, that *Beowulf* includes in considerable quantity those elements that Eco and others consider appropriate, even essential, to the experience of beauty: one more reason yet to value and enjoy the work not just as an artifact, not just as a shining example of Anglo-Saxon didacticism, not just a thumping good tale of our pagan forebears, but—as Tolkien told us, a *work of art* worth studying, and one that rewards study not only with ideas, but also with well-earned aesthetic pleasures. The many subversions contribute not just to the pacing and interpretation of the story, but also to one's aesthetic experience of the whole. As long as the audience feel ready to experience something more than simple, linear story, we will find layers of meaning and feeling well beyond what would come from a simple monster story alone. Subversions of plot and thought turn a simple story of heroic battles into a world of compelling, human, and humane possibilities, a world where storytellers know that one story can lead to or help interpret others, where each story unfolds into a vast tapestry of possibility.

4

Subverting Authority
Dryht, Allegory and Old English Exile Poems

Scholars call many of the Old English poems "wisdom" poems. The term refers to those shorter poems, whether didactic, gnomic, or allegorical, that aim to teach us some concentrated message about how to live. Many Old English poems, often those wisdom poems as well, deal significantly with the problems of travel and exile, whether willing or unwilling. They give sage, sane, and simple advice, necessary wisdom for their time and place: "if you can avoid it, don't become an exile." For instance, "The Wanderer," "The Seafarer," "The Fortunes of Men," "Deor," "The Wife's Message," "The Husband's Lament," and "Widsið," and "Wulf and Eadwacer" all present characters whom fate has caused to "go wandering through many lands" ("Widsið") or "travel the paths of exile" ("The Wanderer") or "face the terrible surging of the waves" ("The Seafarer"). Characters or narrators have lost the status of cultural "insiders" to become "outsiders." In many cases, though, the plaintive tone of lament turns within the poems toward recovery or allegorical potential for redemption: exiled from human contact, the sufferer may renounce the joys and sorrows of the world in favor of the salvation to come or some other hoped-for result, more often than not becoming one of "God's insiders" by enduring a time of grief and loneliness. The exile, the one who has become an outsider, uses deep cultural wisdom to become an insider again, though in a new way. These poems express some wisdom about how to deal with the subversive problem of exile.

The blend of wisdom and exile elements leads to a special kind of subversion common in Old English poetry. Exile may occur simply

4—Subverting Authority

by attrition, but sometimes the lord of the *dryht* (troop or tribe, *comitatus* in Latin), who should have both the loyalty and love of his soldiers and who has authority over them, has either lost his authority (by death, defeat, or incapacitation) or has used that authority to expel or exile a significant character in the poem. In the Anglo-Saxon world exile was the worst of subversions: it takes one from the protected and purposeful life of community and expels one alone into the dangerous and uncaring world. The exile, with no authority above him or of his own, can hardly hope for acceptance elsewhere. The person or persons to whom he had allegiance either have died or have no more use or desire for him. The situation is worth than death, since dying in the service of one's lord implies loyalty and courage, while exile implies failure to keep a promised bond. If one has failed his human lord, probably even God or gods have abandoned him. The thane who has outlived his lord has outlived himself, his purpose and connection to a community. He has no one in authority over him to reward him and make him part of the protective function of a group of soldiers committed to a lord and purpose.

Exile is almost always a significant form of subversion; it was especially so for the Anglo-Saxons, exile being tantamount to a death sentence. Exile subverts the "proper" course of life: one acquires and serves a lord, receives reward, and dies in his service, in battle if necessary but faithful regardless. The relationship to the earthly lord mirrors that with God, one's eternal Lord: courage fidelity constitutes virtuous action in both realms. Exile, either social in the case of one's earthly lord or spiritual in one's relationship with God, produces the most dangerous, frightening, and difficult of plot twists for the individual on a course through life. It provokes an immediate life-change that requires the rethinking of the "plot" of one's own life. The trajectory of life has changed, has suffered a subversion from which it has no likely means to recover. Survival alone isn't sufficient, and only a hero has a chance of dealing sufficiently with the subversion to recover some kind of productive or purposeful life, to return to the safer and productive status of insider.

This chapter will explore the emotional tensions of some Old English wisdom/exile poems as the speakers struggle with the potential horrors (and, occasionally, glories) that their dislocation presents both them as characters and us as readers. A more *affective* reading of Old English poems involves risk, since the poems often have elliptical and elusive metaphorical qualities that, across the distance of so many years, make assured readings difficult. But poems deal not just in ideas, but in emotions as well; finding the emotional center of a poem or poems can lead to a satisfying approach to understanding and linking these poems as part of a fairly unified poetic body, aesthetically moving and rhetorically complete, rather than relegating them to the position of mere mysterious linguistic artifacts.

Let's begin then with "The Wanderer" and "The Seafarer," perhaps the most archetypal of Old English "exile poems." "The Wanderer" begins:

> Oft the solitary one himself finds favor,
> The Maker's mildness, though sad at heart he
> must long stir through water-ways
> with his hands, over frost-cold sea,
> tred the paths of exile: fate is fully fixed.[1]

The speaker continues, remembering trouble, slaughter, and the loss of dear kin: "oft at each dawn I must speak alone my cares; there is no living man to whom I may dare express my mind-sorrows." Thoroughly wretched, the speaker yet creates the utterance, the poem. Experienced and wise of heart, he voices the *ubi sunt*: "Where have the mares gone? Where have the warriors gone? Where have the gift-givers gone, the banquet seats? Where are the hall-revels?" He recognizes and asserts the transitory nature of wealth, friendship, family, life in general, how everything earthly eventually becomes *idel*, "empty," "idle," "useless." "So," he decides,

> good is the one who keeps faith,
> nor should he ever too quickly make known
> the sorrow born in his breast,
> unless he already knows the remedy.
> a man with the courage to bring it about.
> It is well for the one who seeks honor,
> comfort from the father in the heavens,
> where for all of us steadfastness stands.

After a long lament over his exile, the speaker turns in the last few lines to the poem's wisdom: since all earthly things pass, we must *all*

4—Subverting Authority

find comfort where they remain fast, in God. The speaker aims to take us, earthly exiles as well, along, to where we all become insiders again, with God in heaven. God, the one true Authority, allows us authority to accept Grace in our one true Lord. The speaker finds solace and wisdom in the hope of a new *dryht* in Heaven.

Affectively the poem arouses *nostalgia*—literally, from Greek, "home-pain": the speaker longs to return home. As an exile from hall-joys, after a long complaint, he turns abruptly, only in the last five lines, a late penitent, perhaps, to a religious solution. Wisdom, the poem suggests, may appear only late in life, and it may strike suddenly. Fortunately in this case it strikes in time. That, I think, is both the message of the poem and its emotional impact: when loneliness deepens sufficiently, the "wise one" turns "home" to God at last. The delay causes pain, but that pain finds remedy. The subverted story returns to its proper narrative course.

"The Seafarer" teaches the same maxim, but through a slightly different metaphor and emotion and with the addition of an earthly twist. The speaker begins,

> About myself I can make a truth-lay,
> tell of my journeys, how I through toilsome days,
> hard times, sorrowed oft,
> have experienced bitter breast-cares,
> the terrible waves' rolling. There anxious night-watch
> oft occupied me when he drove past the cliffs.

Unlike the wanderer's longing for things past, the seafarer recalls terrifying experiences he'd rather not re-live, and he speaks with a voice like that of the war veteran: "That man does not understand, whom on land the fairest [of things] befalls." While the world grows more lovely, he notes, some people have only the desire to put to sea—not for music nor ring-giving nor for the pleasure of a woman will he stay ashore: "only for the rolling of the waves does he long, who desires to go on the water." When he's on land, the bird calls him back to the whale-road, "because hotter for me are the Lord's joys than this dead life, passing on land." He adds, then, this odd bit: "It is best for each one of men, speaking in after-days, the praise [*lof*] of the living, best of epitaphs"—one does well, even having passed on—to win the praise, and perhaps the prayers, of the living. The poet concludes with a message thematically similar but affectively different than that of "The Wanderer." Twice he expresses the fearsomeness of God, and he calls the one who does not dread God foolish, for "death comes to him unexpected." If one humbly trusts the Maker's might, He will let him live on, that is, bring him to salvation.

The seafarer, even if an insider on land, never feels like one; a member of the *dryht* of sailors, he longs for the sea, where as an outsider he becomes an insider: comfortable with the environment and, even with the sea's vicissitudes, maintaining authority over himself. The poem allegorizes the movement from material life to spiritual life: the self-exiled one becomes the saved one. He may and does place himself in the Lord's keeping. But his text has more "fire" (as well as water) than that of the wanderer, who says it will be well for the worthy one who keeps his faith in the immutable. The seafarer closes with a message of hope mixed with fear and dread, a theme appropriate to the metaphor of the sailor who daily faces the dangers and challenges of the sea. His world is not gone, like the wanderer's, but fearsomely present; his God is waiting immutably ahead, also fearsomely present. No nostalgia for the seafarer: he lives in the wild regions of spiritual seeking, detached from earthly memories, asea in the dangers of the contemplative front lines, committedly poised, joyously, on the unsteady seas between death and salvation.

"The Fortunes of Men" (*Exeter Book* folios 87–88) focuses on what from the human point of view seems the indeterminate nature of life, but what in fact mirrors the presence of God in the unfolding of our destinies. The poem begins with a child's birth, the parents tending and teaching him, but moves within a few lines to the theme that only God knows when his years must end. One may fall prey to the wolf, one to famine, one to the weather, another to war, another to the gallows, any and all subversions—"His name is damned," the poet warns. All sorts of terrible things may, to echo the old hymn, chasten our lives or hasten our end; some may experience misfortune in youth only to turn about and prosper in maturity. God allots talents, tasks, and fame: "artfully the Savior shapes and guides the destinies of the multitudes, of everyone; therefore let us speak thanks for all that He ordains for mercies' sake." Born into the world, we begin as insiders, but fate or just and unfortunate course of events may subvert us, yank us outside human sympathies to suffering or an early death. On the other hand, God may mercifully direct us from youthful errors toward a place in life whence we may find success again, moving from outside back to inside the human—and divinely protected—sphere again, part of the human *dryht* and God's as well.

"The Fortunes of Men" lacks the emotional complexity and humane connections of "The Wanderer" and "The Seafarer," but it expresses another significant aspect of Anglo-Saxon thought: we don't know what direction our lives will take, when or how subversions may come. Our course and adventures often seem fated rather than within our control; we must deal with them as they unfold and hope for the best. The last point of that theme carries the emotional payload of the poem: the warp and woof or our lives suggest the Creator's artistry, but the art that weaves our personal narratives may as well cast us into sorrow as into joy. As humans we have little control but to appreciate the mercies we observe or receive and accept and deal with the sufferings that constitute our portion. This poem, unlike the previous two, takes much out of our control; that fact doesn't, at least I think it doesn't, make the end ring hollow, not from the Anglo-Saxon point of view. Rather, it shows us unflinchingly a truth about the world: we don't know why good happens here and bad there, but we must believe that it all falls within God's plan. We must accept whatever subversions our narratives present us; we can only face them with faith and courage.

"Deor" deals with what we may call a case study of the theory of "The Fortunes of Men." Since this poem is also brief and has an unusual rhythmic pattern for Old English poetry, a complete translation may help the reader here:

> Weland himself knew the worm's persecution,
> hardy man, in hardship experienced;
> he had for companions sorrow and longing,
> wintercold wretchedness, often-felt woe,
> since Niðhad laid him fetters,
> supple sinew-bonds on the better man.
>   That passed; so may this.

> Nor was Beadohilde for her brother's death
> in heart so sore as she was for own suffering,
> once she had clearly conceived
> that she was pregnant. Never could she
> boldly consider how that must work out.
> >> That passed; so may this.
>
> We learn that Mæðhild's moans
> were numberless, Geat's lady,
> that sorrow-love stripped them of all sleep.
> >> That passed; so may this.
>
> Theodorich had thirty winters
> in the Mæring's fastness—that was known to many.
> >> That passed; so may this.
>
> We've learned of Eormanric's
> wolfish thought, widely ruled folk
> of the Gothic kingdoms: that was a grim king!
> Many a man sat bound in sorrows,
> Expecting woe, constantly wishing
> that kingdom were overcome.
> >> That passed; so may this.
>
> The sorry one sits deprived of joys,
> made gloomy in spirit; it seems to himself
> his troubles be endless in number.
> So may it seem that throughout this world
> the Wise Lord wends always,
> to many men shows honor,
> certain fame, to others great woes.
>
> So I wish to say for myself
> that I for a while was the Heodening's scop,
> dear to my lord. *Deor* was my name.
> I had many year a good office,
> a gracious lord, until now Heorrenda,
> song-crafty man, has got the place
> that to me the protector of earls gave before.
> >> That passed; so may this.

Deor, previously an insider as a court bard, alludes to a number of stories in which characters experience a reversal of fortune: Welund the smith, taken captive and enslaved by Niðhad, wrought terrible revenge upon his children and escaped; a symbol of tragic love, Mæðhild's moans were numberless, depriving everyone of sleep; Eormanric, the legendary cruel Gothic king, ruled long and caused great suffering, but even his time passed. Now Deor has found himself replaced by another, admittedly skillful scop. He attaches to his own

4—Subverting Authority

situation the same tag line he has used with all the traditional stories that preceded his own: "That passed; so may this." Discarded by his lord, Deor asserts that his suffering too shall pass. He may win back his post, or he may die—the poem doesn't say—but the suffering eventually must pass. Having become an outsider, has found his position subverted, but he may yet find himself restored among insiders. The poem, through its other examples, suggests that, nonetheless, whether one finds a proper post or not, mortality ultimately claims us all, making us permanent outsiders to any earthly court.

While some scholars consider "Deor" a consolation, I think it may it has greater clarity as a lament, if a somewhat Boethian one. Unlike the previous poems I discussed, it doesn't fall back on salvation or redemption—it hasn't the clear Christian conclusion—though the ambiguous ending doesn't preclude that possibility. Instead, it suggests that, while life assures us that our circumstances will change, whether for the better or the worse, eventually death makes us outsiders to the joys and possibilities of life. Each life faces subversions: we may read the repeated *mæg* as *must* rather than *may*. "Deor" doesn't urge us to seek instead the pleasures of heaven, but it does assure us that the current suffering we too may experience must eventually end—a small consolation, but a serious attempt at such catharsis as lamentation can offer. Though "Deor" is still a kind of exile poem, its emotional complex compares less to that of other Anglo-Saxon elegies and more to many of the quatrains of Omar Khayyám (for example, in Edward Fitzgerald's translation, fifth version, poem number 17):

> Think, in this battered Caravansarei
> Whose Portals are alternate Night and Day,
> How Sultán after Sultán with his Pomp
> Abode his destined Hour and went his way.

Worldly positions and events, both those that we treasure and those that terrorize us, all must, may, will, do *pass*. Life subverts any circumstance, good or bad, sooner or later, and our *dryht* and our earthly lords will pass away just as we do.

Scholars have often preferred to consider "The Wife's Lament" and "The Husband's Message" together. They both appear in the *Exeter Book*, and both have an elliptical, mysterious, riddling quality that makes them nearly impossible to interpret fully and satisfactorily. They may, of course, represent alternating voices, a woman longing for the husband who has sent her away to some kind of hidden sanctuary, and someone speaking to that woman on behalf of her husband to remind her of his love and encourage her continuing fidelity. If we take them as riddles, a plausible religious allegory arises similar to that in "The Wanderer" and "The Seafarer." The "Lament" may express the speaker's sense of loss at Jesus' departure from the world; meanwhile the speaker has died, the body has been buried, and the soul waits for judgment. In the "Message"—more difficult to reconstruct because of problems with the manuscript—the speaker comes to fulfill the Lord's pledge and renew the covenant, to encourage the soul to make the journey across the "sea" of life or death to join Christ. The source of the message and the hearer are "friends" in Christ, a "covenant" they share. But if we read the poems as secular wisdom poems rather than religious riddles and follow their affective concerns, we may watch the characters dealing with insider vs. outsider problems: they have different kinds of subversions, but they struggle with the same issue.

The poems' similarities open another possible reading, one that applies to each separately and to both together. The speaker in "The Wife's Lament" begins by creating ambiguity, calling the narrative both "personal experience" and "riddle." When her lord departs, she becomes a friendless exile in the "kingdom of the world," pining. Her lord commanded her to live in a sanctuary, but her friend has betrayed her, and so she now dwells in a cave or earthen hole, obsessing over her lord in unquenchable anxiety. Her friend, too, shall remain sad: let him be an outcast, too, she says—woe to the one who must wait for longing to turn to love. As with "Deor" we have an elliptical narrative that eschews consolation for lament: the speaker, once an insider, has been left outside her lord's protection, and she is now symbolically or actually buried inside the earth. She hopes to get outside her prison to be reunited with her lord and become an insider again. The poem speaks to any situation in which one has lost a protector or lover, only to be betrayed or at least to lack expected help, ending up imprisoned and unable to act, leaving her with little hope but patience. The poem's wisdom: as Milton would say, "They also

4—Subverting Authority

serve who only stand and wait." It teaches faithful vigilance even as hope wanes, a necessary fall-back for the exile, the sub-verted one.

"The Husband's Message" answers that faithful vigilance. In the voice of a servant the speaker says, "I have come here by ship so that now you may know of my lord's love. I promise that you will find there a permanent, glorious covenant." Take to the ocean, the speaker counsels, and hereafter no one will stop you. "The man has prevailed over his pain.... He has no need of earthly treasures if he may have you, prince's daughter, according to the ancient vow you two made." Then comes the runic passage where the speaker joins sun, road, earth, joy, and man to declare the oath fulfilled. Religious allegory suggests the return of Christ to resurrect the righteous; a wisdom-poem reading offers instead that, if we hold to our vow, a good lord will keep his, even if the payback takes some time. Exile, though a tortuous and torturous subversion, is endurable, and one does best to hope to return among the insiders again rather than merely to bewail the lot of the outsider and die of sorrow.

In "Widsið," the poet-narrator, "who had fared among most of the peoples, nations, and tribes of the earth," is the ultimate outsider who aims by association and name-dropping to become the ultimate insider. Like Johnny Cash's "I've been everywhere, man," Widsið has visited many places, and he rehearses a litany of famous rulers, many of whom we know from other sources, from Attila, Eormanric, Caesar, and Theodoric to Finn, Ongenþeow, Offa, and Hroþulf and Hroþgar. He has sojourned among the Huns, Goths, Swedes, Geats, Danes, Franks, Romans, Saracens, Scots, Picts, Israelites, Assyrians, Egyptians, and Persians—each journey is a sub-version of the whole of his travels. Even Eormanric, the notoriously cruel and stingy king, welcomed him and gave him a golden torque. From his travels he shares these bits of wisdom: princes should live ethically and govern in proper succession; the best kings rule by God's appointment; the best poets say what they want, offer thanks when they get it, and, if they persist, can count on finding someone to appreciate and reward them; good people deserve the fame the bards then give them. The scop experiences the pleasure of travel and knowledge, of meeting the famous, infamous, and accomplished, and of recording their names and deeds—emotionally rewarding, considering alternatives. But the poem, while serving apparently as a teaching tool or mnemonic for poets, concludes with thoroughly practical wisdom. The traveling scop, once an insider as he learned his craft, has become, perhaps as a result of his travels, a perpetual outsider, dependent on patronage. Having found benefactors, he becomes again, briefly, insider, and his words thereafter transform his subjects into the permanent—or at least lasting—insiders of history, from the midst of his words. The poet creates a kind of "dryht of history," a collection of famous persons for his audience to know and understand as significant individuals and as types. Each successive sub-version in Widsið's stories adds an increment to the totality of his accomplishment as traveling bard, as source of knowledge and wisdom.

The final poem I'll treat in this chapter has remained for scholars something of a riddle—in fact many have called it explicitly that. It has a quality that many of the other wisdom/exile exhibit to at least some extent, the sense of something lost and of longing to have it back. Here is the poem, "Wulf and Eadwacer," in translation. I think its "solution" as a riddle—or simply its purpose as a poem—comes down to lexical nuances and an understanding of issues of authority, wisdom, and exile in the poem.

> To my folk it is as if one offers them a sacrifice.
> They will kill him if he comes with a host.
>   It is different for us.
> Wulf is on one island, I on another.
> Fast is that island, surrounded by fens.
> They are slaughter-mad, the men on that island.
> They will kill him if he comes with a host.
>   It is different for us.
> Of my Wulf's wanderings I thought hopefully
> when it was rainy weather, and I sat weeping.
> Then the battle-bold one belayed me with arms.
> There was joy in that; there was loathing, too.
> Wulf, my Wulf! Your hopes,
> so few visits, made me sick,
> mourning in mind, not the least hungry.
> Do you hear, Eadwacer? Our wretched whelp
> Wulf bears off to the woods.
> One easily parts what never was joined,
> our song together.

Scholars have struggled with how to read the relationships among the characters either named or implied in the story. The standard, traditional reading has inferred a love triangle, the young woman caught between the exiled man (and father of her child) whom she loves and the man who has her in his possession (he has qualities both appealing and abhorrent). The woman may also focus on a woman grieving for her lost son. Among some fascinating alternatives, Peter Orton has proposed that the poem really refers to animals, wolves, rather than to humans. Dolores Frese has teased out what I find the most convincing alterative. She finds the poem at the "intersection of pagan and Christian cultures" (1), as an elegiac rather than a lament, with Eadwacer as a "guide from the Christian spirit-world" (14)—that reading fits well with what we understand of the interlaced culture of the Anglo-Saxons.

    The riddle resolves a little differently if we see the "love triangle" as familial rather than romantic. Wulf is most probably the beloved of the speaker, perhaps even already her husband, who has fathered her child. Eadwacer, as other critics have noted, may be a name or an epithet or both: he is perhaps not another romantic lover, but the speaker's brother, the "watcher of the *Ead*," the family treasure, who is the speaker herself. As her brother, he must guard her so she doesn't escape with the exiled Wulf, who, whether he married her or not (we don't even learn her name), is not her family's choice for her spouse. Her family don't want her to be with Wulf, either because he is of lower class or because they have chosen someone else for her to marry. They may want to restrain ("belay") either because of parents' preferences or so that she may serve as a "peace-weaver"—she would be married to someone of the family's choice to end a blood-feud or to secure an alliance. We know that kind of story from other sources, including *Beowulf* and "Deor," and perhaps the more closely related "Wife's Lament," which also comfortably mix pagan-and-Christian and heroic-and-social materials. The woman fulfills a familial obligation by marrying at their choice rather than her own and serving as an ambassador to improve relations. She doesn't object to her brother's embrace, because it shows that her family haven't rejected or exiled her despite her failure to do their will; at the same time she finds her circumstance appalling because she doesn't get to enjoy the embrace of her beloved. Her brother "belays" her, holds her down from going where she wishes to go, to find Wulf—that's where the narrative subversion comes in. She has an idea of a happy relationship, had on her own embarked on it, and now finds herself kept from it by an unwilling family. She still has the dryht of her blood-family, but longs also for the more complete dryht comprising also her husband and child—exile from either causes dread and longing, while the presence of either gives some comfort, though not the comfort of having both. The story presages *Romeo and Juliet* but with a living brother rather than a dead cousin getting in the way of the marriage the woman prefers.

Poems with narrative elements, even brief ones, hinge on subversions as much as do the substantial tales of epics, translations/renderings of biblical books, and modern novels. The narration hints at a likely trajectory and then takes a surprising course relates a compelling story while having no qualms about its didacticism. In the case of the above Old English poems, the subversion may take the form of a riddling hint rather than an explicit fable; it may communicate the transience of life through stories of characters' fall from preferment, imply a worldly story only to turn to religious allegory, or suggest a truncated romance. It will certainly communicate a "moral" or a theme, an idea that the composer wanted to impress upon an audience with as much emotional power as possible. The story allows for the emotional power that comes from dangerous and suspenseful events; the reader's getting caught up in even briefly-drawn characters allows for Eliot's *objective correlative*, the connection to a thought/feeling complex, compassion for suffering characters or joys in their success. Through fable and character-building we get more than a simple homiletic statement of behaviors good or bad. With subversions comes the sadness that cautions audiences about clinging too nearly to what we do or want or even whom we love. The world takes away more than it gives; the virtue comes in our strength and willingness to live anyway and accept the loss with heroic grace.

The dryht will pass, and we will pass; the honor that comes from

4—Subverting Authority

fidelity, plus hope for community ahead—in this life or beyond—supports us as we prepare for the next subversion ahead. The poetic subversions give us mysteries to solve, and the natural subversiveness of poetry urges us to seek sub-version through the pleasure of interpretation.

5

Subverting Ends
Death and the Dead—or Not— in Völuspá *and Some Sagas*

The Norse materials exhibit some intriguing discontinuities in their treatment of death and the dead. Whether in eddas or sagas, writers in most cases treat death matter-of-factly and mythopoeicize afterlife inconsistently. Death, the Dead, and Life after Death appear to represent curiously discrete notions with no clear sense of continuity or absolute boundary, at least in their literary incarnations. Though we're fortunate to have both sagas that treat death in a historical way and eddic poems that treat it in a mythological way, the writers show less interest in "death" as a state than they do in the manner in which characters meet it. They attend to its results in terms of its social implications, but they show the greatest interest in the nature of the events in which death occurs and in the personal traits that distinguish characters as they survive deadly threats or as they face death. In this chapter I'll consider the problem of the liminal boundary between life and death first in the mythological material and then in some appropriate sagas.[1] Perhaps most importantly we find that death as a plot motif both tests and provides space for the next generation—in the literature it points to the necessary fluidity of life in the world and prepares both the departing generation and the one to come for challenges small and great. While death in one way constitutes the greatest subversion of all, the end of life, it is also a natural consequence of living. Avoiding death, though, or turning it into something unnatural, produces a narrative subversion: a change of course of the expected (and usually necessary) narrative. Subverting death redirects a plot into the strange, grotesque,

5—Subverting Ends

horrifying, or, perhaps for the ancient Norse folk, occasionally the humorous.

I

In myth generally, say Classical or Indian, death tends to come by extraordinary means—that's what makes it worthy of a traditional tale. But in most Germanic sources, with their proverbial resignatory gloom, one seldom strays far from mortality in mundane as well as heroic activities: death has a constant presence without receiving either obsessive treatment or embodiment as a god or psychopomp. Any clear understanding of a Norse Afterlife, beyond the little we learn of shades in the cold regions of Niflheimr or Oðin's heroes in Valhöll, remains problematic. In "Gylfaginning" Snorri gives the most complete and sequential accounting of the fate of the dead after Ragnarök—though he too leaves gaps in the story.[2] As the great battle of gods and people against giants and monsters reaches its heroic end, men shall tread the road to Hel, the sun shall fall into the sea, and the earth shall burn, engulfing the last of the old generation of gods. Gylfi asks, "What will happen to them then? Didn't you say that all shall go on living?" The "Third One" answers that many will earn good dwellings and many bad. Some of the righteous will find Brimir, the best of halls, in Gimlé, where they may have plenty of good drink. Other good folk may dwell in Sindri, a hall of red gold, on Niðafjöll. On Náströndir perjurers and murderers must wade through poison in a hall woven of venom-spewing snakes. In the worst of all halls, in Hvergelmir, the great serpent Niðhöggr, who has until Ragnarök nibbled at the roots of the World Tree, shall then chew on the bodies of the evil dead—presumably someone worse than murderers and perjurers (perhaps politicians). A new earth rises out of the sea, and the daughter of the sun will take her place. The younger generation of gods will inhabit Iðavöll at the site of old Asgarð and rule in their parents' stead. Baldr and Höð return from Hel's domain, and the survivors find the old gods' golden game pieces and recount lore of the old days. Two humans who survive by hiding in Hoððmimir's Wood will re-people the world. The story subverts the great apocalyptic subversion by producing a new and better world.

The afterlife does bear an element of justice: those who have done well in life receive reward, and those who have performed evil deeds receive punishment. The description, while spotty, provides more information than simply the chosen warriors of Oðin's hall and a vague underworld of freezing shadows.

Snorri takes some liberties with *Völuspá*, his source—no wonder, if one considers the difficulties of the original—but even he leaves several gaps and uncertainties in his account: who exactly inhabits the new halls—gods, people, or gods and people together? are the old gods not just dead, but gone, and if they can't return, how do people remain? have Oðin's Einherjar privilege or not? have all the dead visited Hel (both the Underworld and the goddess) first? does the new cosmogony reconstitute the old three-tiered pattern? have the new gods enemies, and thus their own Ragnarök ahead? has Snorri christianized the ending of the story, with its evolution toward happiness and renewal, at least for the righteous; is he drawing on an already extant Norse tradition for the ending of the story, or has he drawn a "pagan" ending to rival or parallel that of the new Christian eschaton? He does of course "pull the plug" on the whole story: after the triune Oðin completes his tale with the re-peopling of the world and the birth of a new sun, he adds, "I can't think of how you'll get any more of the course of the world by asking." "*Ok njóttu nú sem þú namt*": so get the benefit according to how you've learned.[3] The whole story is the "Deluding of Gylfi"—seeking wisdom, he's won stories that can make him a better poet and more skilled in lore, but they may not provide objective truths about the world. They do show that the world changes, events follow, old things pass away, and new things replace them—that much Gylfi (and we) may count on.

Völuspá, of course, leaves us with even more questions than does Snorri, as well as some variant details.[4] The golden hall of Brimir the giant and the hall of coiled snakes on Náströndir appear earlier in the poem, after the death of Baldr and the binding of Loki and directly before mention of Niðhöggr gnawing at the naked corpses of murderers and those who seduced the wives of friends. Should we interpret that these less-than-fully-contextualized stanzas describe ongoing rather than apocalyptic options for the dead, or do they represent visions the völva scans on her way to the eschaton? She uses them apparently as images to set the tone for Ragnarök, and then she turns her narrative to Fenrir and his kin, how one will swallow the sun while Fenrir consumes the flesh of the fallen. With the wolf's attack Ragnarök has begun. Again, as Snorri will retell the tale three centuries later, after the fall of the gods and Viðar's avenging his father, a new, green earth arises from the sea. The "Æsir" appear on Iðavöll, Baldr and Höðr return to dwell in Oðin's *sigtoftir* ("victory-place), and the children of the gods shall live on together in the heavens. In the red gold-thatched hall Gimlé the "deserving" will live forever in happiness and ease. Then come a "powerful one," who watches over all, and the dim dragon Niðhöggr, who bears away corpses—at which point either the dragon or the völva sinks down, ending the poem cryptically and abruptly. Are the *Æsir* at the end of the poem the old gods, the new gods, or both? Is the new power who appears a Christian interpolation, a return of Oðin, an unexplained newcomer, or a force that preceded the old gods? Does the dragon do clean-up work and then disappear or die, or does it remain as a plague, as a reminder, or to nibble at some new world tree and recapitulate its work at some future reprise of Ragnarök? May the dragon actually be the force that "resolves" rather than "rules" all? He certainly serves a necessary function in the eschatological process. Further, why does the speaker—either the poet or the seeress or both—state explicitly that Baldr and Höðr return, but leave vague the fate of the first-generation gods? Does the array of punishments and rewards that Snorri places at the end of the story, but that the eddic-poet describes as present before the apocalyptic battle, remain in place, or does the new order replace them, if all soldiers and sufferers except some elite are consumed by the flying dragon?

Here are the final two stanzas of *Völuspá*:

> Þá kømr inn ríki at regindómi,
> Öflugr, ofan, sá er öllo ræðr.
>
> Þar kömr inn dimmi dreki fliúgandi,
> Naðr fránn, neðan frá Niðafiollom;
> Berr sér í fioðrom—flýgr völl yfir—
> Níðhöggr, nái—nú mun hon søcqvaz.[5]

The last line presents a special problem, of course: the manuscripts read *"hann,"* he, instead of *"hon,"* she—the editorial change lies in the assumption that the seeress must be speaking of herself, as her vision ends (or as her ability to see and her influence in the world end with the rise of Christianity). If we accept the original "he," we may translate essentially as follows: "Then comes the power at the Reign-judgment, the 'over-flier' down, he who determines all. Then comes the dim dragon flying, glittering serpent, from underneath Under-Fells: he, 'Undercutter,' bears corpses on his wings, flying over the plain. Now must he sink." The vague "he" may mean the dragon or the one who records the seeress' vision, who must "sink" away when the vision ends because he has no more to relate of it. And the passage does bear the potential for allegorical reading, or it may elliptically refer to the coming of the Christian age. But to me that passage need not imply a Christian interpolation. We may read it as saying that the dragon, a great power, comes from below to fly above the earth (the beginning of the final stanza recapitulates the image of the previous stanza for emphasis); bearing away the dead bodies from the final battle, he must sink down to the lower world, either Nifl-Hell or some other notion of an underworld. Whether the bodies include souls the seeress doesn't hint.

The vagueness of the passage resists a single clear reading, but it does reinforce the idea that the old order passes away—not pleasantly—without specifying what will become of the new. We may read the new generation as a specific metaphor for the new religion or as a general metaphor implying of the natural course of events that no one can alter.

While Snorri gives us a rather fuller picture (including that the dragon torments, *kvelr*, the bodies of the dead), *Vǫluspá* offers perhaps a simpler and more thematically focused one, particularly if we may read the young gods as the new Æsir and the pronoun in the last line as applying to the dragon rather than to the seeress, whether or not we insist on the new power as metaphorizing "the God" or "the new gods." The essential element of the text clarifies that the old generation passes away in favor of a new and better one; a new power (*ríki*) rules over a fresh world, and the sins and sorrows of the old world have been consumed. We need not then read the ending as a Christian sanitization—the generational succession myth serves socially or cosmologically as sufficient rationale for the result—nor need we trouble over human re-population, which in *Völuspá* gets no mention at all. Baldr and his brother, the only named figures to cheat death, do so because they are good, of the younger generation, and belong among their fellows. The text privileges (as does myth normally, though societies struggle with the process) the rising generation rather than any sense of immortality among the old gods. If, however, we take the seeress' final reference to the Æsir to represent the older gods as well as the younger, and the pronoun as a self-reference to the seeress, then we must somehow mythologize the gods' resurrection, upon which the poem spends exactly no effort. That seems a less satisfactory and less likely ending; Norse sagas, while they normally just come to a close rather than alighting on a clear statement of overriding theme, do like to work out what happens to the generations of persons with whom they've largely dealt—that strategy the don't like to subvert.

We may do a fairly satisfying reading of the Ragnarök story, then (whether from *Völuspá* or *Snorra Edda*), given the details we have, to suggest that the Norse "end times" myths deal more completely and directly with succession than with cosmology, much as do the Greek myths concerning Ouranos, Kronos, and Zeus. They imply, not so much allegorically as thematically, that the succession of new, heroic generations may finally lead to peace, prosperity, and happiness, at least for a time. Such a relatively optimistic conclusion falls short of Christian interventionism, but improves on our idea of northern folk as good-naturedly resigned to some medieval notion of "gravity's rainbow." It also supports Paul Schach's idea that the sagas (and I would add here the Eddas as well) are about *hóf* (moderation and self-control) as well as heroism.[6] Heroism *may* produce a better, more successful generation: you never know (*Beowulf* gives us a similar line: *wyrd oft nereð unfægne eorl þone his ellen deah*). Virtue and restraint may help anyone in a pinch, even during such catastrophic subversions as great cosmological events.

II

The sagas actually take an approach to death similar to that of the Eddas: it simply happens—except when it doesn't—and the survivors deal with the consequences. They are normally more concerned with themselves than with the departed, but they courageously press forward, despite the immediacy of mortality, in the apparent belief that their lives may get better. Mortal events fall short of the mysticism of myth, though they may retain a folktalish sense that the results of a death aren't fully fixed. Afterlife hardly enters the picture at all, but on occasion we meet characters in the dim twilight between life and death, characters that may briefly subvert death.

One of the most famous passages to deal with death in the sagas appears in *Egils Saga Skallagrimssonar*.[7] Egil's brother has died as the two fought for King Aðelstan in England. Egil sits in a deep funk, refusing to drink, occasionally drawing his sword halfway out of the scabbard, which lies upon his lap, then thrusting it back in. His facial expression suggests gloom and sorrow at his brother's death: "he wrinkled one eyebrow right down onto his cheek and raised the other up to the roots of his hair," then repeated that action, reversing the eyebrows, over and over (100). After a time of watching him, the king takes a ring from his arm, walks over, and hands it across the fire to Egil. Egil speaks a verse, raises the ring on his sword to honor Aðelstan and show that he has been honored, and thereafter rejoins the conversation of his companions and drinks his fill. What at first seems inconsolable mourning turns out to be besmirched honor: Egil finds satisfaction and resolution in the king's public gift. After the drowning of his son Böðvar, Egil considers starving himself to death, but his daughter Þorgerd talks him out of it. His own death, when it comes, deserves notice, though, mostly for its near banality: one of the greatest sagic heroes, in his eighties and blind, suffers the taunts and follows the orders of the servants, hides his great treasure of silver rather than will it to someone else, and dies not a heroic death, but of a common illness. While appreciating his strength, tenacity, and courage, the saga in no way mythologizes the hero or his death. It does, though, subvert the idea of a heroic death for a hero.

5—Subverting Ends

We may contrast with Egil's story *Bardar Saga Snæfellsáss*, in which the hero apparently undergoes a transformation to become a protective spirit for those who call on him for aid. Bard, believing he has lost his daughter, and having killed his nephews for their part in her disappearance, leaves home, disgusted with the course of the world, and apparently removes himself from the human compass, though later he miraculously reappears in others' adventures at their moments of need. When Ingjald, having taken bad advice from a troll-woman, gets himself lost at sea in increasingly bad weather, Bard suddenly appears, rowing out of the gloom, and saves him, saying that such an intelligent man shouldn't be taken in by such evil folk as a she-troll. At the end of the saga, during the adventures of Bard's son Gest, when Gest finds himself overmatched by Raknar, far from home, off the coast of Greenland, he calls on his father, Bard, for help. Amazingly, Bard appears, but can provide no help. Gest then calls upon King Olaf, who also miraculously appears, and his mere presence has sufficient power to drain Raknar's strength so that Gest may behead him. Sadly, after Gest receives baptism, Bard comes to him in dream and presses his hands against his son's eyes; Gest's eyes burst, and he dies in his baptismal clothes. We learn no more of his father. Bard's apotheosis contrasts with the clear Christian message of the saga as a whole, and Gest's death occurs abruptly: the saga deals not so much with death *per se* as with the problems of a Christian generation succeeding a pagan one.

In its presentation of death *Grettis Saga Asmundarsonar* mediates between the earthier *Egil's Saga* and the more mystical *Bard's Saga*, particularly in the Glámr episode. Glámr, a brave and powerful but temperamental and resolutely unchristian shepherd, meets a violent death at the hands of some unnamed monster, which apparently has also died at Glámr's hands.[8] The shepherd's dead, bloated body resists Christian rites, so Thorhall the farmer must simply bury it in a shallow grave where it lies. Soon Glámr rises from his grave, terrorizing everyone in the district and breaking and crushing livestock or anyone who dares confront him. When Grettir learns of the Glámr's depredations, he undertakes the task of wrestling with him. They duel essentially to a draw, Grettir stopping the monster, but the monster's strange, glowing eyes unnerving the hero so that he temporarily loses his strength. Glámr predicts nothing but suffering and ill-fortune for Grettir before the hero regains his strength and beheads the ghoul. Grettir and Thorhall burn the body and dispose of the ashes, ending Glámr's reign of terror over the night, but the episode leaves Grettir for the rest of his life weaker, more troubled, and quicker of temper than he would otherwise have been: in essence, Grettir through his battle with the un-dead figure acquires Glámr's bad traits and bad luck. The adventure isn't so much about death as about character and how one faces up to terror.

Bard, as a result of his misfortunes, passes from ordinary life into something extraordinary, and he becomes a first benevolent and protective force, and then a vengeful and murderous one—but always an indubitably pagan one. Glámr, apparently through pride and unwillingness to submit to Christian discipline, dies a violent death and then intensifies the violence that preceded him. He proves the greatest test for Grettir, the assurance of the legendary hero's worth, but he also imposes on Grettir the limitations that will destroy him. Grettir gains no good beyond reputation for that battle; Gest, Bard's son, gains no significant help from his father in the battle against Raknar's infernal magic: only the Christian powers of Olaf and the priest with his holy water can subdue it. In both cases death bestows special abilities, either for good or ill, but abilities with limits: in a world where a Christian veneer has clouded our understanding of earlier notions of death, death itself becomes vague and incomplete. Bard is dead, but not; Glámr is dead, but not; Grettir is alive, but moribund: he faces disappointment, outlawry, and death from an adversary armed with pagan magic. Of their fates beyond death we know nothing: Bard never actually dies in the narrative, and the authors say nothing of Grettir and Glámr after their deaths, nor do we know the fate of Egil beyond mortality.

Another of the most famous death passages in Icelandic literature appears in *Brennu-Njál's Saga* (Chapters 126–132) in accordance with a motif common in the sagas: the firetrap where the title character is hemmed in an burnt to death.[9] This scene parallels, and in essence derives from, the earlier killing of Gunnar (Chapters 76–79),

5—Subverting Ends

but with the odd twist that, in the later instance, Kari finds amidst the ashes of their home the bodies of Njál and his wife, Bergþora, lying under an ox-hide thoroughly dead but unmarked by the flames. The couple face death with utter resignation. They are essentially good people—though the sagas seldom get sentimental about such points—and Njál does he best to avoid violence and set right the cycle of blood-feud that circles his family and friends. Fate, of course, takes its course, and when the chieftain Flosi arrives at Njál's settlement, Njál, believing in right and the mercy of God, makes the tactical error of suggesting they defend the house from the inside. His eldest son Skarp-Hedin objects that Flosi's crowd will have no compunction against burning down the building, and he proves right. Njál's sons staunchly defend their home, killing many of the attackers, but they haven't the means to defend against the fire. Flosi offers Njál and his wife leave to come outside to avoid being burnt to death, but Njál asserts that, being old and unable to avenge his sons, he would rather not live in shame, and Bergþora adds that once she was given in marriage, she promised her husband she would share his fate. The odd mix of secular and saintly elements makes the turn of the story, the preservation of the bodies, difficult to interpret as other than evidence that goodness and virtue do matter, and they preserve something essential in the human being. If we find truth in Njál's Christianity, we may read it as a suggestion of the salvation of their souls (Chapter 132 describes Njál's dead body as particularly radiant), but the text doesn't necessitate that reading—we get a symbolic hint of the end (salvation) beyond the end (their death and the subsequent end of the story). Yet the body of their loving grandson, Þord, doesn't survive the flames—curiouser and curiouser.

Gunnar Hamundarson's death makes an instructive comparison. Gunnar, a decent man, Njál's firm friend, and perhaps the greatest of the heroes of this saga, wins not only fortune and glory through his exploits, but also the dubious honor of the hand of the beautiful but untrustworthy Hallgerd. He, too, dies in an attack on his home, though not by burning, brought about partly by his fame and the jealousy of his kinsman Mord, but mostly by the feud created by his wife's ill-dealings. Mord and his band attack the home while Gunnar, unjustly outlawed, sleeps. They kill his dog, but the beast's great howl wakes the hero. The attackers approach stealthily, as Þorgrim the Easterner climbs upon the roof to determine if Gunnar is home. Gunnar strikes him through a window with his halberd, knocking him from the roof. Chieftan Gizur the white asks Þorgrim if he has found Gunnar at home, and in a line characteristic of Old Norse humor, the man replies that he doesn't know, but that Gunnar's halberd certainly is, and he falls dead. The others leap to the fray, but Gunnar fends them off three times with arrows. As they decide if they will make another assault, he, too, against the counsel of his mother, makes a tactical error, picking up one of their stray arrows and wounding one of them with it, leading them to believe that he is short of ammunition. Mord suggests they burn the house down, but the more honorable Gizur refuses. Eventually they renew their attack, wound Gunnar, and split his bow-string. Gunnar asks Hallgerd for strands of her hair to make a new string, but she refuses him because he once slapped her for theft. He continues his heroic defense without the bow, but outnumbered and with no way to keep his enemies at a safe distance, he finally falls to their blows. The people of Iceland mourn Gunnar's death, and Skarp-Hedin later seeks vengeance for it, but Njál builds a burial mound for Gunnar, setting him upright in it. A short time later two servants driving cattle past the mound hear Gunnar happily chanting verses inside it. Skarp-Hedin and Hogni, Gunnar's son, wait outside at night and see the mound open, with fey lights burning inside it. Gunnar is there, his face bright, and he chants that Hogni's father would rather die than yield—then the mound closes. The two men take Gunnar's appearance as a portent, and together they achieve their vengeance—he does not subvert, but approves their vengeance.

The Gunnar episode in a sense foreshadows Njál's death, but more exactly the latter refigures the former; between the two deaths comes the episode of Iceland's conversion to Christianity, and being undead in the old, heroic, ghostly sense has lost its appeal if not its luster. Gunnar's death doesn't keep him from urging vengeance; Njál's death doesn't keep God from using his goodness as a useful way to create a symbol of the significance of faith—even in a world that retains its belief in fate, nominally contradictory to Christian doctrine. The ends after the ends, brief though they be, provoke us to rethink the means, the ways of living and of dying.

The sagas never shirk death—one could treat endless examples of it—but they do regularly enough transgress against any notion that death means simply dead and gone.[10] The dead or otherwise mysteriously gone may return or simply hang about until others, the heroic living or the great cosmological powers, get rid of them. As Miracle Max says in *The Princess Bride*, there's a big difference between mostly dead and all dead, particularly from the viewpoint of the living. But pre–Christian survivors of death don't depend on abstract or divine powers: they follow rather than defy laws of nature that can vary occasionally from quotidian experience, particularly for characters of unusual strength, tenacity, or evil. And death looms as a natural phenomenon, not as prelude to Judgment. The eddic writers likewise maintain the immediacy of mortality, but as in Christian texts, their hints that the course of the universe moves toward cosmological destruction echo constantly.[11] The saga writers largely contented themselves with earthly ends, rather than ends beyond ends, and even the eddic poets turn their ends to elliptical new beginnings with strong hints of earthly experience about them. Imagination takes us to places of sense that help us reflect on the nonsense of the past, what bad choices and bad behavior won for their begetters. The legendary Northern obsession with death may in fact be a myth: it may instead at least partly subvert death, expressing the difficulty of a generation-by-generation struggle as an evolving culture set its sights on a more hopeful future while refusing to abandon its courageous if more reckless past.

6

Grail Quest Romances
Subverting a Happy Ending

The Grail and Tragedy

The medieval Grail quest, with its consummation in a vision of God in the holy relic, should represent the most hopeful of stories, the most satisfying of "happy endings."[1]

It should, given the largely Christian world of medieval Romance, offer an antidote to the equivocal, sad, or even tragic endings characteristic of some of the best "secular" Romances. For example, *Sir Gawain and the Green Knight* has, I think, a "negative" ending, certainly a disturbing one. Gawain returns to court alive, though chastened, but most important, at the crucial point in his adventure, he lost belief in his spiritual defenses, and the court may have missed the point of the experience entirely: they laugh, whether at his failure or in sanguine forgiveness, forget or ignore the implications of how he failed, and decide to wear the green girdle as a badge of honor rather than a symbol of how one fails when earthly fears overcome honor and spiritual commitment. *Le Morte D'Arthur* concludes with Arthur's court and all that Arthur's reign had accomplished destroyed and dissolved, with few characters left even to remember and teach the bits and pieces of good for which Camelot, at its best, had stood. Chaucer's *Troilus and Crisseyde* also comes to a depressing conclusion. While Troilus may safely sit among the clouds and laugh at silly human obsessions, still: he died in sorrow and anger; human love has failed; Crisseyde is doomed, particularly if we believe later additions to the story, to sorrow and abandonment; Troy will fall; even friendship has ended. No good at all has come from what looked to have been a promising mutual love.

6—Grail Quest Romances

Even if we keep those other Romances in mind, the Grail story has a particularly tragic ending: it shows the failure in the earthly sphere of the spiritual quest. Galahad's passing from the world leaves the audience, while not hopeless, hardly hopeful. And, worse, it shows that no matter how hard we try to master our flaws, the best of us who remain after the Best of us have left will continue to betray ourselves and fail. All but the spiritually perfect will subvert ourselves.

That reading may present a problem, but it shouldn't come as a surprise. The story of Christ, until the Resurrection, is a tragedy: God incarnates to teach and save humans, but we in our brutality and pride murder him. Any story that parallels or allegorizes that one, as so many medieval stories do, must turn at least temporarily to tragedy as well.[2]

My point holds true for those French or English versions of the Grail story featuring Perceval as the chief Grail knight, though for this chapter I'll also consider the later French and French-inspired version that appears in the *Queste del Saint Graal*, part of the *Prose Lancelot*, and Malory's redaction of that story as we find it in *Le Morte D'Arthur*.[3]

A word first, though, about the Perceval story, with which I'll deal ahead: it takes up Grail elements with Chrétien de Troyes, but reappears a generation later in the famous, completed German version of Wolfram von Eschenbach and then again in the fifteenth-century English Romance *Sir Perceval of Galles*. The character (as Peredur) in earlier versions is free of such heavy spiritual baggage; magic always tints Romance, but religion colors it variably.[4] In that third incarnation, as in the earliest appearances of the Perceval/Peredur character, the Grail doesn't appear at all. In Chrétien, however, Perceval, having arrived at the Grail castle and having watched the procession, fails his test by neglecting to ask the "Grail questions": "Why does the lance bleed?" and "Whom does the bowl serve?" The Grail then fades from the story, and so does Perceval, the poet turning the remainder of his incomplete Romance to the adventures of Sir Gawain. Wolfram transformed the Grail from a bowl into a stone, probably a figuration of the alchemist's Philosopher's Stone, though sword, lance, and dish remain as Grail-quest icons. The English and especially the German incarnation extend the Perceval story, but only in Wolfram does the knight complete the quest. However, Parzival's Grail—not just the article itself but its nature and value beyond a symbol of purity and a provider of food—while the knight and his family assume guardianship of it, remains beyond our grasp. The audience know it as something worth striving for, but we're not entirely sure why, and we gain no great insight from Parzival's having achieved it. The Grail is his quest, not ours, and its implications the responsibility of his family, not ours.

Nearly Perfect, Not So Perfect and Not at All Perfect: The Perceval Problem

After the emergence into Arthuriana of the Grail story with Chrétien, and Wolfram's subsequent fulfillment of that story's promise, the character Perceval, interestingly enough, soon fades as chief Grail knight. Once the focus of chivalric Romance turns to Launcelot, only Launcelot or his son, Galahad, may for Christian authors prove worthy of ultimate knightly achievements. Because Launcelot can't renounce Guinevere to accomplish spiritual goals himself, he must beget a son matching his own physical ability and lineage, but beyond him in purity and holiness, who can complete the greatest of all quests. Perceval remains in the Galahad-Grail story, but he takes a distant second place in quality and achievement.

While for the French Vulgate-cycle author or for Malory he at least retains his rank among the final, upper echelon of holy knights, another version of the tale maintains the traditions of his rustic education and manners and his eventual rise to significance among Arthur's knights, but drops the Grail element entirely. The fourteenth-century English Perceval Romance (the only medieval English tale to deal fully with that character) presents the familiar background and personality, but omits any pretense to his especial holiness, focusing instead on the character's emergence into potentially responsible adulthood. With Chrétien's Romance unfinished and Wolfram silent in English ears, Perceval in the later stories presents us an interpretive enigma: whom and what purpose does *he* serve? With the beginnings and thematic purposes of the stories much the same, to answer that question we may focus on the variant adventures and especially on their endings.

In this part of the chapter I will briefly explore, not as subversions, but simply as versions, the problematic evolution of Perceval through three Romances: Wolfram's *Parzival* (early thirteenth century), the anonymous *Sir Perceval of Galles* (fourteenth century composition, fifteenth century manuscript), and Malory's *Le Morte D'Arthur* (late fifteenth century). The endings of those Romances issue particular ideas and affective phenomenologies and even poignancies: despite the character's significant achievements, a reader may likely depart Perceval's adventures not with a catharsis drawn from his heroic accomplishments, nor with one from a noble but tragic failure, but instead with a disturbing sense of loss at the limitations that the worlds of the texts impose on his successes and successors. Each story subverts a closing resolution.

Parzival creates interesting metaphorical parallels between its beginning and its ending that I think illuminate Wolfram's title character and thematic purposes, with the goal of drawing from, his point of view, the emergence of a nearly perfect knight.[5] Wolfram begins with a rather cryptic allusion to his themes: "Blame and praise alike befall when a dauntless man's spirit is black-and-white-mixed like the magpie's plumage. Yet he may see blessedness after all, for both colors have a share in him" (Mustard and Passage trans., 3)—the metaphor suggests Perceval's half-brother Feirefiz, whom in Book XV he meets unknown in combat, but with whom he makes peace. Feirefiz converts to Christianity, marries a Christian woman—a Grail attendant at that—and travels to the East to fight paganism; he even begets a holy son, Prester John. As Parzival's (Perceval's) double, he also figures Perceval's own struggles with human potentials for good and evil, accomplishment and failure, immaturity and maturity. And like Parzival, Feirefiz's strength of character leads him to become a nearly perfect knight. Spotted black and white on the outside, Feirefiz represents our human variegated inside. But, inherently good, he turns his life to Wolfram's notion of the proper course for the Christian knight. Parzival realizes in Feirefiz his blood relation to all people and his responsibility to care for his siblings as knight, Christian, and Grail guardian—he makes the turn into adulthood.

Still in the early lines of the poem Wolfram promises a "word of both joy and sorrow" (4), and a "story that speaks of great faithfulness, of the ways of womanly women and a man's manhood so forthright that never against hardness was it broken" (5): happily, Parzival will break his sword over the helmet of Feirefiz, and that chance will lead Feirefiz to chivalric mercy and their mutual discovery of shared blood and shared values. "A brave man slowly wise ... from wrongdoing a man in flight" (5): such a man Wolfram proposes to describe, and those words define Parzival throughout. What, then, do the gradual unveiling of wisdom and flight from evil win him?

Unlike his father, Parzival completes his quest—he asks the question that heals Anfortas and becomes Grail king—and he reunites with his wife. He gains a brother, only to lose him again to Feirefiz's own adventures. Parzival's own son, Loherangrin, will grow to knighthood and win "praise in the service of the Grail" (429). Loherangrin, among his other exciting adventures, will eventually and oddly leave the woman he marries in Brabant because she questions him though he had forbade her to do so—a strange echo of his grandfather, Gahmuret, who also can't seem to stay home. Not only that troubling conclusion to Loherangrin's story, but even Perceval's own end leaves us with a lack of emotional closure: what good has winning the Grail guardianship done Parzival and his family at last? He has won honor and has accepted both mercy in battle and "adult" responsibility, but the Grail in this story offers no explicit spiritual fruits and no assurance that he or his kin will benefit from his achievement. Perhaps the unsettling aspect of this Romance lies in that "realistic" if inexplicit judgment: we must willingly serve, set right our mistakes, learn, accept, and fulfill our responsibilities, strive to know and be good—yet along the way or in the end things may go well or not, as Parzival's varied adventures prove. That prospect may define for Wolfram the perfect—or almost perfect—knight: that he has a good heart, uses it, and responds reasonably to what happens.

Of the three Romances Malory's *Morte* bears probably the greatest familiarity to most English and American readers, and as a part of this central clearing house of Arthuriana, his Perceval story, recapitulating that of the French Vulgate cycle with lesser emphasis on the theology, has emerged as the most familiar Grail story. The questing knights seek the cup of the Last Supper, brought to England by Joseph of Arimathea; most (like Gawain) fail miserably; some (like Lancelot) make earnest attempt and achieve at least glimpses of the holy artifact, which remains tantalizingly out of reach; three knights follow the quest and succeed, though to different levels of fulfillment.

Galahad, chief of the Grail knights, serves in the story really as a Christ-type, Jesus as knight.[6] Unfailingly pure, fully pious, devoted to this quest alone and its apotheotic ending, Galahad achieves the fullest possible experience of the mysteries of the cup, a vision of God tainted only so much as his human limitations necessitate. Despite his bastardy Galahad seems as near as a human can be to freedom from Original Sin. Galahad's having patiently awaited spiritual consummation, God grants his prayer: the great knight, by then crowned king in Sarras, receives the great vision, and he dies in bliss. He has even covered his last earthly responsibility, asking Bors to remind Lancelot of the transience of earthly life. So that we may see the completion of his journey, his comrades have a vision of his spirit's ascent to heaven. Bors, having once experienced sexual intercourse, suffers a taint of the flesh that limits his ability to reach the same the wonders as his spotless comrade—plus we need him to return to Camelot, give Galahad's message to Lancelot, and tell the story of Galahad's end. Bors, the most worldly—though not by much—of our knightly triad, will die years later, after the fall of Camelot, fighting Saracens in the east as part of the Christian effort to retake the Holy Land: notably, the ending of Perceval in our other English Romance, *Sir Perceval of Galles*.

But Perceval in Malory's tale represents a curious middle ground between Galahad and Bors. After Galahad's death here is all Malory blandly says of Perceval's end: "Thus a year and two monthis lyved sir Percivale in the ermytayge a full holy lyff, and than passed out of the worlde. Than sir Bors lat bury hym by hys syster and by sir Galahad in the spiritualités" (607). In addition to that truncated if devotional end, Perceval has probably the least successful and least laudable journey to the final Grail experience. For instance, he nearly falls into sexual sin with the lady in the black ship; by luck, as they lie naked together, he spots the red cross on his sword and crosses himself, ending her enchantment—he then wounds himself symbolically "in the thigh" so that he may remember and do penance for his folly. No wonder: the French tale from which Malory drew his own goes to great trouble to stress the irreplaceable virtue of virginity.[7] Earlier in Malory Perceval has nearly been carried off into the abyss by a demonic horse. Later, on the ship of Faith with his sister, Galahad, and Bors, he attempts but fails to grasp Hurlaine's sword, which is forbidden to anyone but Galahad, the one who shall "pass all other" knights—he should probably know better than to try.

Ultimately Perceval succeeds in the Grail quest because his purity runs deep, his intentions are good, and God grants him the grace of luck when he most needs it. He nearly fails, I think Malory suggests, because of his rusticity: he hasn't the savvy of Bors or the deeply attentive spirituality of Galahad. Finally, he's lovable, but he just isn't that smart. He remains an outsider, not of the lineage of Launcelot, like Galahad and Bors, not reared in the bosom of Arthur's court. He wins salvation, but few people in Arthur's world will remember him. His mother dies soon after he leaves her, his sister dies during the quest, his aunt, whom he meets during the quest and who offers him essential spiritual advice, has probably not survived him. Imagine the power of what he does achieve, a vision of God in the Holy Grail! And yet amidst the magnitude of the other great events of the tale, he recedes into the background, a sub-version, a less-than-perfect knight in a tale about perfection, a rather sad figure at last, I think. Yet he has a significant function: he provides inspiration to those less intelligent among the chivalric class that, with luck, they may still gain spiritual glory though, alas, they'll never be Galahad. But then who else can be?

Though it appeared before Malory's *Morte*, I place *Sir Perceval of Galles* last in the course of this discussion; Malory's tale derived from an earlier, thirteenth-century account, while *Sir Perceval* shows the knight's story entirely denuded of the Grail symbol, a later incarnation, I suggest, in the character's continuing evolution which Malory oversteps on his way back to Chrétien and the Vulgate *Lancelot*. This Romance deals not at all with issues of perfection, but more strictly with the individual's energetic but rather blundering coming of age. No notion of perfection or even almost perfection troubles the knight, nor need it trouble the reader. But like the reader Perceval must learn that actions have consequences and that responsibilities accompany experience. And though many readers may find in this version of Perceval a character with whom they can more easily relate—that *sine qua non* for many of today's students—yet the ending of the poem again begets a lingering, troubling sadness: Perceval dies fighting for something that subsequent generations lost, a fight that with historical perspective we know shouldn't have taken place at all. In the briefest of conclusions the poet explains that after the events of his poem, in which despite his limited upbringing he largely succeeds, Perceval went to the Holy Land and there won many cities, and there was he slain—an abrupt, subversive, and unsatisfying closure after the symmetrical if somewhat cartoonish events the poet has already narrated.

In this version of the story Perceval senior, an accomplished knight, marries King Arthur's sister, who bears Perceval junior after her husband has been slain in a joust with the Red Knight. Secreted away by his mother, Perceval undergoes his traditional rustic childhood, but eventually meets three of Arthur's passing knights. Drawn to their finery (and presumably by his heritage), he leaves his mother for court—she doesn't die, as the character does in Chrétien and Wolfram, but she goes mad, wandering the forest. Perceval meanwhile first finds a sleeping lady and, unbeknownst to her, exchanges rings with her. He then seeks Arthur's court and insists on being knighted. The Red Knight, who killed Perceval's father, appears at court and insults Arthur and his knights. When he leaves, Perceval chases him down, kills him with his rude staff, and takes his armor, gaining vengeance thereby. He also meets and kills the Red Knight's mother, a witch, then finds and defends Lady Lufamore from a marauding Sowdane and his army, killing the Sowdane. He marries Lady Lufamore and receives his knighthood from Arthur, but leaves his wife to complete old business that still troubles him. He finds the lady whose ring he took, returns it to her, defeats the Black Knight and reconciles him with the lady, defeats a giant, recovers his own ring, and rescues his mother from her madness. Whether he returns to his wife before further adventures, the poet doesn't specifically say: having passed the rituals of adulthood and having restored his mother, he takes up the quest of religious war and dies crusading. Without the ring that he took from the young lady, which turns out a magical one that protects the wearer from physical harm, Perceval must face the perils of the world under his own power.

The obligatory tacked-on ending perhaps fits a literary ideal of the time, but that hardly makes a fitting extension of the rest of the poem, given the near absence of religious concerns through the brunt of the narrative. Nothing in the story prepares for such an ending, other than, perhaps, that Perceval junior (as a sub-version or super-version of his father) recapitulates the err-or of Perceval senior: he marries and leaves only to find his death in honorable if unnecessary derring-do. Like his father he leaves behind a widow, and he has in fact proven his mother right: she may have done well to raise him far from the courts of chivalry. And in the long run he causes nearly as much grief as he wins glory—once again we confront the dubious ending. At least in this case his mother is better off, but for how long? And what of his wife? And once again Arthur's court has lost its best champion.

At the conclusion of *Parzival* the title character practically disappears, as the narrator alludes to the later adventures of Feirefiz and Loherangrin. The hero at least apparently remains as guardian of the Grail, whatever good that does. In Malory, Perceval, second of the Grail nights, dies a holy but unremarkable death. The end of Arthur's court remains the same regardless of the Grail Quest, and Perceval seems to have had no particular influence on anyone (beyond his sister's love for him) for good or ill. In *Sir Perceval of Galles* he departs a life of family and court to die crusading—even there, though, the author mentions no apotheosis or even epiphany, suggesting that he saw it as simply an obligatory heroic ending for a hero, a hero who, unfortunately, seems not to have learned all he should about adult responsibilities.

Finally, what or whom does Perceval serve? Sometimes God—not so much king, land, or family: while he does some good deeds, clearly he also causes a fair deal of trouble, though unintentionally. Mostly, I think, he serves himself, as youth must—aren't most of us more trouble than we're worth until we grow up? At last the Perceval stories may be mostly subversions of great knightly tales into bildungsroman and künstlerroman. All three Romances, all three equally balancing versions, thus conclude with the troubling ending that we may come to see as a classic feature of the genre and its time, a turn both realistic and boethian in a world both magical and timeless.

The Emergence of Galahad and the Next Problem[8]

Both Perceval and Gawain enter the French *Lancelot*/Malory tale as well. Perceval of course achieves the quest of finding and looking into the Grail along with Galahad and Bors, but lacking Galahad's intelligence, he doesn't achieve the full spiritual experience, which the Grail offers only to the perfect Galahad. Following Galahad's death, Perceval, having taken religious orders, must wait a year and three days to follow his comrade to death and redemption. After Galahad's death, he has no more epiphanal experiences: the Grail has departed the world with Galahad's soul, never to return again. Bors then has Perceval buried near the bodies of his sister and Galahad, but the author wastes few words on him, the chief Grail knight having achieved the goal and apotheosized. Gawain, unlike the true Grail knights, fails miserably. As a thoroughly earthly knight, and, ironically, the first to avow the quest, he engages in the search as though it involved typical errantry. He fights and even kills other knights along his way, finally learning from a holy hermit that he may as well give up and go home: he has not only sinned terribly, but missed the point of the quest entirely. So Gawain is the first to return home, unwilling to give up earthly errantry for spiritual attainment, having made the attempt, but having failed utterly, no better off for his efforts.

The Grail segment, a sub-version of the story of Arthur's world as a whole, especially in the entirety of Malory's *Morte*, grades or ranks the knights for their spiritual abilities and achievements. Gawain, a fine and worthy gentlemen (in *Sir Gawain and the Green Knight* he is the greatest of knights), yet the most worldly of Malory's knights, ends first and finishes last. Leo Durocher would nod sagely. Galahad, Gawain's super-version, joins the Fellowship of the Round Table late, for this special quest, departs it company almost immediately, ends his life along in human turns but borne up to God by angels.

The later French tale, or Lancelot/Galahad version, circa 1225 for the *Queste* and circa 1470 for Malory, has a different purpose than any of the Perceval stories of the Grail quest, and it has become, I would hazard, except for diehard fans of Wolfram or Indiana Jones, the version most readers associate with Grail Romance. Most important for my argument here: *QDSG* and the *Morte*, as segments of bigger stories, are not strictly about the Grail, nor are they really about Galahad as Grail knight; they are about Lancelot, asserting his primacy as the central knight in the Arthurian canon. The focal character of the French cycle we hardly need doubt. French tales needed a French knight as hero. Galahad, during the Grail narrative, replaces his father, a super-version to him as he is to Gawain, because of his spiritual perfection. But Lancelot again, after Galahad's passing, resumes his pre-eminence as the jewel of Arthur's court until the end of the Romance. He asserts himself repeatedly as the true super-version of *this* tale, and we must relegate the perfect Galahad to sub-version, his the religious story that rises and then fades away.

While Galahad achieves the Grail, the Grail story, like the *whole* story, isn't really *about* him; it is still about Lancelot: in the long run it has more to say about Lancelot's unsuccessful search than about Galahad's successful one. Lancelot learns that he should have achieved the Grail—he has the lineage and the abilities—but because of his failure as adulterer and sexual betrayer of his king with his queen, another knight must appear in his place to win the spiritual honors of which, by choice, he has made himself unworthy.

The only knight not merely to equal Lancelot but clearly to surpass him, Galahad, given cultural concerns of the time, probably shouldn't succeed: he is a bastard. But he is a bastard conceived for a specific, noble, holy purpose by the noblest parents around. Only Lancelot has sufficient inherent nobility to beget Galahad, and only upon the noble lady Elaine, born of the Grail family and who remains chaste after the encounter with Lancelot that results in Galahad's conception, deserves to bear him. Elaine loves Lancelot truly and faithfully, and in a less sinful world, unless he were to adhere to celibacy to win the Grail, Lancelot should marry her. His adulterous yet fully committed love for Guinevere keeps him from allowing his affections to stray even into wedded love, and his body strays from his devotion to the queen only under enchantment: the *felix culpa* that, nominally evil in itself, results in the nominal good of the winning of the Grail.

According to Christian tradition "the Lord works in mysterious ways," but the completion of the Grail quest requires three sins to produce the holy victor. Though the enchanted Lancelot thinks he is making love to Guinevere rather than Elaine, he nonetheless, probably even more, commits a sin in doing so: intended adultery rather than passionate fornication. Elaine sins twice, by making use of the enchantment and in the act of unmarried lovemaking. How does such a sinful event produce a sinless—beyond, of course, the taint of Original Sin—offspring? Despite his inauspicious conception, Galahad appears because the Arthurian authors set up the story such that no real human being, only an idealized figure all but beyond the reach of sin, can achieve the Grail quest.

Galahad's very sinlessness, the trait that allows him to achieve the Grail, removes him beyond audience sympathy, subverts his as human hero. Readers may sympathize more, I think, with Perceval, who nearly fails more than once, who loses his sister along the way, and who because of less than stellar intelligence does not experience the full mysteries of the Grail. He does as well as anyone short of the perfection of Galahad can do. We may also sympathize with Bors, who because he has had sex once may not achieve even so full an epiphanal experience as Perceval—yet we need someone to reach the end of the quest but also to return to court to tell the story. Without Bors the court has no tale, and neither have we. And who doesn't sympathize with Lancelot, in tears for a good part of the journey, able to achieve fleeting hints of the Grail's power, but so devoted to his earthly love that he simply won't give up Guinevere even after he has sworn to do so and when doing so could mean for him the ultimate spiritual experience? The movie hero, the Nobel Laureate, the Super Bowl quarterback of his time, Lancelot wins everyone's sympathy and affection because, despite his flaws, he does his best to achieve, to improve. He remains true to a doomed love, and he strives where we know he must fail, in a quest reappointed to a better soul, but one little able to inspire empathy. He subverts his own success, and in doing so he becomes, despite his almost superhuman abilities, to us fully human and sympathetic.

Galahad we admire, but he eagerly departs the world, leaving us mortals without the hope of his like; Lancelot remains, pressing on to further failures, leaving of hopeless of earthly achievement as well: when the best of us fails, how can the rest of us succeed?

Lancelot ultimately loses in the game of earthly love as well as the game of heavenly love: after Arthur's death, when he finds Guinevere in her convent, she dismisses him without even a parting kiss. He retires to die a holy man, in earthly if not Christian terms a tragic end: in the only pursuits that ever really matter to him, service to Arthur, love of Guinevere, and the desire to free himself of his sins to achieve the greatest of all possible quests, the Grail, he has failed. Lancelot may ultimately receive cosmic or Christian justice, but who can't sympathize with the sense of loss that accompanies the culmination of his life as the World's Greatest Knight? Who wouldn't shed tears, as Lancelot does, in the healing of Sir Urry?

Essentially Christ in mail, Galahad, on the other hand, saves souls, casts out demons, and devotes every ounce of his boundless energy to the holy quest, without flagging or hesitating. He achieves every step of the adventure, from the Siege Perilous to the magic ship with its sword and scabbard to a vision of God in the Grail in Sarras. He doesn't even seem to have his own Gethsemane. His skills, character, and flawless spirituality lie beyond us and beyond his father, whom he inspires only so long as he remains at least theoretically available on earth. Worse yet, having fully achieved the quest, he asks no more than to depart from the world to the presence of God—good for him, but tragic for us. We have lost our human version of Christ in the world, and neither he nor the Grail will return to inspire us. Galahad subverts human life for holy life. If we had hope that every generation or every few generations or even every century or millennium will produce a Galahad, we may wait, preparing ourselves to try to follow the ideals presented in our time to teach us how to deal with our problems. But we haven't that hope. The model, the last antitype-type, has come and gone, the relic that attaches us to the true antitype gone with him. Galahad achieves his Divine Comedy; tragedy consumes the followers of Lancelot who remain not only to fail, but to lack the icon that might otherwise inspire their own search.

Lancelot, too, despite the final act of conversion, remains an enormously tragic figure, in the Aristotelian sense: his errors set in motion the deeds that fell a great kingdom and that undermine the beginnings of an ideal, killing it before it can fully blossom and take root in the wider world.

What must Malory and the author of *QDSG* have wanted to teach us? Did they expect us to strive to imitate Galahad? Wouldn't such a goal in a sense constitute blasphemy, for the sinful soul to expect earthly perfection and the body to end in perfect epiphany? Or did they provide us a hierarchy of models, so that we can find someone with whom to relate, someone who represents an achievable yet worthy model? Without the possibility of achieving the Grail, can I become—probably not a Lancelot—a Perceval, or even a Bors? Where will my subversions take me? Without the talent and skills to become the World's Greatest Knight, I can't become Lancelot or Tristram or even Gareth, but can I get as close as possible, remembering that when I fail, I can still confess, convert, and calm down at the last? Does the Gawain of the Quest narrative, a far different character from him of the Green Knight tale, best of the knights beyond Lancelot, who fails so miserably in the quest, gain redemption at all? On the quest, unlike Lancelot, he procrastinates, puts off penance because he's too busy, and at the end of the *Morte* he falls on the battlefield to the unwilling yet stalwart Lancelot, his former best friend. Do the authors tell us that most of us are more like Gawain, with our own set of skills, knowing ourselves not quite up to the task, giving in to our sinful nature and allowing ourselves to get swept along to destruction, assisting our demise all the way?

I think such questions turn us back to Lancelot, which is where the authors wanted us to go all along. At the end of the story, his story, like that of Coleridge's wedding guest, reminds us to rise tomorrow the sadder and the wiser. I would guess that Malory wrote the story, probably while in prison, as a kind of assignment or penance in response to his own sins, to show that he could at least (and at last) understand what it meant to be a good knight.[9] Having subverted his own life with more trouble than he could handle, her wrote super-versions for his great book. The *QDSG* author may have needed or wanted to show in Galahad and Lancelot some really good reasons for *contemptus mundi*: through them we learn the folly of attachment to fleeting, earthly desires. They needed unhappy endings because they believed we need unhappy endings, at least in our Romances, to turn us from a romance with living to a love of redemption. Even knowing Lancelot's failings, they believed that the knights' bad endings might one day save readers from their own. One may suggest in that sense that the Romances, at least the later or particularly religious ones, must have no ending: the authors, seeing the world through a Boethian lens, turned the narrative gyre and subverted all other endings, awaiting the Second Coming.

7

Plowing, Bowing, Burning, Journeying
Penance and Subverting Penance in Medieval Literature

In Passes VII and VIII of the C-text of *Piers Plowman*, Piers offers to lead the pilgrims on their way to Truth, but he must first plow his half-acre. To speed their progress he requests their help; some agree, and some don't, so Piers calls Hunger upon them to urge their compliance, hoping thereby to find them more helpful to him and to themselves. To find Truth the pilgrims must show willingness to participate in their own salvation and in the general public good: as J.F. Goodridge argues, the primary need of that time, in an age barely surviving the aftermath of plague, constituted staving off famine.[1] When Hunger falls asleep, workers and wasters return to pickiness and idleness: unlike Piers, the model of both social duty and attention to the fair field of personal spirituality, they lack commitment to the physical and spiritual labors that comprise the "good life." Once he has his soil tilled, Piers will then accompany the pilgrims, but he can't acquire a full pardon for them, only a promise that those who do well, who do their part, may ultimately reach Heaven. Piers tears up their general pardon and turns aside to the contemplative life, and thus ends that vision. While the text suggests that penance entails the sacrifice one makes not just for oneself, but for the sakes of others, no pardon, as Goodridge adds, can save a "lazy world."[2] Langland's goal at this point, Derek Pearsall argues, appears rather in his (and Piers's) "endeavour ... to reintegrate the Christian community, to see the potential of the perfected imitation of Christ in every Christian life"[3]; pardon may replace penance only for those already bent on their duty, on their contribution to the welfare of the holistic community, and only if that community as a whole subverts individual pleasures in favor of mutual salvation. For Langland penance and pilgrimage retain public as well as private components. This chapter will take up the consideration of both penance and failure to do penance as subversions of narratives.

Historically and theologically penance follows and requites a subversion of self to sin: it may, for a time, as in Dante's Purgatory, circumscribe a life, containing it, disembodying it to re-embody its better essence through suffering. Purgatorial suffering, sometimes necessary but always transitional, particularly that undertaken as *satisfaction* for sin following *absolution*, led nominally and narratively to a state of bliss. Purgatory for the dead or penance for the living replaced sin, locating it spatially and temporally, for those who committed sin but did not *commit to it*, cordoning a sub-version of a life for a time determined by the sinner.[4]

As *sojourn* penance replaces a more frightening, more formidable *journey* penance: death, with a subversion of justice by *mercy*, but a mercy also subverted by interstitial pain and torment. "Motives behind [traditional] penitential practices," as the *New Catholic Encyclopedia* notes, derive from "a desire to answer the Lord's invitation to imitate Him in carrying a cross,"[5] the notion from which pilgrimage evolves. Religious judgment of penance identifies sin as a dis-ease it must eradicate without analgesic, through bloodletting and penitential amputation of waywardness. Penance as *pilgrimage* subverts penance as purgatorial sojourn: a dangerous but eroticized journey replaces a repeated or extended act of privation or an infliction of suffering by self or other, creating potential problems of *satisfaction* for the sinner.

Penance, often identified also as *reconciliation*, historically has oscillated between public and private event. Private penance increased in the early Middle Ages, and private confession gained greater importance in the process of purging sin; Christian pilgrimages to holy places began as early as the first century, and well before Augustine authorities held a penitent could receive complete remission of sin by meditating at the tomb of a martyr.[6] The eleventh and twelfth Centuries saw an increasing interest in the penitent's intention: in *contrition*, heartfelt sorrow for sin followed by *satisfaction*, the motivated physical act that replaces the eternal suffering of damnation. In the twelfth century further emphasis falls on what some scholars call "radical subjectivism," the focus of contrition fully on the individual's internal experience, plus *commutation*, allowance of individual choice in penitential activity: one may replace the intense and focused corporal punishment of earlier penitential practices with gentler alternatives, such as almsgiving or even pilgrimage.

Of course pilgrimage had its dangers: Morris Bishop paradoxically asserts, "When travel became reasonably safe in Europe, the church encouraged pilgrimages for the spiritual benefits they provided and sometimes as an alternative to punishment for misdeeds; [but] a trip to the Holy Land ensured a troublemaker's absence for a year or two and very likely forever"[7]: pilgrimage ill-timed or ill-executed might subvert life altogether. While "[p]iety and devout reverence for the sites associated with the earthly ministry of Christ had always stimulated pilgrimages," Werblowsky asserts, "there were also voices warning against pilgrimages, casting doubt on their value"— partial-to-firm warnings come for instance from Gregory of Nyssa, Augustine, and Bernard.[8] In the thirteenth century arrives the distinction between *venial* and *mortal* sins, the worst of which, if one died "unrepentant and unreconciled with the church," left one "excluded from salvation,"[9] self-subverted. Scholastics also drew distinctions between imperfect and perfect contrition and temporal and eternal punishment.[10] Duns Scotus (thirteenth century), following the legalistic tendency of earlier Scholastics, specified that the sinner "incurred a liability to punishment which remained even after [one's] receiving absolution: the "remnants of sin" remain until one has physically purged them.[11] Pilgrimage as nominally penitential activity may range from *satisfaction* indulgence to self-indulgence, and individual pilgrims may have intended acts of serious penance, thanksgiving, or self-display. Chaucer's pilgrims nominally travel to seek, thank, and honor the saint "That hem hath holpen, whan that they were seke." The knight, an experienced campaigner, fought among his battles "for our faith at Tramissene," and "Ageyn another hethen in Turkye," and in Alexandria[12]; and as for the Wife of Bath, "thryes hadde she been at Jerusalem. At Rome she hadde been, and at Boloigne,/ In Galice at Seint Jame, and at Coloigne;/ She coude muchel of wandringe by the weye."[13] Too late for Crusades, the knight still does his martial pilgrimage for the good of his faith; the Wife travels, why? perhaps in search of a new husband, perhaps as penance for killing the old ones, perhaps to consult more learned Arabs on means to kill the young husbands she couldn't dispatch with sexual excess. Such sins would of course have required serious absolution, and so a reason for Rome after Jerusalem: only a pope had the authority to grant *plenary indulgences*, those that remit the full temporal punishment incurred through a serious sin.[14] Subversion of suffering comes more happily to those with friends in high places.

Margery Kempe also journeyed on pilgrimage to the Holy Land, Rome, and Santiago de Compostella—she doesn't say why, only that "the time had come that this creature should visit those holy places where our Lord lived and died, as she had seen by revelation years before."[15] On Mount Zion she receives communion, where "our merciful Lord Christ Jesus first consecrated his precious body in the form of bread ... for in this place there is plenary remission"[16]; perhaps the journey serves that purpose, though it may as well serve, depending on how one reads Margery's adventures, as a greater opportunity for self-display on her world's holiest stage—by Margery's time *intention* rests thoroughly and more quietly at the heart of penitence. While "in the 8th and 9th centuries and even later, murderers or other capital offenders were compelled to go on pilgrimages that often lasted years ... [accompanied by] corporal punishments, in the fourteenth century Sir John Mandeville set out for the Holy Land 'to see the world.'"[17] A ninth-century Irish verse exhorts,

> Pilgrim, take care your journey's not in vain,
> A hazard without profit, without gain;
> the King you seek you'll find in Rome, it's true,
> but only if he travels on the way with you.[18]

Thomas More composed a defense of pilgrimage as late as 1529, but for those for whom pilgrimage failed, Purgatory lay ahead, the sojourn that awaited the traveler of the unsubverted and unhealed journey.

7—Plowing, Bowing, Burning, Journeying

Comparison quickly uncovers the unstable nature not only of Purgatory as a place or idea, but of medieval notions of penitence generally. Idea and practice stand at odds. Post-mortal suffering subverts the indulgence in and effects of earthly pleasure, or it may overarch living penance imperfectly done. As permanent or purgative pain, it parallels earthly act: *"Perch' io parti' così giunte persone,"* says Bertan de Born in Inferno, Canto 28, *"partito porto il mio cerebro, lasso!/ dal suo principio ch'è in questo troncone./ Così s'osserva in me lo contrapasso"*— "Because I parted persons so joined, I carry my head, parted, alas! from its source, which is in this trunk; thus one may observe in me the *contrapasso.*" Mandelbaum translates the word as "counter-penalty,"[19] but one can hardly do better than Gilbert and Sullivan's little ditty from *The Mikado*, "To let the punishment fit the crime—The punishment fit the crime." The sub-version of the crime hardly subverts restitution: it hardens the crime into a permanent, terrifying re-placement, a re-embodiment to be fully completed with the re-attachment of the earthly body at Judgment Day. Mortal penance, on the other hand, bears many sorts of sub-versions; Purgatorial penance mirrors Infernal pain in plan and intensity, but a quiet resolution accompanies it: it has its specific purpose and its specific and joyous end.

Contrapasso sub-verts the act of sin, incising the nature of sin rather than re-casting it, re-vising the understanding of its causes and effects, temporarily in Purgatory, permanently in Hell. Its envisioning by those who stand at a safe distance from its enactment, for example Dante and his audience, ranges from the morbidly humorous to the dead-serious, and one's *subjection*—though not *subjugation*—to it depends on interventive influences from the lowly to the blessed: Beatrice can save Dante the Purgatorial suffering he imagines suitable for his weaknesses, but Dante cannot save Vergil the permanent suffering his philosophical orientation has chosen. Penance, whether commuted by almsgiving or a more complete intervention of papal or Divine indulgence, has its own complex politics.

While earthly authorities may dictate penance for the living, Purgatorial penance for the dead swags between Divine Judgment and human free will. In one of the most moving moments in all of the *Commedia* (*Purgatorio*, Cantos 20 and 21), after an earthquake and a polyphonous shout of glory Statius emerges amidst the outstretched souls of the avaricious and prodigal, striding toward Paradise: he departs his penance not at God's command, but when he feels, and as a saved soul knows, his purging complete. The souls in Hell never *purge*, because they do no penance: they dwell in the permanent subversion of their sin, perfectly and horrifically circumscribed by their own choice, the self first defined by and finally enclosed by an exclusive, beloved evil.

Though the intervention of Mary and Beatrice may save him from Purgatory, nowhere in the *Commedia*—not even when he faints at the circumstances of Paolo and Francesca in Inferno—does Dante more fully feel the weight of his own sin than in *Purgatorio* 11 and 12, the terrace of the prideful, those who labor along under great boulders that direct their faces to the ground beneath them. Hearing the voice of Omberto Aldobrandesco and then of Oderisi the manuscript illuminator, Dante the pilgrim bends his own body to the shape of theirs to listen, in physical as well as spiritual empathy. In Canto 12, as Vergil hurries him along, Dante mentions that his thoughts remain behind him: he can't easily escape the sense of culpability and the need for penance, not for a beloved evil, but for one that has haunted him as it always has artists and poets. The desire for fame and to expiate received and perceived political ills lingers, requiring contrition and if not indulgence, penitence. That sin, its practice repeated over years, perhaps outweighs a largely symbolic and unconsummated (if not fully appropriate) love.

Nobody verbally constructed Purgatory more fully than Dante, yet other medieval visionaries, encumbered with frightened and variable notions of doing the time for doing the crime, found subversions of permanent or ultimate suffering in forms of penance ranging from legalistic to creative *quid pro qu*o to firmly fixed faith to rather pleasant pilgrimage to the exchange of simple if vigorous labor.[20] The notion of penance remains constant, ubiquitous; its practice or embodiment varies astonishingly with the power of the individual imagination, the power of fear to generate horrifying images, or the power of inertia to forget, deny, or readily forgive self-indulgence. Those fearsome images hardly begin or end with Dante.

7—Plowing, Bowing, Burning, Journeying

A Revelation of Purgatory by an Unknown, Fifteenth-Century Woman Visionary (1422)[21] provides another excellent example of late medieval notions of post-mortal penance. It shows that even simple peccadilloes such as over-attentiveness to eating, dress, and pets— at least for members of religious orders—constitutes seriously punishable sin. The anonymous *Revelation* relates a brief series of visions characteristic of medieval apocalypses or visions of hell or purgatory. A nun gives to her confessor an account of her dream-vision of a deceased member of her order, one Margaret by name. The dead woman appeared to her to show the seriousness of suffering that takes place in Purgatory and to beg her sisters' prayers and that masses be said for her soul so that she might more quickly find release to heaven. The nun saw three great fires in whose midst appeared "al maner Cristen men and wommen þat lyved in this world," but "men and wommen of ordyr me thogt in þat sygt þay had moste peyne."[22] In the greatest of the fires she spotted the spirit of Sister Margaret, who endured such pains as the young nun feared to describe and the fear of which led her to waken. After rising to say psalms and a litany, she tired and returned to sleep, only to see a second vision of Margaret, her skin rent and burning, fire leaping from her mouth. A small, burning dog and cat followed her steps. Margaret at first seemed to threaten the dreamer, but then she identified herself and asked the young nun to have series of masses sung for her soul to quicken her release from Purgatory, at which point the dog and cat led her back to her punishments. Margaret assured the dreaming nun that she would see her again the next night.[23] Of hell Margaret would tell nothing, other than that both in hell and Purgatory the "worm of conscience" is the worst punishment. She assured the nun that she would ultimately be led to paradise and be "washed in the well of grace and cleansed and be anointed with oil of mercy."[24]

The next night our narrator saw Margaret again, "in her worst clothes as she went on earth and in the greatest fire of the three."[25] Seven devils dressed her in a fiery red gown full of sharp hooks and encircling worms and pitch and tar, and they wrapped a great, hissing adder about her head while the dog and cat tore at her legs. A devil announced that she was suffering so because of earthly pride, presumably love of showy clothing, and from excessive love of her pets. Other devils pulled out her tongue and her heart and tore at them with hot iron rakes, explaining that they were punishing her for wrath and envy, forswearing, backbiting and slander.

Two devils then cut off her lips with razors, struck her heart with an iron hook, melted about her stinking lead and brimstone, and forced her to eat food full of snakes and to drink venom because of her gluttony, misspending, and waste. They cast her into freezing black water and then into fire, then left her covered with worms because of her sloth and gluttony. To reinforce this point two other devils poured down her throat molten gold and silver, which ran out through her stomach.

Margaret was then thrown into a great brass bath full of "al maner of stynkynge thynge"[26] for coveting and lechery, from which punishment she continued to cry horribly. The narrator notes that at that point she saw all sorts of people punished for their sins, particularly for the special sins they loved best, but those guilty of lechery suffered most, especially those of the Church, a hundred times as much as others. She spares no detail in her description of their punishments. Anchorites, both males and females, were thrust into fire, raked with hooks and sprayed with venom, and they had their heads shot through and wrapped round with adders and serpents for their having listened to "idle words" rather than "good words." Even for simply showing their faces publicly, the women had their heads covered with veils of fire.

Margaret emerged from her vessel, saying that those who had prayed for her had helped ease her pains, and she added that one does best to call on Mary and to fast according to Marian rites to win release most quickly from the pains of Purgatory. But Margaret had not yet gained freedom from suffering: flame still flickered from her mouth and heart, and the fiery animals still dogged her footsteps.

The flame, Margaret explained, resulted from her having spoken oaths, and the animals continued to follow her as a result of her too great devotion to her pets, for "sho sett hyr hert to mych on such foul wormes."[27] She added that additional masses said in her behalf and further cleansing in the two great fires of Purgatory would eventually

7—Plowing, Bowing, Burning, Journeying

prepare her for heaven. Penance involves some pain, but the main theme of *A Revelation* lies in its implied comparison of the brevity of earthly penance to the incredible horrors of Purgatorial (or Infernal) suffering. The lesser subverts one's course from the greater.

On the following night the narrator had a final vision in which a devil drew Margaret into the middle fire, where she turned from black to red, and then into the great fire, where she turned from amber to white. She told the narrator that Jews and Saracens and other heathens go directly to hell and never come to purgatory to be saved.[28] Some good Christians, she noted, those contrite folk who have done penance or those too easily shriven on earth, need not suffer the great fire, but are purged by the middle fire alone. A day of penitential suffering on earth, she added, counts for a year of Purgatory. Some pass only briefly through the first fire and then go quickly into the bliss of heaven, and some, already sufficiently cleansed by suffering on earth, may go directly to heaven. Margaret received then one final punishment, the worm of conscience, for a pilgrimage that she promised but failed to make. After that final penance, in the presence of a devil, a "fair lady" and a "fair young man" weighed her in a balance and declared her forgiven of her sins. The lady then invited Margaret to be anointed with the oil of mercy and washed in a well by a white chapel, from which she rose to enter through a golden gate into the joys of heaven.

A medieval audience would likely have seen Margaret's punishments as both just and merciful, given her release—early pardon, in fact—to heaven. Chaucer's Prioress, of whose similar sins we learn in the "General Prologue" to the *Canterbury Tales*, actually undergoes her pilgrimage; that penance—if we may call it so and if we follow Margaret's experience—should spare her that worst of punishments, the "worm of conscience," as long as she does it for appropriate reasons, for penance rather than self-display. Margaret's instruction to her sister extends for the audience a sense of subverting "justice" through penitential activity, particularly that of the living for the sake of the dead. Sadly Margaret confirms and affirms her time's deeply rooted anti–Jewish and anti–Muslim sentiments by referring all "heathens" directly to hell, beyond even the possibility of penance, and it

111

extends the responsibility of non-visionary living folk to make guesses about the status of the souls of the deceased.

Because *A Revelation of Purgatory* in many ways typifies medieval apocalypses that unveil visions of hell or Purgatory, I think one may fairly claim that audiences of the time would have seen Margaret's punishment as both just and merciful. Religious folk must attain higher standards than their lay siblings. Repentance and suffering in life and masses said for one's soul after death could relieve some purgatorial punishment, and as for the remainder, one should willingly suffer pains to cleanse the soul for entry into the eternal joys of heaven. Apocalyptic or eschatological concerns appear prominently in *The Canterbury Tales*—for instance, in the "Parson's Tale," the "Retraction," and in the very notion of pilgrimage[29]—and Chaucer as well as his audience lived in the tradition of Dante: fire-and-brimstone visions, frighteningly illuminated Apocalypses, and of course the specter of the text of the Book of Revelation itself. Keeping in mind that revelations aim to guide us so that we know how to live so that we may avoid punishment in the afterlife, and also that the literature of the Middle Ages is almost universally didactic and apocalyptic, we can read these purgatorial visions through the lens of Bosch-like parallel texts not only as an example of estates satire, but also as encouragement to avoid worldly attachments and focus instead on the joys of the life to come. Ideally one *transcends* rather than subverts suffering to reach salvation—yet an almost prurient interest in the details of the suffering seldom if ever disappears from immediate view. Medieval folk apparently negotiated the pains of pay and payback, whether coyly or forthrightly, in nearly every act of daily living. Those subversive negotiations, both personal in their individualization and matters of religious business in their textual and public representations, godfathered their understanding of the world as a place where dark presences lurked and watched. With luck and grace, or with terror and sorrow, a strong hand intervened at last.

8

Malory's *Morte*
Subverting the World's Greatest Knight

One of the thorny problems of reading Thomas Malory arises from the question of whether we should see the episodes as isolated, merely collected stories (beyond of course their essentially chronological order) or as a thematic continuum. One of the standard concerns of responding critically to or teaching Malory involves deciding which parts to consider or how to excerpt, since the *Works* (as Vinaver terms the book) as a whole rambles through many individual stories with inconsistencies in its details. One of the sticky problems of interpreting Malory requires dealing with what he did with the lives and adventures of his knights: he repeatedly subverts knighthood even as he celebrates it. He always subverts his own characters and his own stories—or, rather, the knights subvert them with unchivalrous behaviors. What was Malory doing, what is he about, and can we find any central issue to use as a guide to his *structure*? His chief concern, I believe, comes in whom he terms "the world's greatest knight" and why he does so; each major knight in turn undergoes a kind of rise followed by a subversion that disrupts the world of the Arthurian text, clipping the individual stories to fit into the scheme of the whole.

As much as one may say that the *Morte D'Arthur* is *about* anything, beyond, of course, the glories and sorrows of Arthur's rise, reign, and fall, it follows the various characters called "the world's greatest knight" in an effort to define, redefine, and solidify our understanding (and perhaps Malory's own) of how a knight attains that title. The episodic narrative recounts the adventures of those knights who receive that designation and ties the changes in what characterizes the world's greatest knight into the evolution of an Arthurian ethos. Death will eventually subvert any knight's standing, but more

Narrative Subversion in Medieval Literature

often before he dies he will self-subvert. The subversions give us almost Shakespearean character fluxes, more often tragic than comic and typically following some kind of narrative comedy with a version of traditional tragedy: a character falls as s result of his own error.

Northrop Frye wrote in *The Return of Eden* that

> [i]n Malory there is a series of graded knights, each knight being better than any other knight he can knock off his horse. Lancelot by this standard is the best knight in the world, "but if it were Sir Tristram"; the pagan knight Palomides is third, and Gawain and Gareth follow. Arthur, though, an able knight and treated with respect as a king, is by no means at the top of the list of seeded players, and if he goes into a tournament disguised and comes up against Lancelot or Tristram, down he goes over his horse's crupper [104].

Those points are true, but only partly true, depending upon at what juncture one picks up the story. Following the divisions in Vinaver's edition, one finds in "The Tale of King Arthur" Balin (and perhaps also his brother Balan) praised by Merlin: "there lyvith nat a bettir of proues, nother of worthyness." Later, even a bit player, Garnysh of the Mownte calls Balin "the Knyght with the Two Swerdis, and the man of moste proues of youre hondis lyvynge." Ironically, at the end of their adventures the two brothers, not recognizing each other, kill each other in a battle they enter disguised, not wearing their regular devices. Their sorrowful mutual fratricide has a touch of the absurd to accompany what we might otherwise call tragedy, and their battle foreshadows those between Lancelot and Tristram, Lancelot and Gareth, and among the Grail Knights. Those later battles, though, end short of the deaths of the participants—the subversion that especially marks their sub-version of the story-motif of the "greatest battle."

In "The Tale of the Noble King Arthur That Was Emperor Himself Through the Dignity of His Hands," which follows the tale of Balin and Balan, Arthur himself is addressed by King Angwysshaunce as "aboven all othir Crysten kynges for of knyghthode and of noble counceyle," and indeed Arthur accomplishes the greatest feats of any soldier in the Roman campaign, briefly earning for himself the top spot as the world's greatest knight, which allows him the respect necessary for a warrior king.

Soon, of course, Lancelot appears in the lists and wins the title

8—Malory's Morte

by general acclaim, and he proves himself *at that time* far beyond Arthur or any of Arthur's knights in prowess, though later he shares the designation of "world's best" occasionally. For instance, in "The Book of Sir Tristram of Lyoness," he labors to a draw with Tristram in the greatest battle ever fought by two knights, foretold in the very first book by Merlin. Lancelot later cedes his "greatest" title entirely to Galahad during the "Tale of the Sankgreal," only to reclaim it after Galahad's passing. Galahad makes all other knights a sub-version of his spiritual attainment, while Lancelot makes all others a sub-version of his earthly adventures, both glories and failings.

This construct explains Malory's devotion of a whole tale to Sir Gareth, a tale which appears to be of his own composition, not drawn from a source, as are so many of the stories that make up the *Morte D'Arthur*. Gareth at one point fights Lancelot to a draw and mutual truce, thus making him, at least temporarily, the equal of the world's greatest knight, worthy to be knighted by him, and worthy of at least a share of the title of world's greatest knight. Otherwise, "The Tale of Sir Gareth" may seem almost superfluous, a strange though entertaining break in the tale of Sir Lancelot or an odd but moral preface to "The Book of Sir Tristram." Yet Gareth is a sub-version of Lancelot: a better version in that he finds a proper marriage partner and remains true to her. As faithful-lover knight his story creates the super-version of Lancelot's, though in the *Works* as a whole he soon recedes to a distant sub-version of the knight of greatest prowess.

"The Book of Sir Tristram of Lyoness" is by far the longest in the *Morte D'Arthur*, perhaps oddly since Tristram has less impact than any of the other major knights on the trajectory of the *Morte* as a whole. It relates the adventures of many knights, but chiefly those of Tristram and Lancelot and how for a time they share the title. For instance, though Tristram is felled by Lancelot at the tournament at Lonezep, Lancelot on the second day gives up the prize to Tristram, arguing that Tristram has on that day performed worthier deeds. In this book also Lancelot, by means of enchantment, is induced to beget Galahad upon Elaine, who calls him the best knight in the world. Later, when Elaine visits Camelot, Lancelot is again enchanted to lie with Elaine, who he thinks is Guinevere. When Guinevere finds out what has happened and scolds him, Lancelot goes mad and disappears from court for more than two years. Presumably during that time Tristram is the world's greatest knight, and as his book closes, Sir Palomydes adjudges, "I dare sey I felte never man of youre myght nothir so well-brethed but yf hit were sir Launcelot du Laake."[1] Lancelot's "infidelity" with Elaine parallels with Tristram's with Isode: Tristram marries another Isode, "Isode of the White Hands," a subversion of his own true love, which he never loses despite his marriage. But Tristram as fully "earthly knight" never engages in a Grail Quest or its equivalent. For all its length, Tristram's tale, despite its many interesting facets, remains in the *Morte* a narrative sub-version of Lancelot's.

The stories of the loves and jousts of Lancelot and Tristram are followed, of course, by the "The Tale of the Sankgreal," which features Sir Galahad and shows him the most perfect of all knights because of his perfection as spiritual knight, the knight whom even Lancelot cannot unhorse. Having achieved the quest of the Holy Grail and having experienced its mysteries to the full, Galahad prays that he may be delivered of this earth, and, commending himself to his comrades and his soul to God, he realizes his proper end: "And so suddeynly departed hys soule to Jesu Cryste, and a grete multitude of angels bare hit up to hevyne in the syght of hys two felowis.... And sythen was there never man so hardy to sey that he hade sey[ne] the Sankgreal" (607). As the chief grail knight, Galahad shows the perfect combination of holiness, courtesy, and prowess; together they make him the greatest of the world's greatest knights. One gets the sense that the combination is one of Malory's main points for the whole of the *Morte*: a knight does not succeed by martial ability alone. Gawain may be the first of Camelot's knights to commit to and set out on the quest, but he is also the most miserably, because the most ill-suited to that quest. A martial rather than spiritual knight, he never quite gets its purpose. Even the other knights who achieve the quest, Perceval and Bors, are sub-versions of both Galahad and Lancelot: they show what lesser beings than the perfect earthly or spiritual knight can still attain, if they have commitment, faith, courage, and luck.

"The Book of Sir Launcelot and Queen Guinevere" follows the Grail quest. Sir Tristram having been treacherously killed by King

Mark, and Galahad having ascended to Heaven, Lancelot remains as sole title-holder. Bors, while he returns from the Gail quest to tell the story of it, has never ranked with those other knights Malory termed "greatest." Lancelot re-confirms himself both in his rescue of Guinevere in the story of "The Knight of the Cart" and also in another story which is apparently, despite his attributing it to a "Freynshe boke," one of Malory's own additions to Arthuriana, "The Healing of Sir Urry." This brief story has great importance in the development of Lancelot's character and for our understanding of what makes the world's greatest knight.

In Spain seeking renown Sir Urry of the Mount undertook a battle with a Sir Alpheus "for verry envy," that is, probably, because of mutual wrath. Urry kills Alpheus but receives himself "seven grete woundis, three on the hede and three on hys body, and one uppon hys lyffte honde." Because of enchantments placed upon him by Alpheus's mother, "a grete sorseras," Urry's wounds will not heal "untylle the beste knyght of the worlde had serched hys woundis." Urry's mother, sister, and page cart him through many lands with no success. He arrives ultimately at Arthur's court at Pentecost, and Arthur declares, "[H]ere shall youre son be healed and ever ony Crystyn man [may] heale hym." Arthur tries first, "nat presumyng uppon me that I am so worthy to heale youre son be my dedis, but I woll corrayge othir men of worshyp to do as I woll do." Then Malory rehearses the list of the one hundred ten knights then at court, each of whom tries unsuccessfully to heal Urry's wounds. It is no slack list, including Sir Bors, one of the Grail knights, and Sir Severause le Brewse, who promised the Lady of the Lake never to do battle with Lancelot, and who never fought against other men, but only against giants, dragons, and beasts, and Sir Lamorak, "the moste nobeleste knyght one of them that ever was in kynge Arthurs dayes as for a wordly knyght" (note *wordly*). Arthur bemoans Lancelot's absence, but then Lancelot is spotted and brought to the task. Lancelot too responds humbly to the idea that he may succeed: knowing his own failings, he feels that he dare not assert himself beyond other knights. But at Arthur's beseeching, he prays devoutly and touches each of the wounds, and each heals immediately as though it had never existed. Sir Urry rises from his bed ready for a joust, and Lancelot weeps "as he had bene a chylde that had bene beatyn!" Here Lancelot becomes, as is Galahad, Christ-like, achieving briefly a purer version of ideal knighthood. While he can't rise to Galahad's level of spirituality, the test of Urry's wounds shows him the power of the power of spiritual knighthood, which for a moment he gains, a glory beyond his other achievement—not enough, though to keep him from returning to Gwenevere.

That tale is followed almost immediately by the treacherous discovery of Lancelot and Guinevere *in flagrante delicto*, which of course touches off *Le Morte D'Arthur*, in which tale Lancelot once again and finally proves himself the world's greatest knight, finally to die a holy man. He does not match his son, but in some senses he doubles him; as Galahad doubles Christ, or becomes him to the degree that any earthly knight may, Lancelot doubles his own son, but falls back to his ways as earthly rather than spiritual knight. With the downfall of Arthur's court and the deaths of the king, queen, and the world's greatest knight, the world descends into the chaos whence it came, with only a vague hope remaining for the someday return of the king whose court harbored and encouraged legend's greatest chivalry.

In looking back over the tales of the knights, we find an immitigable pattern, beginning with Balin, whose dolorous stroke wounds King Pellam and creates the need for Galahad's accomplishing the quest of the Grail, to Lancelot, who finally abjures his sins and becomes a hermit. Balin, a wordly knight, seeks only to serve King Arthur and win honor, no mean goal, but certainly an earthly one. He dies from wounds received in a battle with his brother, Balan, when they fight not recognizing each other. The point of the equation of the names of the brothers, the fact that the names sound alike, is the suggestion that Balin figuratively kills himself—Balan serves essentially as a character double or another self—probably because his focus is earthly rather than spiritual. He does not even recognize the "mervaylous spere," with which he wounds King Pellam, for what it is, the spear with which Longinus pierced Christ's side. Balin, the most earthly of the "world's greatest knights," holds the title only briefly and falls in the youth of his service.

8—Malory's Morte

The next book—or collection of books, Works—focuses on Arthur, whom we see as a much more Christian knight, though he accomplishes his ends through battle. The *Morte* serves to point a direction for the character of the world's greatest knight and to establish Arthur as a great knight worthy to be the world's greatest king, and thus worthy of the service of the world's greatest knights. Once he has achieved his empire and essentially retired from knightly deeds to kingship, he can no longer do the deeds necessary of the world's greatest knight, and so a new figure must replace him.

There Lancelot enters, and in the next book he achieves deserved recognition as the world's greatest earthly knight. As Larry Benson points out, Malory needed "to invent a new tale of Lancelot, one that would in brief compass raise him from the relatively minor role that he plays in "Arthur and the Emperor Lucius" and establish him as the greatest of knights and best of lovers" (81). R.M. Lumiansky similarly aims to make "indisputably apparent" the book's "general unity in theme, structure, and characterization" (4) with the organizational principle being, as Mary Dichman specifies, "the pattern of Lancelot's supremacy" (75). Malory closes this third book by announcing that "at that tyme sir Launcelot had the grettyste name of ony knyght of the worlde, and moste he was honoured of hyghe and lowe." Until the very end of Malory, that is Lancelot's position: world's greatest *earthly* knight. Only at the end of the final book, "The Most Piteous Tale of the Morte Arthur Saunz Guerdon," does he become the holiest knight living as well. Having subverted himself, a sub-version of Galahad, the returns to the super-version of himself, the better version, one with earthly prowess but heavenly direction.

In the fourth book Gareth briefly matches Lancelot for martial prowess and for courtesy, and in a sense surpasses him morally and ethically, as well as according to religious law, for he successfully completes his quest and marries his beloved, dame Lyonesse. Oddly enough, marriage and settling down, retiring from errantry, seems to disqualify a knight from holding or striving for the title of world's greatest knight, and Gareth serves no important function in the remainder of Malory's work (other than that his death provokes battle between Arthur's court and Lancelot's followers). His brief stint as co-holder of the title does, though, exemplify what we might call the ideal of the "world's greatest earthly knight," someone who achieves his quest, marries his love, and remains (as far as we know) faithful to her. Gareth, both brave and true, succeeds as a knight and as a Christian, but the marital tie disqualifies him from the greatest test for a Christian knight, the quest for the Holy Grail, and it seems to sap him of the power necessary to continue to vie martially with Lancelot for the title of world's greatest earthly knight. Gareth may also serve, though, as the exemplar of married love, which is killed by adulterous love; Lancelot's killing Gareth during the rescue of Guinevere provokes Gawain's seeking revenge, which ultimately brings about the battle in which Arthur is killed and the fellowship of the round table dispersed. In that sense, one may say that Lancelot, in killing Gareth, kills a part of himself as well. Alternatively, one may argue that Lancelot, or Gareth, or even Galahad represents the problem of divided loyalties: to remain the world's greatest knight, the soldier's first loyalty must be to knighthood and his king.

Following next, "The Book of Sir Tristram" creates a major subversion or character double for Lancelot as greatest of Arthur's knights. Tristram like Lancelot possesses (and is possessed by) both great martial prowess and the love of his king's wife. But in Tristram's story I find no hint of Christian concern: he is Lancelot's *earthly* double. Lancelot at least strives to experience the mysteries of the Grail, and he fathers the knight who accomplishes the quest. Tristram, while he tries to act courteously, gives in to a moment of weakness and marries Isode of the White Hands, who was good enough to heal him, though he marries her out of gratitude rather than love and claims that as far as he knows, she remains a maid. Tristram pursues no Christian quest, though, and he apparently dies an unshriven adulterer. Perhaps that circumstance accounts for the preference that Malory seems to show for Lancelot even as the two knights share the title of world's greatest for the duration of Tristram's book. The Tristram/Lancelot double echoes Malory's theme nearly as significantly as does the Lancelot/Galahad double.

The sixth book recounts the quest of the Holy Grail, in which Sir Galahad surpasses all knights living, dead, or to come. As the perfect warrior and Christian, he fulfills, supposedly, Lancelot's potential, though I wonder if Lancelot would have been Lancelot without Guinevere. In this book we see a realignment of the graded knights according to Christian virtue rather than martial prowess. Gawain, for instance, passes out of the story quickly and brutally. We also see the greatest knightly achievement: the completion of the Grail quest, a quest for God rather than for earthly fame, though, as the greatest of the world's greatest knights, Galahad wins both, largely through freedom from anger, lust, or any other sin. The earlier "Christian knighthood" that seemed doomed by divided loyalties achieves its ideal in Galahad. Galahad embodies the super-version of the stories of knightly quests.

With Galahad's Christ-like departure from this world, Lancelot regains his old title, firmed up by King Mark's assassination of Tristram and solidified by Lancelot's healing of Sir Urry. The seventh and eighth books offer no serious challenge to Lancelot's title, and his turn to holiness following the death of Arthur and Guinevere's retreat to the convent brings him as close as an earthly knight may come to the knightly perfection of Galahad. Malory and Arthur are at last earthly rather than spiritual heroes, and while Galahad falls at the center of the *Works*, Arthur and Lancelot book-end it and draw the vast majority of human interest.

Thus we travel in our history from the earthly Balin to the earthly but holier Arthur, to the greatest of all merely earthly knights, Lancelot, to the courteous but married Gareth, to the courteous but adulterous Tristram (strange: this Christian low-point is by far the longest book in Malory), to the greatest of heaven's knights (in contrast to Tristram), Galahad, and back to Lancelot. Their concerns move from earthly to more spiritual, back to earthly, to their least spiritual point with Tristram, to their holiest point with Galahad, and back to Lancelot, who vacillates, to become holy at last. As Benson mentions, Malory's "method of invention is simple enough: a common pattern of action—a proof-of-knighthood theme—provides the shape of the narrative" (71). Malory does seem to balance his interest in romance with a dose of *contemptus mundi* or at least of the transience of this life and an interest in preparation for the one to come. I find somewhat curious that he concludes by predicting Arthur's someday return, and not Galahad's or Lancelot's, but perhaps with Arthur come all the rest, or perhaps Arthur's presence and accomplishments will always draw to him the world's greatest living knights. Perhaps Malory's own career led him to reflect on the nature of true knighthood and good kingship, especially if he saw himself as the "ill-framed" (*mal oret*) knight aiming to serve the proper king against the historical background of the War of the Roses.[2]

The construct "the world's greatest knight" provides a thread that sews together Malory's tapestry and connects each tale to the other thematically. It offers the general reader a doorway through which one may both enter and depart Malory's labyrinth, and perhaps more usefully it allows for a series of build-ups and subversions that provide a periodicity to the question of greatness: we create the idea by increments. "King Arthur and the Emperor Lucius" establishes Arthur as Christian knight and king, but once Arthur was king, Malory had to replace him as knight, following with Lancelot, and Tristram (briefly with Gareth), culminating the sequence with Galahad in "The Tale of the Sankgreal" then re-establishing the dominance of Lancelot (especially in "The Knight of the Cart" and "The Healing of Sir Urry"). The presentations of Galahad and Lancelot clash: the two knights most commonly associated with the title and best representing the struggles of the world's greatest knight as earthly and heavenly cannot long linger together. With the death of Arthur, and then with the passing of Sir Lancelot and the fellowship of the Round Table, comes the final subversion of Arthur's court as *the realm* of the world's best. Lancelot, Malory's focus even more than Arthur (probably because of his heavy reliance on the French prose *Launcelot* as well as his interest in knightly behaviors), dominates the later books. He finds parallels in Tristram, whose long book largely recapitulates and expands on the Lancelot-style love dilemma, and in Gareth, a favorite of many readers because of his virtues of patience and fidelity as well as martial skill and courage, and Galahad, too good to live as a knight of this world for long. Though this construct may oversimplify a massive and complex work, it makes as a useful reading tool, and it holds an otherwise episodic narrative together as a complete and unified work of art—despite, or perhaps because of—the repeated and powerful subversions.

Malory's *Morte* makes a curious composite of the subversive and the conservative. The most subversive of narratives in its presentations of so many versions of the Arthurian knight, it returns to thoroughly traditional themes addressing proper conduct and the supremacy of divine love and the spiritual quest (while still affirming the value of earthly quests and loves as well). Much as in Shakespeares's plays, the characters all reflect on one another in their desires and struggles and in the mortality that claims them all at last.

9

Troilus and Cressida and Subverting Genre

Here we return briefly to Derrida's "Law of Genre"; subverted Romance makes a perfect genre for experimental mixing, since Romance already blends so many elements of its own and because it easily invites parody. Postmodern notions of genre almost assume subversion as part of the process, but writers choose genres because of what the genres allow them to do: Chaucer chose Romance as his medium for the Troilus and Cressida story because of what he could do both in and with it; Shakespeare, too, would choose genre because of his company's performance needs, not merely by his own preference. In *Troilus and Cressida* Shakespeare, working out of his medieval sources, used the degradation of character, manipulation of plots and subversive elements, and the undermining of possibilities for humor to create the ultimate subversion of story, character, and moral purpose. He aimed to disrupt easy notions of romance, fidelity, and honor and mercilessly subverted artistic boundaries to bring us to a troubling distrust of stories: what if they lead us astray rather than to virtue, to doubt rather than to belief in the potential for human good? Building on Chaucer and Robert Henryson, he seems to have made a particular effort to subvert the ending of those previous versions of his story. He created a sub-version of the combined super-version he got from Chaucer and Henryson. Considering Shakespeare as medievalism-ist, this chapter will begin with discussions of Chaucer's version of the Troilus and Cressida story, then move to Henryson's addition to Chaucer's tale, and then stray into the Renaissance to conclude with Shakespeare's subversion of medieval construction of a subversive Classical story in a drama where everyone is bad and no one at all seems redeemable.[1]

9—Troilus and Cressida *and Subverting Genre*

Character Problems, Typical Scurrilous Behavior and the Subversion of a Tradition

In *Shakespeare's Problem Comedies* W.W. Lawrence suggests that the "acid brilliancy of its character drawing" in part "compels instant attention" to *Troilus and Cressida* (122). He finds Troilus and the Greek chieftains "powerless ... before egotism, selfishness, and lust" (165), and he sees in the play Shakespeare "rather analyzing life than satirizing chivalry" (170): an accurate view, I think, of a play more cynical yet than its sources. While Lawrence's metaphor implies more about how the playwright drew discrete and distinctive characters, it also suggests to me a useful term for them as dramatic characters, as subversions of anything admirable or good. What G. Wilson Knight called the "hate-theme" in Shakespeare—"cynicism toward love, disgust at the physical body, and dismay at the thought of death ... [and] a revulsion from human life" (15) plays a big part in how this play subverts the old story. Lawrence's poetic image, "acid character," fits especially well with what Shakespeare did with Chaucer's and Henryson's works; the affective qualities of the play for the reader come from the characters' selfishness, cowardice, faithlessness, and general hatefulness, and their persistent failure to do something *good.* They have plenty of others ready to subvert them, but they also have complete willingness to subvert themselves and anyone else. While the play has too limited a scope (and too distant a setting) to express a *general* hatred of life, it does collect a cacophony of "bad" characters none of which earns audience sympathy. Further, the subversion of any sort of satisfying ending troubles notions of honorable battle or love; deriving mostly from their repellent natures, the play ends not only with Pandarus plea for disease for his audience but also with a sense that everyone in the world of the text can't have gone mad because they must already have been—they were merely waiting for opportunity to leak the acid that had already tainted them beyond their ability to survive any test of quality.

David Bevington observed that *Troilus and Cressida* "ends anticlimactically, in utter disillusionment, with the senseless death of Hector, the drifting apart of Troilus and Cressida, and the continuation of the war in a spirit of blind fury"; worse yet, perhaps, Troilus laments, "The bonds of heaven are slipp'd, dissolved, and loos'd" (Act V, scene 2, line 156): the setting and content of Romance have lead to nothing, or something worse than nothing, in that the characters learn nothing, gain nothing, and can hope for nothing (Bevington 147). Acid character and bad behavior have subverted any hope for recovery in this world, turning the play away from comedy or Romance and toward tragedy. The original title calls it a *History*, probably the best choice for an audience who believed in the Trojan War as a fact even while they felt willing to allow contemporary writers a great deal of latitude for adjustment and addition. But Shakespeare subverted modern understandings history with the latitude of his adjustments and his unwillingness to allow the textual world significant admirable qualities, and he subverted the idea of tragedy by building scurrilous characters underserving of pity except as one can offer it to any suffering creature.

Those "acid" or bad characters in *Troilus and Cressida* repeatedly hoist any expectations of worthy or honorable behavior, subverting themselves and their text from comedic happy ending or cathartic tragic ending—can an audience feel better simply because the world will soon shake off the last of a bad generation? So we have any sense that the next generation will do better? The characters corrode any other characters with whom they come in contact: no one in the play makes anyone else any better, and nearly everyone makes other characters worse, and no one looks kind or sensible enough to give the world children who will improve it. The reputation not only of Cressid, but also of nearly every character in the play, plunges, leading Bevington to judge that "Shakespeare's task, as dramatic artist, is to deal with this fallen reputation" (34). Fallen reputation is a common kind of subversion—Shakespeare focused on it again specifically in *Othello*—but then we must wonder where it leads. If the characters lack sufficient grandeur or appeal, it doesn't make for tragedy or Romance; if they're not funny it makes for melodrama rather than comedy, and so it will have difficulty building any long-term effects. In the simplest terms, tragedy is scary, Romance is exciting, comedy is funny, and history is true: this play subverts every one of those options.[2]

9—Troilus and Cressida *and Subverting Genre*

Shakespeare's work often affirms Horace's notion of poetry as "sweetly useful," but we may wonder about the useful of a play with no redeeming characters. Can we find it in an acknowledgment of the bitter truth of scurrilous actions? Anne Barton has observed, "Its unconventional form, neither comedy, tragedy, history, nor satire, its intellectualism, savagery, and disillusion speak forcefully to contemporary audiences naturally skeptical about ideas of honor, nobility, and military glory" (443)—practices common enough in modern or postmodern art—but Shakespeare's audience still devoured work that taught the value of moral lessons, patient suffering, redemption, exemplary behavior, even if cast in relief by their opposites. They and the next few generations firmly believed in following traditional form and genre: note for instance that Dryden called Ben Jonson the more correct poet because he more exactly followed Latin models, and Samuel Johnson condemned Shakespeare's pleasure in puns regardless of the vehicle. We must wait until the eighteenth century for extensive experimentation in genre, but Shakespeare as a playwright had already grown to feel comfortable subverting genre for the sake of what he wanted a play to do. He must have found from experience that his audience cared more about the complexity of thought and character than they did about Classical correctness. He may have wondered, too, how far he could push the idea of hateful Classical characters and still compose a play worth an audience.

With the exception of Thersites Shakespeare used noble characters in *Troilus and Cressida*, but they all think poorly and act badly, even worse than in his antecedents, and in his play we don't see their endings. Chaucer shows Troylus dead but happy, and Henryson shows Cresseid alive but diseased and rotted beyond recognition. In Shakespeare the rascally Thersites serves better than anyone else as a voice of wisdom in the play, since he unabashedly lampoons the other Greeks about their flaws, but his wisdom suffers from cynical meanness, perpetual cowardice, and a nearly exclusive reliance on insults to make his points. He may seem funny (in a Don Rickles sort of way) until we realize that he slices right through the façade of nobility straight down to nasty truths about violent, arrogant, adolescent bullies and shameless, faithless women and men. He falls into sarcasm rather than satire: the characters are so bad that the audience can hardly use them as a means to improve our own moral fiber. The Classical sources were supposed to have given us at least a sense of positive growth: Achilles grows from a pouting boy to a man with the capacity for compassion, and Odysseus applies his ability to think and scheme to return to the family who still love and need him. Shakespeare subverted our too easy willingness to see goodness in a ten-year war that, coming from a kidnapping, should never have happened: even once the war has begun, the return of Helen could have ended it. Shakepeare's time knew too well the horrors of war into which men eager for gain or glory so easily throw themselves and others.

Chaucer and Henryson

The Cressid story comprises only a small part of Benoît de Sainte-Maure's *Roman de Troie*, and Chaucer takes up the story at a different point and added considerably to what appears there. Chaucer followed the plot of Giovanni Boccaccio's *Il Filostrato* pretty closely, but he changed the tone, the themes, and the kinds of virtues and failings that he wanted to treat. From Benoît, Boccaccio had built a superversion of the story; from Boccaccio, Chaucer created a parallel version: less misogynistic, more humane. He must have admired both sources, but wanted a poem with a very different feel—not a positive as opposed to a negative result, but one that allows for a redemptive spiritual turn.

Chaucer had treated Criseyde's character a good deal more gently and sympathetically than does Shakespeare: Troylus must win her, and the fourteenth-century version hasn't quite the rapid and obvious responses to him and to the Greeks as does the seventeenth-century Cressida. While not *saying* strictly so, Chaucer, less sympathetic to Troylus than his sources, depicts Troylus both in action as a liar and by metaphor as a rapist (*raptus*), a hawk that grasps an innocent lark (Cressid) in its talons (Book 3, lines 1191–92). He shows Criseyde's problem largely and to some extent reasonably as *fear*, which more

9—Troilus and Cressida *and Subverting Genre*

than any other thought or emotion guides her actions. As the Romance ends, she is in the process of failing in both loyalty and chastity: circumstance and fear have subverted her loyalty and fidelity. Troylus acts throughout, though, on what we may call violent attraction. Having at the beginning of *Troylus and Criseyde* made fun of love and lovers, he falls irresistibly for Criseyde: fate, chance, or the gods subvert his pride in his own chaste thoughts. Troylus achieves Criseyde's body in an image of violence, and at the end of the poem he dies in the mindless violence of battle. The poem ends in an incongruous but hopeful lesson, in Troylus' looking down from heaven and laughing at the sad absurdity of human folly—the poet hints by extension that we may learn the same lesson and save ourselves a good deal of trouble, subverting our own potentially violent and feckless affections. Chaucer's narrative is gentler—both gentler and more gentile—than his sources or those works he influences.

Henryson's *Testament of Cresseid* deals with the aftermath of what both Chaucer's and Shakespeare's works show us. Where he picks up the tale, Troilus has recovered a bit of his soul if not his heart, while Cresseid has lost heart and body and retains only the merest hold on a thread of soul. The gods have punished her for failing to sacrifice to Venus and Cupid and for bewailing how they have failed to reward her devotions. They curse her with leprosy, and so she loses both the quality that attracted Troilus to her in the first place, her beauty, and any hope that the Greeks, who have just used her anyway, will give her further notice. Henryson's Cresseid has failed in troth, chastity, and piety, and she has no expectations. Her former lover's failing to recognize her when he sees her, as she searches the battlefield for trinkets left on the dead bodies, constitutes the moral power of the poem: for divine and human alike, she has dissolved away, any hope subverted by her failure to keep troth. In his approach to Cressid Henryson went back to Boccaccio more than did Chaucer, and he re-set a course that Shakespeare continued, of subverting any notions of good in the story. Henryson concentrates attention on "fals Cressid and trew knicht Troilus" (145), as Haydock shows, and his poem "weds the repletion, disfigurement, and infamy of ancient satire to penitential regimes for the satisfaction of sin"

(150).³ Henryson's Cressid still attracts some sympathy, but hardly what Chaucer aims to arouse: Chaucer saw her as pitiable and cast her story much more as a horror in the midst of a pitiless war.

Where Shakespeare takes up the action, Troilus and Cressida have already fallen in love, or what in the play must pass for love. Troilus complains about their situation, and Cressid refuses to admit to it—she simply does not want to deal with it. Quickly we learn that neither has a particularly admirable character, and neither attracts much if any sympathy. Shakespeare, however callously he depicts the characters, packs the play with nominally comic scenes, but they only darken the world of the play further. The Prologue identifies the "princes orgillous" (line 2), recalling Spenser's prideful giant in Book 1 of *The Faerie Queene*, and notes how "their high blood chaf'd" has caused the circumstance of war—not a very good reason, thoroughly subvertable by logic, though we are more than two and half millennia too late for that. After we meet an unappealing Troilus and Pandarus, scene 2 shows Cressida repeatedly saying insulting things about Troilus as Pandarus tries to broker their love. Cressid even calls Pandarus a "bawd" (line 281), but that doesn't stop him, and it doesn't stop her. The third scene takes us to the Greek camp and Ulysses' overzealous defense of degree. We learn that Patroclus does funny imitations of the Greek commanders, that Hector has medievally challenged the Greeks to send a single combatant against him, and that Ulysses will adopt wiles similar to those Pandarus uses to win Cressid for Troilus so he can help the Greeks get Achilles back into battle again: a series of subversion that have little if anything to do with the problem that has caused the war in the first place.

Act II begins with Thersites railing at Ajax, literally proclaiming him "fool" (line 25); most versions of the Trojan War story show foolish elements in Ajax's personality, but this one has Thersistes to make them public and obvious. In II, 2, Hector argues that the Trojans should simply let Helen go and so end the war, but Troilus argues him into believing that honor should prevent them from doing so—even Cassandra's warning cries don't reach through their courtly dispute. The third scene again features Thersites' insults, this time directed at Achilles and Patroclus rather than at Ajax. Ulysses whips

9—Troilus and Cressida *and Subverting Genre*

up Ajax's anger at Achilles' pride. These scenes subvert expectations of mutual respect or heroism.

Act III, scene 1, begins with silly "comic" dialogue between Pandarus and a servant and continues with a sickeningly satirical exchange between Pandarus and Helen and Paris. In the course of a little over a hundred lines the word *love* appears eighteen times and the word *sweet* nineteen times; some of the language echoes that of Shakespeare's sonnets, but in this context it rings of insincerity. The scene ends with the opposition of love and thought, an idea with a history, but one that subverts them both. In III, 2, as Pandarus leads Troilus to Cressid, Troilus asks him, "O, be thou my Charon,/ And give me sweet transportation to these fields/ Where I may wallow in the lily-beds/ Propos'd for the deserver!" (lines 10–13)—the metaphor subverts a love encounter with a death image.

No one has behaved well enough to deserve something good; Troilus, too, is clearly thinking of himself and not Cressid. Pandarus begs, or requires, of Cressid that "if my lord get a boy of you, you'll give him [to] me" (lines 104–105), as if he were some sort of Merlin preparing for Troy's better future: his motives are also selfish. Cressid admits that "to be wise and love/ "Exceeds man's might" (156–57), reinforcing the theme of the previous scene. Each character subverts anything we could reasonably call love. Scene three shows Calchas arranging for the exchange that will bring Cressid from Troy and the Greek princes showing their mock-scorn for Achilles. Ulysses observes that virtue is its own purpose, but we don't learn it, since no one in the play shows any virtue. With the subversion of plot and character comes the subversion of virtue as well.

Act IV begins with dialogue between the Greeks and Trojans about the exchange, including jokes about Helen as whore and Menelaus as cuckold. Aeneas indicates pretty clearly that everybody already knows about Troilus and Cressida's "secret" romance. IV, 2, has Pandarus joking with Cressid even as she's about to be exchanged and Paris in a horrifying irony telling Troilus he should willingly give up Cressid for the good of Troy: he subverts his own circumstance without even realizing it. In scene 3 Paris hurries Troilus to give her up and adds, with teeming irony, "would, as I shall pity, I could help" (line 11). In IV, 4, Troilus and Cressida repeatedly exhort each other to remain faithful, and they exchange favors in a reverse of chivalric tradition: he gives her a sleeve, and she gives him a glove. They reverse roles. Troilus will later see Diomed with that sleeve, sparking in him a monomaniacal hatred. The glove, normally a symbol of the knight's strength and martial endeavor, serves here as a symbol of Cressid's pledge of fidelity, which immediately fails. The sleeve, normally a sexual symbol in that it shows the woman's devotion to the man, passes from the sexually faithful man to the disruptor of fidelity, Diomed. And even though we must call Troilus sexually faithful to Cressid, he still exploits her and turns from loving her to lusting for battle. Love, promise, custom: everything in this world falls in a series of subversions as all turns to emptiness and chaos.

The notorious scene 5 shows Cressida arriving at the Greek camp and immediately exchanging kisses with the Greek princes. "[H]er wanton spirits look out/ At every joint and motive of her body" (lines 56–57), Ulysses observes, and eight lines later, at the sound of a second trumpet flourish, all the men exclaim together, "The Troyans' trumpet," an obvious pun hinting that they all see Cressid as Troy's strumpet, their lower-class version of Helen. They will subvert her love for Troilus and for Diomed, and later, according to Henryson, they'll pass around as they please, a narrative turn subverts Romance and History into modern tragedy.

Hector arrives for single combat with Ajax, and the two men make one pass. Hector doesn't try very hard, and Ajax appears to be winning—he even says that he would willingly have killed his adversary—but Hector subverts the fight, arguing that cousins shouldn't harm one another. Once Achilles has sized up and threatened Hector, they all repair to dinner, except for Troilus: he asks Ulysses to take him to see Cressid at Menelaus' tent.

As Achilles plots Hector's death for the next day, and Thersites harangues Patroclus, Achilles, Menelaus, and even Cressid (the "Troyan drab," Thersites calls her in 5.1.96), Diomed is already seducing Cressid with Troilus and Ulysses looking on. Ulysses fans the flames of Troilus jealousy: this brief moment of peace is no more than a sham. Even Cressid notes that "The error of our eye directs our

9—Troilus and Cressida *and Subverting Genre*

mind" (line 110), and Troilus in a long lament suggests that "This is, and is not, Cressid!" (line 146): she is a subversion of the self he knew, no longer his idealization of her, and Troilus is also now himself, neither her nor his idealized Troilus. Cressid laments that the mind is too easily swayed even as Troilus hopelessly suggests that the heart must believe despite the evidence of eyes and ears. Even Ulysses' nominal comfort serves only to weaken another of Troy's greatest soldiers. In scene 3 shows Troilus receives through Pandarus a letter from Cressid; he shreds it without reading, and what he mutters recalls Hamlet: "Words, words, mere words, no matter from the heart" (108). He subverts all the words he has spoken of his own love and care for her even as he fails to recognize that she is living in a hostile camp and has no control over her own safety.

In a brief scene 4, Thersites on the battlefield continues his torrent of insults, is confronted by Hector, and begs off fighting because he is only a "filthy rogue" (line 29): he must subvert his own honor before the Trojans just as he does before the Greeks. In scene 5 Diomed has won Troilus' horse on the battlefield and, speaking to his servant, reveals that he knows of Troilus' love for Cressid: he thereby subverts his own honor, too, identifying himself as a cad. In scenes 6 and 8 Hector and Achilles meet in battle, and Hector gains the upper hand, but when he pauses to rest, the lurking Achilles and his Myrmidons slaughter him; like the other characters, they have no honor, either. Those scenes sandwich another of silly comedy with Thersites again begging off battle, this time because he has met a "bastard" like himself, and bastards should stand up for one another. Few if any honorable actions interrupt the miserable behavior; subversion takes over the battlefield as it does the bedroom.

Scenes 9 and 10 show the retreat from battle, the spreading news of Hector's death, and Troilus' dismissal of Pandarus with a slap. Pandarus gets the last word, bequeathing to all who like him "trade in flesh"—and perhaps to the audience in general—his sexual "diseases." Actors and even the author himself subvert the relationship between play and audience—would anyone return for a second performance after an epilogue like that? Any audience member—not just those with sexually transmitted illness—who believes in the glories of battle, the acceptability of faithlessness, the propriety of secret love affairs, the willingness to put aside honor for political purposes, and the intelligence of those who insult others for pleasure suffers from the diseases that Pandarus bequeaths. Those diseases subvert the world of the play, and Shakespeare makes that subverstion the central topic for public discussion. Each scene presents its own kind of subversion, undercutting love, wit or humor, courage in battle, nobility—anything the play offers.

The coarse humor of the play, the greater cruelty than we find in Chaucer's tale, the seeming abysmal pessimism with respect to human nature: all turn on the pun that identifies Cressid as strumpet and subverts her as a woman. Her acid character doesn't in itself ruin Troilus, but it certainly does not save him from his own contemptible rashness and selfishness. Thersites has verbal wit and identifies the problems of the world: he makes plain its perversions and subversions. Hector's death at the hands of a dishonorable Achilles and his mob undercuts any potential humor in the Greeks' plottings: it subverts the notion of achieving honor as a reason for battle. We fight more for our own vanity than for any honest cause. Once we believe Cressid a simple strumpet and no more, and reflect in the same sense on Helen, we subvert the entirety of the Trojan War epic ethos; we subvert Romance, we lose tragedy, and we make comedy impossible. The play provides a positive theme only in the form of an opposite to all that is says and shows: all we can do in this world is to try to behave more bravely and generously, stay truer, avoid dissembling and others' wiles, and show compassion rather than egomania. The play, which proudly and almost obnoxiously subverts all genres, tells us that in a world of problems we can't avoid confronting them, and we may not have the strength even to mitigate them; we can prepare for them and resist giving in to them, and we *can* act better than we do.

In a recent and excellent book on Henryson's *Testament of Cresseid* and its analogues, Nick Haydock observes in *Troilus and Cressida* an "elimination of catharsis" (249) and s persistent attention to a "degrading [of] rank and deflating [of] overblown egos" (263), a "suppression of the distinctiveness inherent in particular examples of

9—Troilus and Cressida *and Subverting Genre*

generic errantry" (247).[4] The play shows clearly where the human problem lies and exactly how powerfully it can act; in this case the subversion of genre appears also as a subversion of each successive character. Shakespeare's play proves troublesome emotionally as well as interpretively because even what we thought we knew of his story and characters suffers moral and affective subversion. Louis Wright and Virginia LaMar assert that "[t]he Elizabethans, who thought of the Trojan War as a genuine episode in ancient history, probably regard *Troilus and Cressida* as a chronicle play" (255); that idea makes good sense generically, but Shakespeare charts a more complicated emotional course that extends to subvert the whole of the Troy story. So different from its sources, it can't be history; it lacks moral instruction except in its briskly negative examples; its heroes don't behave admirably. Beyond that, even, this little sub-version, to turn even the traditionally admirable parts to vulgarity, subverts the whole of the ongoing Trojan literary enterprise. Harold Goddard notes its "debunking" (i.e., subversion) of the heroic and romantic ideal, hardly appropriate to its likely audience (probably the "barristers at one of the Inns of Court") (2), suggests the "annihilating power of this play" (3–4), and calls it "the most intellectual play [Shakespeare] ever wrote" (4) and, along with *Measure for Measure*, one of only two Shakespeare plays we may call "didactic" (3). Didactic, yes, but in what it doesn't show rather than in what it shows. Whatever *Troilus and Cressida* teaches, it does so in a peculiarly difficult way. It foregrounds out-of-control excesses, making it typically Ovidian, and it sucks the substance out of naughty jokes and insults. Faith and honor give way to the weakest cajoling, making them all the more important in life—and all the more valuable and admirable. Chaucer's Romance and even Henryson's portrait of a lost and decaying Cressid disappear in the language of lies and vituperation: railing replaces love-language, convenience replaces love and heroism, and icy pragmatism replaces compassion and even genuine sexuality.

Probably partly because of the switch from textual Romance in Chaucer and moral epic-epilogue in Henryson to stage production in Shakespeare, no stirring adventure occurs in *Troilus and Cressida*. The soldiers bollix the battle scenes, and the lovers immediately subvert the love scenes, and this world has no magic of any sort. No prayers, services, or religious appeals redeem this world from itself. The play parodies Romance in the vision of an empty world with nothing worth doing, no one worth loving or fighting, and no means to transcend the horrors of how human frigidity. It thoroughly subverts ideas of goodness in human character. It may, though, catch the conscience of its audience: this hardly sweet diversion has the usefulness of showing a world and a species with a potential for good and an unwillingness to express it. Neither Troilus nor Cressida acts lovingly or nobly. Achilles is a pampered, murdering gang leader with no sense of honor. Ajax is even dumber than he is in Greek and Latin sources. Hector, a minor character in the play, subverts his own sense of honor in battle or in policy, and he dies after stupidly disarming to rest right in the midst of battle. Cassandra warns characters of their danger and folly, but they ignore her, subverting the amazing opportunity to take advantage of trustworthy foretelling. Repeated subversions of any hope we may have for goodness retard any likelihood of catharsis, so the play has little purpose beyond making fun of tragedy, Romance, comedy, history, and anyone willing to believe in any of them. Shakespeare's straying from the story's history and its precedents subverts the play's Classical roots, dumps it into the slough of early Renaissance modernism. As a subverstion of comedy the play also hits a significant mark: as with *A Midsummer Night's Dream*, *Much Ado*, *Measure for Measure*, and even *Twelfth Night*, subversions of a happy ending undercut a comic catharsis, too. The almost exclusively nasty humor shows how joking doesn't fit the seriousness of the subject matter: prolonged war, dishonorable behavior, destruction, infidelity, extreme egotism, and loss followed by loss find no relief or alternative in humor that doesn't aim to heal. The play comprises the ultimate subversion of what drama "should" or can do. It presents unpleasant plot, characters, and setting with no thought of or hope for redemption for any of them. It gives us humans at somewhere near our worst. It subverts us almost as much as it does itself.

    Troilus and Cressida shows how we take insufficient advantage of our potential for good and maximize our potential for evil; such choices we can chock up to the lingering horrors of war, or we can face the evil aspects of our nature, subdue them, and make moral and ethical choices instead. This play deals with how we subvert ourselves in ways far worse than difficult situations subvert us; we must fall back on poor us of free will and subsequent bad behavior as the cause of most of our ills, and we must attribute the subversion of the better parts of ourselves and our world to our own weakness and sinfulness. Here the "moral" comes from exclusively bad examples.

Shaping Shakespeare's *Troilus and Cressida*: Subverting Antecedents

The evolution of the medieval to the Renaissance Troilus and Cressida story, from Chaucer to Henryson to Shakespeare, produced not only the obvious changes in genre, plot, and tone, but also some notable differences in what and how it subverts. With broadly stroked yet significant emotional shifts, even something as simple and direct as theme or didactic purpose changes significantly. All three texts address the problems of failed courage and *trawþe*. Because of changes—toward greater extremes—in plot and character, and because the three works take up the plot at different points, the developing dramatic tensions vary quite a lot. Henryson's *Testament* adds to while Shakespeare's play strays from their source in Chaucer, and each creates in its own way an especially disturbing emotional and aesthetic experience. Having read the poem, who can forget the scene of the oblivious Troilus tossing a bag of gold to the mutilated Cressid? The play, though it comes last in chronological order of composition, falls in the middle of the plot; it aptly fills the gap (interverts?), showing how and why the kinder Cressid of Chaucer could become the moribund, disease-riddled shadow of the *Testament*. Chaucer shows the sorrows of clinging to this brief and undependable life; Henryson shows a memento mori of the passing of sexual love; Shakespeare subverts the entirety of the human endeavor when we miscolor it with war—we have much more to worry about here than winter and rough weather.

Together the three pieces yield an unexpected but certainly a worthy consummation to thoughtful explorations into how broadly a single story can change in the smithy of writers with the same material in hand but different motivations at heart. Given a genesis in sexual frailty, a subject as sure to raise consternation in Shakespeare's time as in Chaucer's, the Troilus and Cressida Romance deconstructs courtly love expectations, but for Shakespeare it allowed room to subvert his tradition and so leave his audience with rather different moral, aesthetic, and philosophical problems to solve.

Though the "story" began properly with Benoît de Sainte-Maure's *Roman de Troie*, it gained no significant steam until Boccaccio's *Il Filostrato*, where a strong autobiographical influence of youthful disappointment laces it with male complaint at female infidelity—a product far less worthy of detailed attention in its simplicity and relative puerility than Chaucer's more compassionate version. Its thematic focus and narrative rhythms change markedly in subsequent incarnations, Chaucer's by far exhibiting the most varied and generous sympathies and most thorough and nuanced character development, at least for the two principles.

Chaucer's characteristic subversion of simple readings helps his refiguration of Boccaccio by means of expanded emotional incongruities, a turn that Shakespeare later intensified. As he begins, Chaucer's narrator observes (Book I, lines 13–14 and following) that it suits well "A woful wight to han a drery feere,/ And to a sorwful tale, a sory cheere": a woeful person will probably have a gloomy companion and a sorrowful tale shall have a sad tone—that tone subverts any joy the reader may bring to the work at its outset. He tells Troilus's "double sorrow," yet asserts that if his telling may "don gladnesse/ Unto ony lovere," that Cupid has his thanks—how can a gloomy tale possibly bring joy? The Muse he invokes, oddly enough no Muse but the Fury Tisiphone, "the punisher," in Greek myth, sees to it that spirits enter the Underworld, particularly Tartaros when appropriate—an authorial choice that better fits a curse than a request for aesthetic inspiration. "By his contrari is everything declared," says Pandar, and the tale functions by a series of opposites, doubles, comparisons, and subversions. Weakness tames pride, and the plot turns on no emotion

9—Troilus and Cressida *and Subverting Genre*

so much as fear: Troilus fears telling his love, Cressid fears returning it, Pandar fears if she doesn't, Cressid fears the Greek camp, Troilus fears she won't return, and one has a hard time believing that Calchas has left Troy for the sake of prudence rather than fear. Chaucer begins with a symbol of terror and subverts a would-be love story into a debacle of loss the echo of adolescent melancholy.

The middle of Chaucer's tale, Book 3, invokes a seemlier Muse, Venus, and then follows with a second, of Calliope, the Muse of Epic poetry—an odd second choice, too, as the subject deals with a nascent and somewhat adolescent relationship: Troilus begs only a kind glance and Cressid's willingness to accept his service, and Cressid begs that Troilus respect her honor. Odder yet for a Romance, the whole of Book 3 leads through male trickery to what amounts essentially to Cressid's rape, a clear subversion of Troilus' supposed willingness to protect her honor. Cressid then ironically pledges her fidelity, subverting what should be outrage for what Troilus has done. By the end of Book 3, one has a hard time retaining sympathy for anyone in the text: the love affair has reached physical consummation, but at the expense of everyone's honor. Book 4 begins with a turn of Fortune's wheel. Again the narrator invokes Furies—all three this time—as well as Mars, Venus' less appealing consort. The plot turns to Cressid's exchange for Antenor, who according to medieval tradition later betrayed Troy, a subversion of an action the Trojans thought to their advantage. Cressid will fall to infidelity through fear, and Troilus will tumble into despair through loss, both damnable sins to Chaucer's audience. No respite eases the general infidelity of this world that tolerates if not builds the foundation of its art on the kidnapping of Helen.

Troilus and Criseyde ends with more subversion, with a further downturn of Fortune's Wheel: Hector is killed through Achilles' treachery, Cressid fails to keep her troth, shame silences Pandar, and Troilus dies at Achilles' hands. Then comes an improbable turn: Troilus ascends to the happy Seventh Sphere of Heaven, where he looks down on the vanities of human life and laughs.[5] "Go litel bok," says the narrator, in both a tonal and factual irony, as he asks that next time God send him a comedy instead of a tragedy to write. Seek divine rather than human love, says the voice, though fidelity to either seems to produce desirable results in the next life if not in this one. The closing subversion turns the story from hell to heaven, as the poem turns about-face from the narrative and emotional trajectory that has come before. Even the brief love scenes lack any sort of emotional satisfaction; they lack any sense of chivalry because they derive from schemes and pimping rather than any dependable demonstration of love. Yet Chaucer manages sympathy for everyone: he explicitly excuses Cressid because of the frightful subversion of her circumstance—how could anyone feel anything but terror there, a lone woman being turned over to a camp of bitter, angry, lonely soldiers? He shows Pandar recede into his own shame, his scheme, whether to help his friend or gain influence with him, subverted—though Pandarus doesn't turn as bitter as does Shakespeare's version. He redeems Troilus despite his dishonorable wooing and battlefield anger. The same loopy congeniality of the *Canterbury Tales*' narrator appears in the Romance, omitting Boccaccio's bitterness and falling well short of Henryson's stricter moralizing. Chaucer's tone never subverts the sense that we may find some good in this world and certainly in the next; Shakespeare's never subverts the sense that we may not find good anywhere.

Henryson's unabashed didacticism gives way occasionally to hints of compassion, but their emotional effects never subvert his sense of moral judgment. The sorrow of the final confrontation between the two former lovers places the poem emotionally midway between Chaucer's and Shakespeare's, without Chaucer's explicit urging to forgive, but short of the general condemnation Shakespeare's play demands. Critical responses to "The Testament of Cresseid" have varied widely, particularly with respect to how harshly the pagan gods judge Cressid: they curse her for her complaints by infecting her with leprosy. The disease allegorically punishes her blasphemy and her sexual excess. In Christian terms we may see Cressid's error as a self-subversion, a failure to accept fully the sacrament of confession: as Robert Kindrick observed, Cressid "does not look inward to find the cause" of her woes.[6] Henryson asserts that "Ane dooly sesoun to an cairfull dyte/ Suld correspond"—a mournful poem should fit a sad

9—Troilus and Cressida *and Subverting Genre*

season (or situation)—and he proclaims his poem a tragedy. The narrator reflects for a time on the nature of romantic love, especially for old men, though he claims to know well what it means to both old and young. He sits by the fire and takes a drink of "spirits," reads first from Chaucer's *Troilus and Criseyde* and then from a second book "In quilk I fand the fatall desteny/ Of fair Cresseid, that endit wretchedly." So he begins his narration with how Diomed satisfied his appetite for the lady, then sent her off, after which she became a "court commoun." Henryson adopted a Chaucerian motif, how the sorrowful one finds comfort in a sorrowful story, but then built his own addition partly from Chaucer's foundational sub-version and partly from Boccaccio's. Unlike Shakespeare, whose plot begins with trepidation and moves to erotic passion with little if any love behind it, Henryson begins in sorrow, after his characters have used or been used up. His mood and tone lament his own sorry, human infidelity, the personal tragedies wrought by war, and sad and sometimes horrific afflictions that life casts on the weak and fearful.

The movement of Henryson's poem increases Cresseid's misfortune: he deals with her more fully than do either Chaucer or Shakespeare. "Quha sall me gyde?" she asks, then curses the gods: "O fals Cupide, is nane to wyte bot thow/ And thy mother, of lufe the blind goddess!/ 3e causit me alwayis understand and trow/ The seid of lufe was sawin in my face.... Bot now, allace, that seid with froist is slane" (ll. 133–39), and so she sets up the curse that follows. In nearly the exact center of the poem, Saturn and the Moon reply: "For the dispyte to Cupide scho had done/ And to Venus, oppin and manifest,/ In all hir lyfe with pane to be opprest,/ And torment sair with seiknes incurabill,/ And to all louers be abhominabill" (304–308.) They have no need to "change her mirth to melancholy," since her life has already fallen apart, but, being pagan gods, they subvert her further. The greater sorrow, however, may attract more pity and reinforce the need for the patient suffering that must follow sin and subversion of worldly hopes.

For Cressid one further subversion awaits. One day on the field Troilus passes her and other lepers, who call out for alms; neither recognizes the other, but Troilus sees something in her face that

141

reminds him of Cresseid, and so "For knichtlie pietie[7] and memoriall/ Of fair Cresseid," he tosses her a small purse of gold. Cressid must ask of another there the name of the soldier, and when she learns it, she bewails her woe, "O fals Cresseid and trew knicht Troylus!" She passes judgment on herself and then makes her will and testament: her corpse to the worms, her gold to the lepers, her ring to Troilus, and her spirit to Diana—chastity at last. Troilus later builds a her tomb and inscribes it with the words "Cressid of Troy, once counted the flower of womanhood, under this stone, late a leper, lies dead"— a succinct epitaph, somewhere between merciful and unfathomably cold.

Cressid may reach some redemption in her last speech, but Henryson omits Chaucer's scene of a dead but redeemed Troilus. Denton Fox suggests that Henryson "takes a weak, selfish, and unfaithful, even lascivious, woman and manages to make her into such a pathetic and much-abused beauty that we are tempted to comfort her,"[8] but kindness may have been more a temptation than reasonable judgment for Henryson's readers. The ending reflects the subversion not only of physical beauty, but also of one's ability to recognize the suffering of another in our sorrows. Even the moral narrator need repeat no moral judgment, since the penalties of the gods and the passing of time have done what damage they can, and the time and its sufferings have passed. Henryson's ending more than Chaucer's foreshadows the direction Shakespeare will take with his re-vision of the story, where, unlike his two major predecessors, Cressida—along with all the other characters—will lose what sympathy the audience may have felt.

"Shakespeare's play," Heather James argues, "systematically repudiates its predecessors"; it "exhibits an exasperating pleasure in rousing audience expectations based on an anticipated genre or text"[9]—it subverts tendencies to pity and so becomes even more strongly and limitingly moral than Henryson's *Testament*. Troilus ends the play a mad, friendless combatant lusting only for blood, Pandar wills the audience the diseases distributed by the children of his profession, and the audience must wonder if we have found anything redeeming in this incarnation of the Troy story: disgust and futility have subverted and replaced the glory and grandeur of the ancient Greek world.

Shakespeare begins quite differently than does Chaucer, with the latter's call upon the Fury; Shakespeare's Prologue brings immediate focus to the Greek princes' pride. Less a sin for the Greeks than for medieval and Renaissance Christians, deadly pride comes in this play before a domino-sequence of falls. Shakespeare's Prologue terms himself

> A prologue armed, but not in confidences
> Of author's pen or actor's voice, but suited
> In like conditions as our argument,
> To tell you, fair beholders, that our play
> Leaps o'er the vaunt and firstlings of those broils,
> Beginning in the middle....
> Like or find fault, do as your pleasures are,
> Now good or bad, 'tis but the chance of war [lines 23–31].

The Prologue scorns audience approval as out of his control, a matter of the fortunes of war rather than something in his, the author's, or the audience's hands. More like an epic—or Epic Romance—it begins *in medias res*, specifically in the midst of *war*. Yet it quickly subvert epic tone and intent because it shows no productive heroism or any laudable actions. Whatever Greeks or medieval or Renaissance audiences may have wanted to see of or about themselves, they wouldn't find it in this play.

Contrary to a likely epic move, Act I takes us immediately not to war, but to a potentially (and terribly flawed) romantic encounter. Troilus has already fallen for Cressid (with no sub-version of love-disdain). "Why should I war without the walls of Troy,/ That find such cruel battle here within?" he asks, subverting already our appreciation of him as soldier. Since we have here no epic here, no comedy, and no Classical tragedy, we must look for something else: sorrow, conflict, and joking with no laudable goal. If Shakespeare knew Henryson, that echo may have made tragedy impossible. He knew Chaucer, but wrote a Cressid influenced more by lust than by fear. Characters' actions hinge on momentary self-indulgence and explosive arrogance with no concern about where such extremes may lead—Shakespeare makes plain that they all subvert themselves. "I tell thee I am mad/ In Cressid's love," says Troilus in I.1.51–52, foreshadowing his and the general madness at the end of the play, and then "she is stubborn-chaste against all suit," he adds in line 97: he fails to note that, while he has no responsibility for many of her choices, he is subverting her life in such a way as to allow her no means to retreat from ignominy. In I.2 we learn in a soliloquy that Cressid conceals her love for Troilus, and in III.2.117–18 she admits, "I was won, my lord,/ With the first glance"; war may produce impatience, but Troilus does not provoke her to a feeling she hadn't already experienced. She bears responsibility, too, despite Troilus inappropriate wooing, and the war neither quickens nor subcues her feelings.

In III.1 Pandarus, in an exchange with Helen and Paris, uses the word *fair* or *fairly* ten times in five lines (in conjunction with the aforementioned repetition of *sweet*): Cressid may be *fair*, but she is not *sweet*, and Troilus may claim to treat her sweetly, but he is hardly fair. In scene 2, as Troilus stalks Cressid's door, he asks Pandarus, "O, be thou my Charon," to beg admission. Charon, again, conducts souls not to Paradise, but to the Underworld, the land of the dead, and, if Shakespeare thought of Dante rather than the Greeks, to eternal torment, a torment that souls in the *Commedia* seek willingly. While Dante's quest moves from Hell to Purgatory to Heaven, the characters in this play simply move further into Hell. When the lovers meet, between them they use the word *fear* six times in eight lines, and over the course of forty lines Troilus, Cressida, and Pandarus use the word *faith* five times, and when Cressid pledges, she uses *false* or *falsehood* eight times in twelve lines: the verbal echoes convert quickly from fair and sweet to fear and faith and then to false: what begins as sexual attraction turns quickly to fear of faithfulness and simple falsehood at last. "Well, uncle, what folly I commit, I dedicate to you" (III.2.102–103), warns Cressid, and soon come the famous echoes in their pledges: "As true as Troilus" (line 182) and "As false as Cressid" (line 196), again foreshadowing the conclusion. Yet the famous line overstates Troilus' faith. Troilus' second sorrow, the treacherous killing of Hector by Achilles and his Myrmidons, trumps his loss of Cressid, and he will commit a kind of suicide on the bat-

9—Troilus and Cressida *and Subverting Genre*

tlefield by facing all foes, including Achilles, in exclusively pitched battle. By then the fear that so marks Cressid in Chaucer's Romance and that marks both characters in Shakespeare's play has disappeared, subverted by other emotions.

In Act III, scene 2 Troilus and Cressida meet and agree to a "bargain," as Pandarus puts it, "to press it [a bed] to death"; in III.3 Ulysses arranges a single combat between Hector and Ajax, with the intention of inflaming Achilles with the desire to fight so that the Greeks can have hope of victory. The parallel events show the quick movement to sex as a subversion of love and the quick movement to ritual combat as a subversion of war. Ulysses acts as pander for a false fight designed as another kind of wooing. The fight, in Act IV, ends "sweetly," though not "fairly" (with Ajax probably winning), and with no bloodshed because Ajax and Hector are cousins. It helps subvert Troy, moving events toward Hector's death and toward Cressid's departure. Act IV begins with Diomed's arrival in Troy at night to receive her in exchange for Antenor. Anything resembling love, if anything does, takes place offstage, and the onstage exchange occurs in the dark, lit only by torches, in a metaphorically subversive reversal of a marriage ceremony, the turning over of the bride. In III.3 Ulysses observes, "beauty, wit,/ High birth, vigor of bone, desert in service,/ Love, friendship, charity, are subjects all/ To envious and calumniating Time": the characters need very little time for all such virtues to fail them. "I care not to be the louse of a lazar, so I were not Menelaus," says the scurrilous Thersites in V.1, perhaps echoing Henryson, but certainly verbalizing the sense that the world of the characters has been decaying long before the events of the play began. Thersites refers to Cressid as "the Troyan drab" in V.2, echoing Ulysses' sentiments and Troilus' worst fears; far worse for Troy, in V.3, asserting his honor, Hector departs Troy for the battlefield despite the pleas of Cassandra and Andromache, and in V.8 he foolishly disarms on the battlefield, subverting himself as soldier and allowing opportunity for the treacherous Achilles. "Hope of revenge shall hide our inward woe," laments Troilus, who has devolved into little more than a berserker, in V.10, before he turns over the stage to Pandarus, who has the play's final words, subverting the practice that the person in charge should get them (or confirming that the worst possible person has charge).

The closing tone contrasts starkly with Chaucer's and Henryson's: Chaucer hints at redeemability in the desire to love faithfully and in the opportunity to gain distance from and perspective on the folly of human experience; Henryson has Troilus build a marble tomb for his dead sometime-love, his narrator warns women of deception, and he hints at respect for even the dishonorable departed ("Sen sho is deid, I speik of hir no moir"); Shakespeare has subverted the possibilities for redemption.

Chaucer's narrator in his early poems claims sleeplessness and sorrow in love: "For both I hadde that which I nolde,/ and I ne hadde that thing that I wolde,"[10] probably a characterization to attract sympathy to the narrator in a Courtly-Love influenced world, but also perhaps a state of mind that leads to both lament and consolation for lost love real or imagined. Henryson's narrator, too, claims the pains of love-longing, perhaps in honor and echo of his beloved mentor, but perhaps because he felt romantic sorrows as well: he does seem to have had an issue with faithless women. Boccaccio reputedly wrote *Il Filostrato* as a response to spurned love. Of Shakespeare's romantic feelings we know little, other than that the plays often take a rather realistic view of such concerns. Chaucer and Henryson to some extent subvert or at least sublimate their feelings through their narrators and via their stories; Shakespeare deepens the bitterness of the story, though the target of any satire may have been political rather than romantic: look what silly wars can do to otherwise potentially good people—it turns them all to monsters. The horror of loss comes not merely by chance, and not merely by war, but also by the rapidity with which we often give in to weakness. Shakespeare may have struggled more than did Chaucer or Henryson with the fear and loathing associated with pledges of truth and subsequent infidelity, a theme that pervaded his world politically as well as individually. He concludes with a strong sense of irresolution, mixing in his use of sources a painful matrix of life-lessons and leaving his audience troubled by providing no simple solutions to the problems of bad thinking, rash choices, and cowardly actions.

9—Troilus and Cressida *and Subverting Genre*

Thersites and the Subversion of Humor

In the Old World humor probably served much the same purpose as tragedy, to purge unbalanced emotions but also to point a way to virtuous behavior. We don't see as much of it as in the Modern world, and it often addresses more personal than political concerns. Chaucer used some gentle humor in his Romance, Henryson little if any in his postscript to Chaucer. Shakespeare turned his wit to Thersites, who takes up quite a good deal more of this play than he deserves. His humor relies on insults as its conveyance, and while he may utter truths about the problems of the world, he never does anything to make the world or its characters better. His victims listen when they find him witty, and ignore him if they find him right, subverting the power of satire to change us for the better. Only Cassandra actually tries to help; she appears only briefly, and no one pays her any attention either. Thersites' humor adds no insights that we didn't already have, and it falls more into sarcasm than satire: he uses it for his own entertainment rather than their improvement. Cressida and Pandarus also provide some humor in the play, but their humor, too, causes more annoyance than pleasure, and even an audience who responds briefly to it will quickly see its emptiness—again it serves no useful purpose, and it isn't funny enough on its own to entertain.

Shakespeare uses humor in his plays—humorous characters, language, situations, repartee—not for that silly cliché notion of "comic relief," but to reveal characters' errors, flaws, and obsessions (and sometimes their intelligence), to clarify and deepen themes, and to show where received ideas bring harm rather than good. In *Much Ado About Nothing*, Dogberry, insulted by the villain Conrade, who calls him an ass, insists that the insult become part of public record: "O that I had been writ down an ass!" (5.1.87) Dogberry, guilty of all sorts of hilarious malapropisms and perhaps even of some degree of cowardice, actually serves, along with his fellows among the Watch, as the *ass* of the play: he carries the burden of truth and justice in the world of the play. In *Troilus and Cressida* Thersites should serve that purpose, but he fails, willing to exercise his wit but unwilling to carry the burden that goes with it. Why is he in the Greek army at all? Certainly no soldier, he begins as a kind of "voluntary" servant to Ajax, with whom he immediately trades insults and whose company he leaves for that of Achilles and Patroclus, to receive beatings there instead—he too self-subverts.

Thersites' humor should help Ajax know himself, as that of the Fool in *King Lear* does for Lear. It doesn't. Ajax remains strong and stupid. I anything, he gets worse, becoming more proud and dull. Ajax doesn't learn; he beats. With Achilles and Patroclus he does the same thing: instead of calling a traditional curse upon Patroclus, "thyself upon thyself!" he shouts; "[t]he common curse of mankind, folly and ignorance, be thine in great revenue!" he adds (2.3.27–29). That curse comes true for all the characters in the play: they condemn themselves and one another to foolish and ignorant behavior throughout. In the dialogue following among Thersites, Achilles, and Patroclus, the word *fool* appears ten times in the course of thirteen lines: anyone listening or reading carefully at all will notice that Shakespeare calls our attention to the mutual foolishness we see throughout the play, from the most noble to the most ignoble. In *Lear* the Fool at least does the king some good; in *Troilus and Cressida* Thersites can point out others' foolishness, but fully participates in it himself, showing no greater purpose than do the fools around him. We hardly need him: we can see well enough the ubiquitous foolishness without him. Unlike *Much Ado About Nothing*, this play doesn't have the ass it needs to carry the events to some sort of useful resolution. Even Troilus, who has at least some good traits to recommend him in Chaucer's poem, and Aeneas, usually a positive figure for English poets, lack a sense of the seriousness of their situation: In Act I, scene 1, when Aeneas returns from the field of battle to report that "Paris is gor'd with Menelaus' horn" and adds, "Hark what good sport is out of town today" (i.e., the fighting), Troilus responds, "But to the sport abroad—are you bound thither?" (lines 112–15): to them the war implies not the struggle for the survival of their city, but *sport*. Their dialogue subverts the seriousness of war, and their lack of awareness subverts their purpose and their lives.

In Act I, scene 2, Cressida observes to her servant that the behavior of Ajax should produce smiles rather than anger. She then engages

9—Troilus and Cressida *and Subverting Genre*

in a long dialogue with Pandarus: he tries to win her to Troilus' love, and she fends him off, even though we learn later that she loved him already. "I swear to you, I think Helen loves him [Troilus] better than Paris," Pandarus, obviously lying, asserts, and Cressid replies, "Then she's a merry Greek indeed" (lines 107–108). She makes fun nominally of Helen, but really of both Pandarus in his praising and Troilus in his loving, ironically since she has fallen for Troilus easily enough and will do the same again with Diomed. The humor turns quickly from witty to sad and ironically subversive. Pandarus suggest that Troilus esteems Helen "no more than I esteem and addle egg," and Cressida replies, "If you love an addle egg as well as you love an idle head, you would eat chickens i' th'shell" (lines 130–34): both Pandarus and Troilus suffer from an idle brain—neither Cressid nor Troilus nor anyone else anything more than an addled mind. Their jokes subvert only themselves.

In Act I, scene 3, Ulysses delivers his famous "degree" speech. He claims that Troy hasn't yet fallen to the Greeks because they fail to observe social place: "[d]egree being vizarded/ Th'unworthiest shows as fairly as the mask./ The heavens themselves, the planets, and this centre/ Observe degree, priority, and place" (lines 83–86). He hopes to subvert Achilles' pride and get him back to his proper "place," leading the fighting. Then, almost as a response to Ulysses' speech, through the course of seven scenes Shakespeare unleashes Thersites, who to insult not just Achilles, but everyone, including himself. He proclaims Ajax a fool and a dog, and he won't even stop when Ajax beats him: "no man is beaten voluntary," suggests Achilles after Thersites insists he serves there of his own will. Thersistes does, undercutting his own wit, showing it no more than wordplay. Apparently Achilles is wrong, and we do take voluntary beatings: the Trojan War is such an instance for both the Trojans and the Greeks.

Thersites' says in II.3 that the walls of Troy will fall by themselves before Achilles and Patroclus can get the job done. As so often happens in Shakespeare's soliloquys, the character speaks as he believes, and here he happens to be right: neither Patroclus nor Achilles will bring down Troy; only the Trojans' own foolishness can do that. Thersites continues to call Patroclus, Agamemnon, Achilles, and even himself a fool: they all serve unreasonably, partly because the reason for the war, "a whore and a cuckold" (72–73), hardly merits their suffering and certainly does not deserve the name of honor. "Why do we fight?" makes an awfully compelling question, but nobody bothers to answer it (only Menelaus actually could), and nobody changes—except to get even worse—and nobody escapes the pattern of subversions, self-generated or otherwise.

In III.3 Patroclus urges Achiless to fight: "Sweet, rouse yourself" (line 222), and Patroclus, too, with a "sweet Patroclus" (*sweet* subverts the proper forcefulness of the message by making it seem like an appeal to a child). Achilles observes selfishly in reply "I see my reputation is at stake,/ My fame is shrowdly gor'd" (lines 227–28). *Shrowdly* puns, as a portmanteau, on *shrewdly* and *as if in a shroud*: Ulysses has acted shrewdly to try to get Achilles to fight, trying to subvert his childish pride. Degree, as Ulysses has warned, is failing.[11] Thersites then appears to comment on Ajax's behavior as he prepares for the one-on-one combat with Hector, but his lines apply equally well to Achilles: "if Hector break not his neck i' the' combat, he'll break it himself in vainglory" (258–59). "I had rather be a tick in a sheep than such a valiant ignorance" (311–12), he adds, but he has no one left to subvert, as the soldiers have already subverted themselves. Having observed Cressida with Diomed in V.2, Thersites says that the gossipy Patroclus "will give me any thing for the intelligence of this whore," and he concludes, "Lechery, lechery, still wars and lechery, nothing else holds fashion. A burning devil take them!" (lines 192–96) Lechery and battle-lust define and subvert both peoples, Greeks and Trojans.

In V.4 Thersites convinces Hector not to fight with him; he refers to Nestor as a stale old mouse-eaten dry cheese," to Ulysses as "dog-fox," to both Achilles and Ajax as curs, and to the Greeks in general as barbarians (lines 1–16). He even calls himself "a rascal, a scurvy railing knave, a very filthy rogue" (28–29). Hector immediately replies, "I do believe thee," and leaves him alone. Thersites subverts everything we think of as proper military manliness. In V.7 he begs off another fight, this time with Margarelon (a bastard son of Priam), who appears in the play only for this instance. He argues that as bastards they should respect each other and do each other no harm.

9—Troilus and Cressida *and Subverting Genre*

Margareleon calls him "coward" and curses him, but also leaves him alone; Thersites may call the attention of the audience to the fight between Menelaus and Paris: "The cuckold and the cuckold-maker are at it. Now, bull! now, dog!" (lines 9–10) Once again none of the ostensible humor enlightens the characters, but it does tell the audience something about the world of the play: the characters will subvert truth no matter how or from whom they get it.

Pandarus, the remaining source of humor in the play, offers little more: his humor falls flat, and in the last lines of the play it turns into sarcasm and curse. In I.2, as he tries to charm Cressida for Troilus, he mentions an incident where "there was such laughing," but apparently Pandarus has no talent for telling jokes: he actually says nothing funny to make Cressida laugh, and she lampoons his ineptness with her own jests. In III.1 Pandarus attempts to get help from a servant of Paris, but the servant jokes at Pandarus' expense, and Pandarus misses the content of the jokes entirely: "Friend, we understand not one another; I am too courtly and thou too cunning" (lines 27–28). When he does meet Paris and Helen, Pandarus addresses them with a nearly incoherent mix of courtliness and familiarity—he even calls Helen "Nell," reducing her to little more than a typical servant girl, and they make fun of the silliness of his locutions. In III.2, having just come from Paris and Helen, he taunts Troilus and Cressida for their blushing and their hesitancy to jump into bed, suggesting they get busy and "press it to death" (line 209). They can't see the danger in kind of precipitous act of lechery that Shakespeare, through Thersistes' speech, pairs with war in V.2. The odd, though traditional and ubiquitous pairing or war and lust subverts them both. Shakespeare suggests war is lust, and lust initiates a kind of war, each on incongruous passion, and in the world of this play one leads to the other. War is, in a sense, the ultimate example of excess. Both the Troy story generally and its Troilus and Cressida biproduct highlight excesses and the ease with which excess produces subversion. Having subverted ourselves by excess, we may not have a chance to go back and fix the problems that excess creates: Shakespeare, and probably Chaucer and Henryson, too, learned that lesson from Ovid if not from practical experience.

"[P]leasure and revenge/ Have ears ears more deaf than adders to the voice/ Of any true decision," says Hector (2.2.171–73). Shakespeare's audience, with its taste for revenge tragedy, must have found a particularly potent but evil kind of pleasure in such stories. They subvert us from proper Christian choice and humility, but they can also suggest a satisfying sense of justice. The Trojans consider returning Helen to the Greeks and her lawful husband, which would constitute a moral, sane, and just act; it would probably end the war and saving Troy and many lives on both sides. But the desire to keep Helen, to avoid dishonor in returning her (and lose the honor of fending off the Greek heroes), outweighs the clarity of thought in which Hector has just argued for her return. Shakespeare shows how the desire for pleasure and pride make us unwilling to follow wisdom even when we find it before us in the clearest possible terms, even when we speak it ourselves.

As the Greeks try to find a means to get Achilles back on the battlefield, Ulysses asserts, "The amity that wisdom knits not, folly may easily untie" (II.3.101–102). Universal folly is the great subverter in this play. If we fail to apply wisdom to make a friendship work, or if that friendship isn't a wise one to begin with, it will fail: our subsequent foolishness will undoubtedly ruin it. The same point applies to "love": Troilus and Cressida's relationship will fail just as Paris and Helen's will, and Cressid's realignment with Diomed has no hope at all. Real friendship could save us from many sorrows, but false friendship subverts all relationships: Pandarus' services to Troilus have immoral bases, so they must lead to no good; Hector and Ajax's friendship is weak and useless to begin with, since they are enemy combatants. "He that is proud eats up himself," Agamemnon says at the end of the scene, ostensibly about Achilles, but it applies to nearly everyone in the play: pride subverts them where humility could save them. "He will be the physician that should be the patient," Agamemnon adds in III.3.213–14, referring this time to Ajax, who is just as proud as Achilles but even less self-aware. In battle Avhilles shows no sense of honor, just the desire to kill. If we would find and cure destructive faults in others, we must excise them from ourselves first—but this play suggest we will subvert both and allow neither.

9—Troilus and Cressida *and Subverting Genre*

In III.2, as Cressida prepares to meet Troilus, "giddy" with expectation for their sexual encounter, Troilus warns her, "This [is] monstruosity in love, lady, that the will is infinite and the execution confin'd, that the desire is boundless and the act a slave to the limit" (lines 81–83). Troilus undercuts his own sexual prowess by warning Cressid that a man's performance often doesn't live up to a woman's expectations or to his own promises. Ironically deflating and sadly true, that warning subverts lust even as it does love. Cressid has already prepared herself, though: "To fear the worst oft cures the worse" (line 73): she hasn't awfully high expectations for their relationship anyway—she thereby subverts her own amorous adventure. Shortly she will make that point even more clearly: "to be wise and love/ Exceeds a man's might; that dwells with the gods above" (lines 156–57). She identifies the cause of the war in the play, and she foreshadows their falls, but she mistakes with respect to the Classical god: they subvert themselves with poor amorous choices, too. The play subverts all hopes for wisdom just as it subverts humor—it is a kind of anti–*Lear*, which uses humor to spotlight the failure of wisdom.

In III.3 Ulysses tries to subvert Achilles' tantrum and win him back to battle with two gems of manly wisdom: first, that a "man ... [c]annot make boast to have that which he hath,/ Nor feels not what he owes, but by reflection" (96–99); second, that "no man is the lord of any thing.... Till he communicate his parts to others" (115–17). The first maxim asserts that nothing has meaning of itself, but rather we come to understand it by perspective, because someone else must observe and judge it in comparison to something else we mutually value; the second says that someone may have skills or intrinsic value, but no one will know about it until we see that virtue on display. Though it won't work on Achilles, here we get a useful thought with theological implications that respond to critical Christian analysis. But the point isn't quite right: virtue comes not merely in thinking about good and right actions, but in doing them; however, doing them is the important thing, whether someone else observes them or not. In the Fallen world tests separate assumed virtue from demonstrable virtue.

Ulysses will second these thoughts with "Perseverance, my dear lord, / Keeps honor bright" (150–51), and "Love, friendship, charity, are subjects all/ To envious and calumniating Time" (173–74). Not wanting to fall short—to prevent subversion by means of piling on old wisdom—he adds, "The present eye praises the present object" (180) and "things in motion sooner catch the eye"(183). With elements of both the medieval and the modern world, Ulysses not so subtly asks Achilles, "Look, time passes to nothing before you know it, and so do we, so what have you done for us lately?" Later, in Act IV, scene 5, Hector will recapitulate the sentiment: "The end crowns all,/ And that old common arbitrator, Time,/ Will one day end it" (224–26). They must make the most of the strengths and virtues the gods have given them—but they don't, and they won't. Patroclus warns Achilles, "Those wounds heal ill that men do give themselves" (229); he at least speaks more out of love than utilitarian purpose (Ulysses' warrant), but ironically Patroclus' death, not his words, however well intended, will bring Achilles back to the fight. More ironically (and subversively for the Trojan War tradition) Achilles will neither kill nor die honorably.

In Act IV, scene 4, Troilus warns Cressida, as she is about to leave for the Greek camp, that "sometimes we are devils to ourselves,/ When we will tempt the frailty of our powers" (95–96)—nearly everyone in the play and nearly everyone in life believes we are stronger than we really are against both temptation and enemies. Hector tests the frailty of his own powers when he arms to fight despite the warnings of Cassandra and Andromache right before Achilles' men will kill him on the battlefield. "Mine honor keeps the weather of my fate," he proclaims, and "Life every man holds dear, but the dear man/ Holds honor far more precious-dear than life" (5.3.26–28). Hector echoes traditional notions of honor that this play fully subverts, and Shakespeare subverted his traditional story in the manner of his death. The speech about honor does him little good, and it leads to disaster for his family and Troy. Shakespeare may well have wanted his audience to wonder about it, too, though perhaps more seriously than when Falstaff questions the value of honor in *1 Henry IV*. Honor, of course, has great value, but one must know how to separate it from

9—Troilus and Cressida *and Subverting Genre*

pride and foolhardiness, and one must be willing to practice it rather than subvert it. And in this play Shakespeare subverted not only honor, but everything.

As early as Act I, scene 1, Troilus observes, "Fools on both sides!" (line 90). That is the clearest and most exact statement of the situation of this play, and it specifies the problem in the world of *Troilus and Cressida* and why it will fall to a series of subversions. A world full of fools can teach us nothing. A species who learn from opposites and opposition, we humans must have the wise as well as the foolish to benefit from the contrast. Thersites' humor, all of the humor, fizzles; any hint of courage or wisdom immediately fails; the characters fall short of tragic nobility; all the adventures turn sordid. We have neither the joy of comedy, nor the relief from tragedy, nor the excitement of adventure, nor the illumination of history. We find only doubts about heroism, love, honor, fidelity, truth and wit: subverting genre, subverting character, subverting humor, we have subverted all those virtues as well.

Postscript—*Meta-, Para-, Neo-, Socio*-phrase
Gavin Douglas's Sub-versive Eneados

As an allegory is a sub-version that points to some kind of super-version of a story—an invitation to leap from *Everyman* to the story of everyone or anyone—so a translation serves necessarily as a sub-version (if not a dangerous subversion) of its original. It re-creates its original, recreates the reader, and creates a new original, something the language may not have had before and on which it may build further.

Before John Dryden's technical distinction of metaphrase, paraphrase, and imitation come into critical parlance and changed the landscape of what *translation* may mean, we may do well first to consider why a translator took up the task. In his "Preface" to *Ovid's Epistles* Dryden suggests that, with respect to an original, one may stay too slavishly literal, find a middle ground between accuracy and poetic license, or allow too much freedom in poetic rendering. The chosen course, though, comes most directly from the genesis of the translation, its motive and *motif*. While Gavin Douglas was asked by a politically powerful cousin, Henry, Lord Saint Clair, to undertake the rendering of Homer or Vergil into Scots—and so he did it partly as a response to a direct request—Douglas's accomplishment in his *Eneados* represents an enormously difficult, time-consuming, and self-sacrificing labor.

Douglas must have had, in addition to the request—or, perhaps even *command*—some sense of personal or national investment in the prospect as well. The fourteenth-century *Sir Gawain and the Green Knight*, for instance, directs its audience to a comparison with

Postscript

Troy—especially its destruction—and to Britain's desire to legitimize itself internationally through a connection to what was *heroic* about Troy, but *lasting, exploratory,* and *productive* about its prodigious child, Rome. Gavin Douglas, as inheritor of Gawain as well as Chaucer and Vergil, must complete a literary quest for a stable narrative and linguistic foundation, to establish a new tradition impervious to the vicissitudes of personal or national sins, to the ebb and flood of assertion, invasion, and identification. He flexes the Scots *langue*—along with his audience's notions of righteous living—by adding to it the prodigious *parole* of his translation of the *Aeneid*, the book that best expressed Roman notions of virtue with lasting and powerful effect. As Haydock succinctly puts it, "Douglas adopts the persona of a classicizing poet of the 'auld fassioun' within a distinctly Scottish setting" (66).

A scholar's method, as we move on from Dryden, may direct a translation toward anything from anthropological and paleographical homage to contemporary political and idiomatic immediacy to personal poetic virtuosity. The quality of Douglas's product, along with his considerable adjustments of and additions to Vergil's *Aeneid*—probably the most influential single poem on the Middle Ages and Renaissance—mark his *Eneados* as a move to legitimize, expand, and limber Scots as a literary language, to give it place among European languages and to invigorate and empower its own speakers. As Robert Henryson's *Testament of Cresseid* and his beast fables connect both the writer and his country first to literary fathers Chaucer and Aesop and second to established linguistic authorities in English and Greek, so Douglas made a firmer, more foundational connection by bringing Scotland to Rome and *vice versa*: as Vergil provided Rome the spectrum of its essential virtues through the *pius* Aeneas, so Douglas adopts those virtues, particularizes and specifies them in Scots for his own contemporaries.

Even more than Chaucerian efforts in English—Chaucer's works range more widely in their issues and sway more readily between *sentence* to *solace*—Douglas's *Eneados* establishes a cornerstone of moral instruction, a weighty center from which Scots literature can readily expand, and a vector by which to conduct a language into interna-

Meta-, Para-, Neo-, Socio-*phrase*

tional discourse. As T.R. Steiner has asserted, medieval translations had not only their own didactic purpose, but more explicitly a "*moralisatio* overriding other considerations"; as we move into the Renaissance with its nascent ideas of nationhood, a new "patriotic strain" arises "whose primary function was enrichment from foreign stores of the developing vernacular and its literature."[12] More recently translators have taken particularly public and political aim at their texts: note for example Seamus Heaney's iricizations in his *Beowulf*, hius translation popular partly because of the license he assumes as poet and as Irishman rendering, even colonizing, a fundamental Old English work.

Focusing on the Prologue from Book 1 of the *Eneados*, with a brief nod to translation in Book 1, this brief postscript to the study of narrative subversion will explore how through translation Douglas may have aimed, in addition to traditional moral and social implications, to expand both his own poetic language and the range of linguistic potential in Scots. I would like to suggest that those language considerations represent a significant achievement and a fundamental purpose in the choices and methods that Douglas employed in the creation of a great Scots poem from a Latin über-classic. Dryden declared of his own translation that "I have endeavored to make Vergil speak such English as he would himself have spoken, if he had been born in England, and in this present age."[13] Douglas sought by means of deep grounding in an irrefutable Classic a means to create vibrant literary space for Scots in which it could readily exhibit both lexical liveliness and social seriousness. In Saussurean terms he sought at once to ground and extend the *langue* and legitimize and enliven the *parole*. His sub-version of, to his mind, the greatest of *superversions*, serves as a foundation for subsequent Scots literature and language development. Whereas Willis Barnstone distinguishes between translator as "freely creative person" or "erroneous slob" (117), he also notes that translation "not only transforms other literatures, their authors and translating authors, but in repressive [or any] societies serves specifically as an instrument to educate, inform, and alter political and hence literary values" (123)—the old work in the old language becomes a new work in the new language. I would add that translation

Postscript

need not repress; it can, at its best, at least to some extent, liberate as well: Douglas particularly—in approximately 2,200 lines of prologue plus the thirteenth book, which he drew from the fifteenth-century Italian poet Maffeo Vegio—sought to establish something authoritative in literary history but also something fully immediate in Scots and Scottish society in its effects: how doubly ironic that the Battle of Flodden occurred just six weeks after the *Eneados*'s appearance. The thirteenth book adds the account of Aeneas's marriage and apotheosis: it rehabilitates Aeneas after his abandoning Dido and confirms the quality of the hero's character for which Douglas argues so strongly in the Prologue to Book 1, affirming social and religious values of fidelity and piety that Douglas, as a churchman, wanted to inculcate.

While Douglas's poem in many ways deals with notions of virtue, it does not exclusively focus so, and while it lionizes Vergil and his poem, it does not limit itself so. Marilynn Desmond[14] argues that in the *Eneados* "we can witness the formation of modern attitudes toward a monumentalizing view of Vergil's text" (164), but Douglas's translation also "demonstrates an ideological aim in his attempt to claim Vergilian eloquence for the Scottish language and Scottish identity" (165). Mary Jane Scott[15] noticed that "Douglas enhanced Vergil's *Aeneid* descriptions of storms, flood and mountain with realistic details from his Scottish experience" (107), essentially re-localizing a poem that itself had apotheosized in European literature generally. Gordon M. Kendal[16] has remarked on the importance of Douglas's "involving the reader in [the *Aeneid*'s] retelling" (ii); that isn't a small point, because it foregrounds the idea that the literature serves more than an archival or educational function: it connects readers indelibly to the evolution of their language through the addition of text that rebuilds their national foundations. Lois Ebin[17] calls further attention to the imbedding of the narrator in the Prologues, asserting that they "define a poet-narrator whose role is central to our understanding of the translation. In his guises as poet, priest, and translator, the narrator introduces a series of conflicts which question the value of poetry and qualify the *Aeneid*'s central themes. His activity establishes a movement from doubt and uncertainty to renewed creativity which complements the larger journey of Aeneas within the poem" (353)—the poet connects, adds, affirms, linking his own audience to the original, to the threat of the characters' failures, but also to the power of their virtues. As critics unfailingly notice, Douglas packed the Prologues, from the very first in all its 511 lines, with purpose.

The first Prologue serves not only as *apologia*, but also as a means to place the translation rhetorically, linguistically, morally, and religiously in his own particular context; it reverentially acknowledges both patron and source and creates a tone at once highly serious, highly personal, and highly national. Concluding his dedication of the book to Saint Clair, Douglas writes,

> Quharfor to hys nobilite and estait,
> Quhat so it be, this buke I dedicait,
> Writtin in the langage of Scottis natioun,
> And thus I mak my protestatioun [lines 101–104].[18]

Since Saint Clair asked for the poem (a Scots translation either of Homer or of Vergil), what makes it worthy of dedication is its language and the clearer moral weight that accompanies Vergil's rather than Homer's heroes. More than labor, affection, the value of the source: the work creates a space, a retro-fit beginning, a center of gravity from which new literature may grow and expand with authority.

Douglas begins his poem with effusive praise of Vergil, offering "Lawd, honour, praysyngis, thankis infynyte" to "Maist reverend Vergill," the "Gem of engyne and flude of eloquens; Vergil serves as both lantern and mirror—matching the two great traditional images of the poet, the first Romantic and the second Classical—and his works prove "Plesand, perfyte and feilabill," since "our all rung is thyne hevynly bell" (lines 1–13). The passage both recovers Vergil, Augustine-like, for the Christian reader and specifies his work as pleasing, perfect and feel-able: one not only learns from it and hears the music of the heavens in it, but one can feel it deeply—a point that critics don't always specify with epic poems and their translations. He then asks why he should translate Vergil's "dear" and "perfect" Latin into his own "harsk spech and lewit barbour tong" and "ignorant blabryng imperfyte" with illustrative anaphora:

Postscript

> For quhat compare betwix mydday and nycht?
> Or quhat compare betwix myrknes and lycht?
> Or quhat compar is betwix blak and quhyte? [lines 25–27].

But he quickly answers his own question:

> And netheless with support and correctioun,
> For naturall lufe and frendely affectioun
> Quhilkis I beir to thy warkis and endyte—
> All thoct God wait tharin I knwa full lyte—
> Sand that thy facund sentence mycht be song
> In our langage alsweill as Latyn tong... [lines 35–40].

Then he adds that it is impossible he will do as well, but with Vergil's leave he will "wryte sum savoryng of thyne Eneados" in "my rurall wlgar gross" (lines 43–44). Affection for both patron and poet, I think, move the effort, which he cautions with his own humility, taking care to catch himself from soaring too high: As well? No, no, he says, but his point is not so much to do as well as Vergil as to bring the best available poetry into Scots: the rural vulgar tongue thus expands by acquiring and imbedding the best poetic matter available to it from any time or anywhere. And though that matter be secular, it yet has divine imprimatur and no equal: "Bot thy wark sall endur in lawd and glory.... Nane is, nor was, ne yit salbe, trow I/ Had, hass or sal haue sic craft in poetry.... For thou art all and sum, quhat nedis more/ of Latyn poetis" (lines 49, 55–56, 65–66). As Douglas worked, he decided he did best by "Kepand na sudron bot our awyn langage,/ And spekis as I lernyt quhen I was page./ Nor yit sa cleyn all sudron I refuss,/ Bot sum word I pronounce as nyghtbouris doys" (lines 111–14); he's willing to use "Sum bastard Latyn, French or Inglys oyss/ Quhar scant was Scottis— I had nane other choys" (117–18) because he wants to get the "cullour of his properte" as exactly as he can. He will keep out "Southern," or English, and even French and vulgar Latin as much as he can, and will stick to Scots as much as he can while keeping strictly to Vergil. Strict, of course, he does not remain: witness the matter of the Prologues and the thirteenth book, the decasyllabic couplets, and the occasional indubitably northern lilt: "Our land and sey kachit with mekil pyne" (line 4, "O'er land and see tossed with great suffering").

The Prologue moves from multi-faceted paean and humble but energetic linguistic commitment to comments on the faults of William

Meta-, Para-, Neo-, Socio-*phrase*

Caxton's 1490 translation of the *Aeneid* from a French intermediary: with that man "of Inglis natioun" Douglas has little patience:

> In proyss hes prent ane buke of Inglys gross,
> Clepand it Vergill in Eneadoss....
> It hass na thing ado tharwith, God wait,
> Ne na mair lyke than the devill and Sanct Austyne [lines 138–43].

A bad translation, apparently, constitutes an aesthetic, an intellectual, and a religious error. He continues at Caxton,

> Hys ornate goldyn versis mair than gilt
> I spittit for dispyte to se swa spilt,
> With sych a wyght, quhilk trewly be myne entent
> Knew neuere thre wordis at all quhat Vergill ment... [lines 149–52].

The caustic jibe, part of a 126-line passage, merits the addition of extra syllables for the poet to spit his contempt; one must never take any part of a work lightly, Douglas specifies in his own note following line 192, for "Vunder derk poetrye is hid gret wisdome and lerning." He must "twiching Vergillis honour and reuerens,/ Quha euer contrarly ... stand at defens" (277–78), for he is bound to Vergil: "Quha is attachit ontill a staik, we se,/ May go na ferthir bot wreil about that tre," especially so with Vergil, who "euery vertu belangand a nobill man" (line 325) teaches through Aeneas.

The next passage of about ninety lines deals with issues of language and literary history. He discusses his translation method in lines that echo King Alfred's Preface to Gregory's "Pastoral Care," which come out, roughly "I translated sometimes word for word, sometimes sense for sense, as I thought best rendered the meaning":

> Sum tyme I follow the text als neir I may,
> Sum tyme I am constrenyt ane other way.
> Besyde Latyn our langage is imperfite
> Quhilk in sum part is the causs and the wyte
> Quhy that of Vergillis verss the ornate bewte
> Intill our tung may nocht obseruyt be... [lines 357–62].

Because he sometimes simply couldn't find the right word, "Diuersyte in our leid to seik I cess" (line 372). The advantage that accrues to Scots, though, is that he then expands both *langue* and *parole*, the whole and the ready language, by adding from other sources, however reluctantly.

Postscript

Douglas finds some offense even in Chaucer, though "as he standis beneth Vergil in gre,/ Vundir hym alsfer I grant my self to be" (lines 407–408): for "My mastir Chauser gretly Vergill offendit" (line 410), for instance in saying that Aeneas, leaving Dido, was forsworn. Douglas can't admit the hero a traitor, as he was both bound to his mission by the gods and chose of his free will to follow that mission: both laudable elements in his experience. Finally, Douglas concludes the first Prologue by affirming "In Criste is all my traste, and hevynnys queyn" (line 462), asking Vergil's pardon if he too offends, and asking the reader not to pass judgment too quickly on his work, but to continue to the end and find the good in it: "Beis not ourstudyus to spy a moyt in myne e,/ That in your awyn a ferry boyt can nocht se" (line 500)—Douglas mixes humor with his morality, and morality with example. The Prologue turns the translation also into an *essay*: an attempt, fully conscious, with its own rhetorical purposes not replacing, but adding to or occasionally inflecting those of the original.[19]

Translation is first of all a linguistic act. I think we have always known that it is a very personal act, too, intrusive yet honorific—though sometimes, as with Seamus Heaney's *Beowulf*, it can be a politically subversive act, too. Postmodern thought has taught us it is always a political act, but Douglas would I think replace *political* with *national*. Douglas teaches us most, I think, that it is also a moral act, not merely in the sense of the famous Italian pun on translator/traitor, but also in range of ethical concerns that trouble the task all the way from the selection of the text to changes one makes in it to the commentary one adds to it. And for Douglas each literary, moral act has potentially national consequences. By working as he did, Douglas gave Scots more freedom to paraphrase, render closely, acquire new words, and build a more socially, artistically, and morally energetic language: a great deal to accomplish from a subversion. The task of translation is so difficult that perhaps one must begin with a sense of *ought* to feel willing to begin in the first place, and one must have a motivation greater than the personal to finish.

This postscript doesn't aim at any sort of complete or even adequate comment on Gavin or his *Eneados*. I intend in it only to offer some transitional thoughts, to subvert the reader away from my sub-

Meta-, Para-, Neo-, Socio-*phrase*

versions toward his or her own. The act of reading or of creating criticism is inherently sub-versive and subversive. Each time we read or write, we subconsciously or intentionally translate a work into a new sub-version that fits what we get from that work at the time or what we need it to do for us. As the "Scottish Chaucerians" channeled Chaucer to build a national literature in Scots, Douglas rebuilt, brick by brick, Vergil's epic, adding a book of his own, to establish a foundation for that building-in-progress. Scottish national sentiment, the willing and unwilling influence of a burgeoning English literature, and the perennial and powerful tug of Classicism drew Douglas and his fellow Scots to their own re-vision and helped draw their world into a renaissance. Classical and Renaissance literary subversion require their own study: beyond what I have said about the solutionless problem, the necessary aesthetic of subversion, character issues and character comparisons, translation concerns, dealing with penance and with exile, death, and other endings, the subversion of genre and Classical heroism, and the general practice of subversive reading and writing, they have vast and interesting histories of their own. Subversion went on, goes on.

Chapter Notes

Preface

1. Eco's novel includes a number of subversive elements, including explorations of the monastery library, a discussion of laughter, and a brief romance, but mostly in the brilliant William's failure to solve the mystery by other means than mistakes and accidents—not by Sherlockian brainpower alone. The Rose has no name, and, like all material things, must fade. Critical response to the film version of the book often turns on the fact that it isn't the book: it must lack some of the book's textual richness to maintain a nominally understandable plot. Yet one should hardly fault a film for being a sub-version of its source, which it must inevitably be. Eco's *The Role of the Reader* (1979) explores the idea of "open" and "closed" texts, those that invite energetic reader response and those with limited "play" that discourage it—the notion can apply to recastings as well as to readings, and *The Name of the Rose* certainly invites cinematic and other interpretation.

2. See A.J. Gurevich's chapter on time (e.g., agrarian, genealogical, cyclical, biblical, historical) in *Categories of Medieval Culture*, trans. G.L. Campbell (London: Routledge & Kegan Paul, 1985), 93–151.

3. Donald R. Howard makes this argument in *The Idea of the Canterbury Tales* (Berkeley: University of California Press, 1976). We may as we read get a varying sense of order and fragmentation. Paul Ruggiers in *The Art of the Canterbury Tales* asserts that "[t]hese tales, so variously ordered, obviously, may give the surface impression of discontinuity. They may, however, be seen as a series of intellectual discoveries, involving the audience's passage from ignorance to knowledge," especially as one considers the movement of tales from the Knight's to the Parson's (xiv).

Chapter 2

1. We may make the pretty direct "Russian formalist distinction between *fabula* (the chronological order of a narrative's events) and *sjuzhet* (the order in which a narrative presents those events)," as it appears in Scholes, Phelan, and Kellogg (288), or we may seek something more esoteric, such as the leaping and lingering method of ballads, the incremental repetition of apocalyptic narratives such as the Book of Revelation, or "widening gyre" spiral that Yeats observed of history.

2. In "Narrative and Hermeneutics" Ricoeur suggests, "I assume that it is the task of an hermeneutic to disentangle from the referential claims of any literary work the kind of world that the work displays," and "what is to be interpreted in a text is a proposed world, a world that I might inhabit and wherein I might project my own possibilities" (149), and the concept of "emplotment" structurally connects everything from fiction to history to epic to drama. The world of the text mediates between tex-

tual plots and readers' own plots. Bal argues that we accept as mythos, story, fabula "a series of of logicaly and chronologically related events" regardless of nominal genre: plot crosses generic and thus textual boundaries: we may study plot wherever we find sequences either described or challenged. Derrida, questioning notions of both genre and mode (in the context of Genette's arguments regarding form and content), argues that a text may not respond to critical notions of mode and genre, "especially when the text does not seem to be written sensibly within their limits, but rather about the very subject of those limits, and with the aim of disrupting their order" (209): in a kind of dissemination the world of a text self-deconstructs, or self-subverts, the subversive act itself a plot. Building a world, regardless of genre, requires some notion of plot, but the world will inevitably self-deconstruct—suffer subversion—either within the boundary of its covers or outside them. We re-read then because the world of the text attracts us to reconstruct it. Genette will argue about Proustian narrative of *Recherche du temps perdu* (in *Narrative Discourse*) that while the "specificity of narrative taken as a whole is *irreducible* ... that specificity is not *undecomposable*" for analysis (22–23), inviting any number of sub-versions, and "the real author of the narrative is not only he who tells it, but also ... he who hears it" (262), inviting infinite subversion. Or as Culler explains plot and character fluctuation in his discussion of Echo and Narcissus, the "task of interpretation is to understand the displaced parallelism that the narrative establishes"—Shakespeare's characterization similarly and always depends on such interpretive moves, as do postmodern notions of discursiveness, directing thought to variations, alternatives, uncertainties, sub-versions. We read character and plot, regardless of genre, through an act of continual pairing and re-pairing, to our own world or to other textual worlds we know.

3. Language, Roland Barthes explains, means the "concurrence of ... articulation, or segmentation, ... and integration." Narrative depends on two powers: "distending its signs over the length of the story and ... inserting unforeseeable expansions into these distortions" (*Image—Music—Text* 117). Thus in any utterance, plotted or not, clarity and distortion collaborate in the construction of order. Medieval readers found order in disarticulation: the fourfold exegetical method explained by both Aquinas and Dante: simultaneous reading on the literal, moral, historical, and anagogical levels. In the modern or contemporary world we build readings around character: in *An Intimate History of Humanity* Zeldin builds a chapter on the stories of a brother and sister whose lives twist and turn around the idea of escape: Gérard Colé, vowing not to follow his poor alcoholic father, escapes from poverty by establishing a riding stable, escaped to become journalist, broadcaster, and public relations worker, escaped from the world of money to that of power as a political organizer, and escaped from that to organize an international gambling operation; his sister, Michéle Blondel, escaped from home to young motherhood, from that to the life of an artist, first as a painter, then a sculptor, then as a designer of fountains. In each case the escape subverts the old life, and each in turn becomes a sub-version of something unknown which neither may ever find. Bakhtin makes a point similar to Barthes' in his discussion of discourse in the novel, with respect to clashing speech types: The "distinctive links and interrelationships between utterances and languages, this movement of the theme through different languages and speech types, its disper-

Notes—Chapter 2

sion into the rivulets and droplets of social heteroglossia, its dialogization—this is the basic distinguishing feature of the stylistcs of the novel" (263); I would add that the point holds true for any plot that crosses significant boundaries in its subversions to create sufficient contrast that the reader can imagine many possible turns in the story or the characters. In *Structuralist Poetics* Culler considers from Greimas' *Du Sens* three types of narrative syntagmemes: *performanciels* (performing tasks), *contractuels* (one accepts a task or refuses it), *disjonctionnels* (displacements to or from tasks); whether or not one takes exception to the terms, they provide a useful model for narrative and character movements in *Hamlet*, as the protagonist at once takes dead aim at and scrupulously avoids the task the out-of-joint times have appointed him to set right.

4. See, for instance, Barthes' *The Pleasure of the Text* for an eroticizing of reading and thus a seduction or at least sexualization of plotting.

5. One may make a case that the first solutionless problem, though of a different kind, appears in perhaps our earliest extant substantial narrative, the *Epic of Gilgamesh*. Episodic, caught between the "artless plotting of folk tradition and the consciously artful or consciously empirical plotting of romance and history" (Scholes, Phelan, and Kellogg 208), *Gilgamesh* presses toward a terrifying but necessary end. With the slim but sufficient taint of a mortal mother within him, he seeks immortality, but cannot and will not find it. He hasn't a choice to make, but a fate to accept. He cannot solve his problem because his nature does not contain a solution: mortality, not tragedy, binds him.

6. Susan Stanford Friedman observes that plot moves "horizontally" through time, but also "vertically" through space, both intertextually and intratextually—the result may provide a matrix of subversion possibilities.

7. This problem occurs, for instance in *Beowulf*, where Hæðcyn, son of Hreðel, accidentally kills his brother Herebeald with a stray arrow: the father suffers because he can't get compensation for a killing within the family, thus leaving his son unavenged. See lines 2430–43.

8. *Hamlet* as a play is of course more about character than it is about plot, and most of the other characters represent sub-versions of Hamlet as he tries to find some means within his character to deal with his problem. Hamlet as prince had some autonomy, but Hamlet as nephew and avenger has none with respect to action, only what he can voice to himself or his friends. In that sense he represents that struggle of self-fashioning upon which Greenblatt elaborates, the Renaissance's awkward attempt at growing a balance between rising notions of "personal order" and a social structure of "bounded desires" (1).

9. Peter Goodrich makes a fascinating argument that in addition to the poem's obvious Christian content, Gawain represents a pagan, Frazerian "year-king," with the beheading game figuring a human sacrifice (65), and so the "girdle and its reception suggest that Gawain and Camelot have humanly failed both old and new modes of sacrificial perfection" (79). The subverting in both a "primary" reading and a that of veiled tradition adds weight to the apocalyptic suggestions of Gawain as follower-son of Solomon (and thus of David and thus of Christ) and as priest-shaman whose failure to provide the crossover sacrifice attracts the wrath of vengeful, destructive gods.

10. Arthur traditionally waits for a miraculous event before beginning a holiday meal, and the Green Knight

calls what he offers Arthur's court a "gomen." Games in the pre-modern world often had instruction as their basis—even those with potentially deadly outcomes—and this one achieves no less. A game serves as a sub-version of some serious endeavor, as jousts at tournaments rehearsed knights for actual combat in their lords' behalf.

11. The solutionless problem idea also provides a useful means to stimulate class discussions: students usually find the idea troubling but intriguing, and they will try very hard to find solutions, even if they must manipulate elements in the stories to allow them to do so. Such discussion often led to productive connections between their studies and their lives—especially helpful in these days of "relevance."

Chapter 4

1. For the sake of the more general reader, I have included only Modern English translations in this chapter rather than the Old English originals. Old English texts appear, for instance, in the Krapp and Dobbie series *The Old English Poetic Records*, though one can find many of them online with a simple search for titles.

Chapter 5

1. For the foundational theoretical work on the importance of liminalities, see Victor Turner, *The Ritual Process: Structure and Anti-Structure* (Chicago: University of Chicago Press, 1969).

2. For Old Norse text see Anthony Faulkes' edition, *Edda: Prologue and Gylfaginning* (Viking Society for Northern Research, Oxford University Press, 1982, reprinted by Short Run Press, Exeter, 2000); for a translation see Jean I. Young's *The Prose Edda of Snorri Sturluson: Tales from Norse Mythology* (Berkeley: University of California Press, 1965).

The most important critical discussions of Snorri and the *Prose Edda* probably remain Sigurður Nordal's *Snorri Sturluson* (Reykjavík: [n.p.], 1920), Fredrik Paasche's *Snorre Sturlason og Sturlungerne* (Oslo: H. Aschehoug, 1922), H. Kuhn's "Das Nordgermanische Heidentum in den ersten Christlichen Jarhhunderten," *Zeitschrift für deutsches Altertum* 79 (1942): 133–66, Anne Holtsmark, *Studier i Snorres Mytologi* (Oslo: Universitetsforlaget, 1964), and Óskar Halldórsson's "Snorri og Edda," *Snorri: Átta alda minning* (Reykjavik: Sögufélag, 1979), 89–111.

3. Faulkes' edition, page 54.

4. Decent, easy-to-locate editions of Völuspá are now available online, but for a standard print edition see Hans Kuhn's *Edda: Die Lieder des Codex Regius Nebst Verwandten Denkmälern* (Heidelberg: Carl Winter Univeritätsverlag, 1983). The best translation may still be Lee M. Hollander's in *The Poetic Edda*, 2nd ed. (Austin: University of Texas Press, 1962), 1–13. See also Ursula Dronke, *The Poetic Edda* 1: Heroic Poems (Oxford: Clarendon, 1969). For studies of the poem one does well to begin with the work of Sigurður Nordal, "Three Essays on Völuspá," trans. B.S. Benedikz and J.S. McKinnell, *Saga-Book of the Viking Society* 18 [1971]: 79–135, and *Völuspá*, trans. B.S. Benedikz and John McKinnell, Durham and St. Andrews Medieval Texts 1 (Durham: Dept. of English Language and Medieval Literature, 1978), and Paul Schach, "Some Thoughts on Völuspá," *Edda: A Collection of Essays*, ed. R.J. Glendinning and Haraldur Bessason, University of Manitoba Icelandic Studie 4 (Winnipeg: University of Manitoba Press, 1983), 86–116. See also Ursula Dronke, "*Völuspá* and the Satiric Tradition," *Annali dell-Istituto Universitario Orientale, Napoli, Sezione Germanica* 22 (1979): 57–86, and "*Beowulf* and Ragnarök," *Saga-Book of the Viking Society* 17 (1969): 302–25, as

well as Elenore Cole Pritchard's doctoral dissertation "The *Völuspá*: A Commentary," University of Pennsylvania, 1972 (AAI 33.4, 1694-A).

5. Taken with a slight format adjustment from Anthony Faulkes' edition of Snorri Sturluson's *Edda: Prologue and Gylfaginning* (London: Oxford University Press, 1982/1988, reprinted Exeter: Short Run Press Limited, 2000).

6. Paul Schach, *Icelandic Sagas* (Boston: Twayne, 1984).

7. For Old Norse texts see Guðni Jónsson, editor, *Íslendinga sögur*, 2nd ed., 13 volumes (Akureyri: Íslendingasagnaútgáfan, 1953). Jónsson also did a four-volume edition of the *Fornaldar sögur* (Akureyri: Íslendingasagnaútgáfan, 1954). My translations here come from *The Complete Sagas of the Icelanders*, trans. Bernard Scudder, ed. Viðar Hreinsson (Reykjavik: Leifur Eiriksson Publishing, 1997). *Egil's Saga* appears in Volume 1, pages 33–177. The five-volume set is perhaps the best available source for English readers.

8. We might call Glámr, in a sense, a poor-man's Beowulf.

9. Dean A. Miller discusses this point in *The Epic Hero* (Baltimore: Johns Hopkins University Press, 2000), 144–45. He notes the close tie to another motif in which a hero visits a grave mound or similar feature to confront a dead/undead inhabitant. The firetrap motif appears widely, with slight variations, he notes, for instance in *Landnámabók, Hænsa-Þoris saga, Vatnsdæla saga, Hallfreða saga, Eyrbyggja saga, Guðmundar saga dyri*, and *Hrafns saga Sveinbjarnarssonar*. For additional theoretical background see Georges Dumézil, *The Destiny of the Warrior*, trans. Alf Hiltebeitel (Chicago: University of Chicago Press, 1970).

10. In an odd but telling case at the beginning of Volsungasaga, Sigi, the grandfather of Volsung, murders Breði, Skaði's servant, out of jealousy for the servant's having had a more successful hunt than Sigi has had. The murder doesn't diminish the heroic traits of his line, but it does perhaps linger among them, sometimes subverting their endeavors as thread of bad luck.

11. For an extremely helpful study of the range and relationships of Icelandic literary texts, editions, and critical bibliography, see especially *Old Norse-Icelandic Literature: A Critical Guide*, edited by Carol Clover and John Lindow, Islendica XLV (Ithaca: Cornell University Press, 1985). Two particularly useful English-language studies of sagas are Theodore M. Andersson's *The Icelandic Family Sagas: An Analytic Reading*, Harvard Studies in Comparative Literature 28 (Cambridge, MA: Harvard University Press, 1967), and Carol Clover's *The Medieval Saga* (Ithaca: Cornell University Press, 1982). For a thorough study of Ragnarök see John Stanley Martin, *Ragnarök: An Investigation into Old Norse Concepts of the Fate of the Gods*, Melbourne Monographs in Germanic Studies 3 (Assen: Van Gorcum, 1972). For student-friendly introductory guides to Norse myth, see E.O.G. Turville-Petre, *Myth and Religion of the North* (London: Weidenfeld and Nicolson, 1964), and Kevin Crossley-Holland, *Norse Mythology*. For a recent general introduction of particular use to students, see Heather O'Donoghue's *Old Norse Literature: A Short Introduction* (Oxford: Blackwell, 2004).

Chapter 6

1. Northrop Frye in *Anatomy of Criticism* suggests that romance as mode "is nearest of all literary forms to the wish-fulfillment dream" (186), and as a mixture of private/public experience it "has analogies to both rituals and dreams" (193), to "experiences that should be positive or 'happy.'" In the definition of "Medieval Romances" in

A Handbook to Literature, a handy place to start for such things, Harmon and Holman assert "the epic has weight and solidity, whereas the *romance* exhibits mystery and fantasy; the tragic seriousness of the epic is not matched in the lighter-hearted *romance*" (310). I'd like to call that understanding of Romance into question without entirely disagreeing. Ker wonders if "Romance be the name for the sort of imagination that possesses the mystery and the spell of everything remote and unattainable" (321); that notion of unattainability suggests the likelihood of problematic or even tragic endings, more akin to my argument here.

2. We always have the problem of how seriously the audience would have taken Romance endings. As Auerbach points out, in the High Middle Ages "the heroic epic *is* history ... however much it may distort and simplify" (122), but a "fairy-tale atmosphere is the true element of the courtly romance" (133). I respond to many of the romances as tragedies because they encompass elements by which Aristotle defined tragedy: a high-ranking hero who falls by his own error, committing some atrocious violence, recognizes (except perhaps in Perceval's case) the enormity of the error and must (along with the audience) experience cleansing for the subsequent suffering.

3. For the French text see Albert Pauphilet's 1949 edition; see P.M. Matarasso's *The Quest of the Holy Grail* for a translation. For Malory the easiest source is Eugene Vinaver's edition of Malory's *Works*.

4. See the excellent concluding chapter on the influence of magic on the upshot of Romances in Mickey Sweeney's *Magic in Medieval Romance*, pages 146–169.

5. For readers without easy access to Lachmann's 1926 edition of *Parzival*, see the 2003 De Gruyter volume based on the Lachmann with a modern German translation by Peter Knecht.

6. Ihle suggests reasonably that Malory's "guiding principle" is "the attempt to produce a coherent story from the diverse sources" (172), to make a super-version of a collection of sub-versions. Frye's suggestion (1965) that Malory's adventures follow a "series of graded knights, each knight being better than any other knight he can knock off his horse" (104), allows for a series of sub-versions culminating in the glory of the Grail. Wolfram periodically subverts Parzival's search, but the superversion that culminates the story lacks a sense of useful closure. For anyone but Galahad, the Grail quest always will.

7. Ihle observes that Malory's tale focuses more on Perceval's "obligations to others" rather than on the "peril to his own soul" (130): Perceval's is therefore already a sub-version of the Grail quest.

8. Taylor argues that "romance was the literature of feudalism," and "[f]eudalism was the practical basis of chivalry, and medieval romance is romance of chivalry," so "[w]hen feudalism died, the real spirit of chivalry died also, and medieval romance ... ceased to exist" (254). Galahad more than Perceval turns Romance subsequently to a construct most often either explicitly or metaphorically Christian, which subverts it to add an enormous dimension to its feudal foundations.

9. While scholars still debate Malory's life, see particularly P.J. Field's biography.

Chapter 7

1. William Langland, *Piers the Plowman*, trans. with introduction by J.F. Goodridge (Harmondsworth: Penguin, 1959), 21.
2. Langland, 23.
3. *Piers Plowman by William Lang-*

Notes—Chapter 7

land: An Edition of the C-text (Berkeley: University of California Press, 1978), 15.

4. For a useful collection of medieval documents on penance see John T. McNeill and Helena M. Gamer, *Medieval Handbooks of Penance: A Translation of the Principal Libri Poenitentiales* (New York: Columbia University Press, 1990). The introduction points out, "While the penitentials were primarily intended for the use of priests, it was sometimes found convenient to provide them in the vernacular ... to make their contents comprehensible to the people." The editors add, colorfully, that the "ideal [of penitential theory and practice] was founded in monastic asceticism; the reality in primitive brutality" (3).

5. 2nd ed., edited Berard L. Marthaler, et al. (Detroit: Thomson Gale, 2003), Volume 11, page 66.

6. *New Catholic Encyclopedia*, pages 69–70, 343, and 346. Readers interested in the textual history of early penance from the ancient Church to the beginning of the eighteenth century may want to consult *Medieval Handbooks of Penance: A Translation of the Principal libri poenitentiales and Selections from Related Documents*, by John T. McNeill and Helena M. Gamer (New York: Columbia University Press, 1990; first published 1938).

7. Morris Bishop, *The Middle Ages* (1968; Boston: Houghton Mifflin, 1987), 149.

8. R.J. Zwi Werblowsky, "Introduction" to *In Praise of the New Knighthood* in *Treatises III*, from the *Works of St. Bernard*, Volume Seven (Kalamazoo: Cistercian Publications, 1977), 116–17.

9. Joseph Martos, *Doors to the Sacred: A Historical Introduction to Sacraments in the Catholic Church*, expanded edition (Liguori, MO: Triumph Books, 1991; first published 1981), 291–92.

10. Martos, 292.
11. Martos, 296.
12. "General Prologue," lines 51, 62 and 66.
13. "GP," lines 463–67.
14. Martos, 298.
15. *The Book of Margery Kempe*, trans. B.A. Windeatt (London: Penguin, 1985), 96.
16. *The Book of Margery Kempe*, 108.
17. *New Catholic Encyclopedia*, Volume 11, page 348.
18. From the *Codex Boernerianus*, translated in James Carney's *Medieval Irish Lyrics* (Dublin: Dolman Press, 1985), 80–81.
19. Allen Mandelbaum, trans., *The Divine Comedy of Dante: Inferno* (New York: Bantam, 1982), 263. The Italian text is on the facing page, 262.
20. Medievals, Martos explains, thought of God as a "king who issued commands for the welfare of his subjects, [and] sin was a violation of God's law that demanded punishment" (287). As the practice of sacerdotal assignment of penitential activity expanded, penalties "were not the same everywhere but generally speaking they tried to make the punishment fit the crime, at least in intensity if not in kind" (286). Later, fasting, abstinence, recitation of psalms, almsgiving, and pilgrimage replaced corporal punishments, the outward act a sign of inward contrition (288–91).
21. For the text see *A Revelation of Purgatory by an Unknown, Fifteenth-Century Woman Visionary: Introduction, Critical Text, and Translation*, ed. Marta Powell Harley (Lewiston, NY: Edwin Mellen, 1985).
22. *A Revelation*, 60.
23. As the *New Dictionary of Theology* somewhat backwardly notes, "While there is no scriptural evidence that contradicts the doctrine, the scriptural basis for the doctrine remains unclear" (edited Joseph Komonchak, Mary Col-

lins, and Dermot Lane [Wilmington, DE: Michael Glazier, 1987]). Purgatory as part of the Christian cosmos has gone in and out of fashion. For a complete study of its history, sources, linguistic background, and implications see Jacques Le Goff, *The Birth of Purgatory*, trans. Arthur Goldhammer (Chicago: University of Chicago Press, 1984). Of the ultimate reason for the imaginative creation of purgatory, Le Goff asks, "Wasn't the point of introducing a temporary Purgatory mainly to throw the inextinguishable fires of Hell into sharp relief?" (359). Purgatory thus models what we may suffer briefly but most hope to avoid perpetually.

24. *A Revelation*, 66.
25. *A Revelation*, 66.
26. *A Revelation*, 68.
27. *A Revelation*, 78. The reader may note similarities to Chaucer's Prioress.
28. The narrator apparently suffers from the same anti–Semitic or simply xenophobic prejudices as Chaucer's Prioress.
29. See Richard K. Emmerson and Ronald B. Herzman, eds., *The Apocalyptic Imagination in Medieval Literature* (Philadelphia: University of Pennsylvania Press, 1992), 153–54; and D.W. Robertson, Jr., *Preface to Chaucer: Studies in Medieval Perspectives* (Princeton: Princeton University Press, 1962), 373.

Chapter 8

1. See D. Thomas Hanks, "Malory's *Book of Sir Tristram*: Focusing *Le Morte D'Arthur*," *Quondam et Futurus* 3.1 (1993): 14–31.
2. For interesting discussions of Thomas Malory's identity, see William Matthews' *The Ill-Framed Knight* and P.J. Field's convincing *The Life and Times of Sir Thomas Malory*. For an especially useful study of the biographical and historical context as well as a consideration of how Malory may have identified with Lancelot, see Christina Hardyment's *Malory: The Knight who Became King Arthur's Chronicler* (2006).

Chapter 9

1. This chapter draws partly on my approach to *Troilus and Cressida* in *Shakespeare and the Problem Play: Complex Form, Crossed Genres, and Moral Quandaries* (Jefferson, NC: McFarland, 2012), but it highlights the playwright's use of subversion rather than his penchant for creating problem plays.
2. The 1609 Quarto labeled the play a "Historie"; the First Folio calls it "Tragedie"; *The Riverside Shakespeare* places it among the comedies; it uses the subject matter of medieval and Renaissance Romance. The confusion draws us to the idea of intentional subversion of genre.
3. See also Lee W. Patterson, "Christian and Pagan in *The Testament of Cressid*, *Philological Quarterly* 52 (1973): 696–714.
4. Haydock suggests that we may see *Troilus and Cressida* helpfully as a "parodic and satiric reaction to the composite genre that had come to embody the highest aspirations of Renaissance poetics, the romance epic" (249); in some ways it responds more, I think, to Spenser's *Faerie Queene* than to Chaucer or Henryson. Spenser shows both good and bad knights, but focuses on the good finding virtue; Shakespeare undermines that virtue as a realistic constituent of the behavior of ancient heroes.
5. D.W. Robertson considered the poem another instance, in greater magnitude, of Chaucer's *de casibus* tragedy, informed by Boethius ("Chaucerian Tragedy," Chaucer Criticism, Vol. 2, ed. Richard J. Schoeck and Jerome Taylor [Notre Dame: University of Notre Dame Press, 1961], 86–121; reprinted from

English Literary History 19 [1952]: 1–37). I see it more as Romance Epic, a grand tale of subverted love amidst war, lacking any character sufficient to experience the kind of fall and recognition necessary for tragedy.

6. Lee W. Patterson, "*The Testament of Cresseid*: Introduction," *The Poems of Robert Henryson*, ed. Robert Kindrick (Kalamazoo: Medieval Institute Publications, 1997).

7. I find an interesting pun here, as the word suggests both "pity" and "piety."

8. "Introduction," *Testament of Cresseid*, ed. Denton Fox (London: Thomas Nelson, 1968), 23. Fox observes later, considering the leprous Cressid, that Henryson has "skillfully introduced a walking corpse onto the stage" (45); the dramatic allusion may have influenced Shakespeare's treatment, subverting all the characters as *memento mori*: exemplars of exclusively worldly appetite and so already spiritually dead.

9. Heather James, *Shakespeare's Troy: Drama, Politics, and the Translation of Empire* (Cambridge: Cambridge University Press, 1997), 95 and 92.

10. *Parlement of Foulys*, lines 90–91.

11. The same pun occurs also in 1.2.190, where Pandarus describes Antenor as a good man of "shrowd wit." Having captured him, the Greeks will exchange Antenor for Cressida at Calchas request, and the exchange will fully subvert Troilus and Cressida's romance.

Postscript

1 T.R. Steiner, *English Translation Theory 1650–1800* (Assen: Van Gorcum, 1975), 7.

2. Quoted in Barnstone, *The Poetics of Translation: History, Theory, Practice* (New Haven: Yale University Press, 1993), 28.

3. Marilynn Desmond, *Reading Dido: Gender, Textuality, and the Medieval Aeneid* (Minneapolis: University of Minnesota Press, 1994).

4 Mary Jane Scott, "James Thomson and Gavin Douglas: Some Continuities in Scottish Augustan Verse." I could locate this article only online at www2.unca.edu/postscript/postscript/ps.1.15.pdf; the pages are numbered 106–14.

5. Gordon M. Kendal, *Translation as Creative Retelling: Constituents, Patterning and Shift in Gavin Douglas' Eneados*, PhD thesis, University of St. Andrews, 2008.

6. Lois Ebin, "The Role of the Narrator in the Prologues to Gavin Douglas's *Eneados*," *Chaucer Review* 14.4 (1980): 353–65.

7. Full text of the *Eneados* appears in Gordon Kendal's edition of 2011, or the reader can find online the Bannatyne Club edition of 1839 in two volumes.

8. He concludes the Prologue to Book 2 with a nod to *contempus mundi*, to remind us that whether our arts succeed or fail, mortality gets us, work and all, at last.

Bibliography

Albus, Anita. *The Art of Arts: Rediscovering Painting.* Trans. Michael Robertson. Berkeley: University of California Press, 2000.

Andersson, Theodore M. *The Icelandic Family Sagas: An Analytic Reading.* Harvard Studies in Comparative Literature 28. Cambridge, MA: Harvard University Press, 1967.

Auerbach, Erich. *Mimesis: The Representation of Reality in Western Literature.* Trans. Willard R. Trask. Princeton: Princeton University Press, 1953.

Bakhtin, M.M. *The Dialogic Imagination: Four Essays.* Ed. Michael Holquist. Trans. Caryl Emerson and Michael Holquist. Austin: University of Texas Press, 1981.

Bal, Mieke. *Narratology: Introduction to the Theory of Narrative.* 2nd ed. Toronto: University of Toronto Press, 1997.

Barnstone, Willis. *The Poetics of Translation: History, Theory, Practice.* New Haven: Yale University Press, 1993.

Barth, John. "Lost in the Funhouse." *Lost in the Funhouse.* 1967. Toronto: Bantam, 1969. 69–94.

Barthes, Roland. *Image—Music—Text.* Trans. Stephen Heath. New York: Hill and Wang, 1977.

———. *The Pleasure of the Text.* Trans. Richard Miller. New York: Noonday Press, 1975.

———. *S/Z: An Essay.* Trans. Richard Miller. New York: Farrar, Straus and Giroux, 1974.

Barton, Anne. Introduction to *Troilus and Cressida. The Riverside Shakespeare.* Ed. G. Blakemore Evans, et al. Boston: Houghton Mifflin, 1974. 443–47.

Benson, C. David. *The Canterbury Tales: Personal Drama or Experiments in Poetic Variety? The Cambridge Companion to Chaucer.* 2nd ed. Ed. Piero Boitani and Jill Mann. Cambridge: Cambridge University Press, 2003. 127–42.

Beowulf: With the Finnesburg Fragment. Ed. C.L. Wrenn and W.F. Bolton. London: Harrap, 1973.

Beowulf and the Fight at Finnsburg. Ed. Frederick Klaeber. 3rd ed. Boston: D.C. Heath, 1950.

Bevington, David. *Shakespeare's Ideas: More Things in Heaven and Earth.* Maldon, MA: Wiley-Blackwell, 2008.

Bishop, Morris. *The Middle Ages.* 1968. Boston: Houghton Mifflin, 1987.

Bonjour, Adrien. *The Digressions in Beowulf.* Oxford: Blackwell, 1950.

The Book of Margery Kempe. Trans. B.A. Windeatt. London: Penguin, 1985.

Carney, James, trans. *Medieval Irish Lyrics.* Dublin: Dolman Press, 1985.

Chaucer, Geoffrey. *The Complete Poetry and Prose of Geoffrey Chaucer.* Ed. John H. Fisher. New York: Holt, Rinehart, and Winston, 1977.

Clover, Carol. *The Medieval Saga.* Ithaca: Cornell University Press, 1982.

The Complete Sagas of the Icelanders.

Bibliography

Ed. Viðar Hreinsson. Trans. Bernard Scudder. Reykjavik: Leifur Eiriksson Publishing, 1997.

Cooper, Helen. *The Structure of the Canterbury Tales*. Athens: University of Georgia Press, 1984.

Crossley-Holland, Kevin. *The Norse Myths*. New York: Pantheon, 1981.

Culler, Jonathan. *On Deconstruction: Theory and Criticism after Structuralism*. Ithaca: Cornell University Press, 1982.

_____. *Structuralist Poetics: Structuralism, Linguistics, and the Study of Literature*. Ithaca: Cornell University Press, 1975.

Deimling, Barbara. "Early Renaissance Art in Florence and Italy." *The Art of the Italian Renaissance: Architecture, Sculpture, Painting, Drawing*. Ed. Rolf Toman. Köln: Könnemann, 1995. 238–307.

Deleuze, Gilles. *The Fold: Leibnitz and the Baroque*. Trans. Tom Conley. Minneapolis: University of Minnesota Press, 1993.

Derrida, Jacques. "The Law of Genre." Trans. Avital Ronell. *Glyph* 7 (1980): 202–32.

Desmond, Marilynn. *Reading Dido: Gender, Textuality, and the Medieval Aeneid*. Minneapolis: University of Minnesota Press, 1994.

Douglas, Gavin. *Gavin Douglas's Translation of the Aeneid* (1513). Ed. Gordon Kendal. London: MHRA, 2011.

Dronke, Ursula. "*Beowulf* and Ragnarök." *Saga-Book of the Viking Society* 17 (1969): 302–25.

_____. *The Poetic Edda*. 1: *Heroic Poems*. Oxford: Clarendon, 1969.

_____. "*Völuspá* and the Satiric Tradition." *Annali dell-Istituto Universitario Orientale, Napoli, Sezione Germanica* 22 (1979): 57–86.

Dumézil, Georges. *The Destiny of the Warrior*. Trans. Alf Hiltebeitel. Chicago: University of Chicago Press, 1970.

Ebin, Lois. "The Role of the Narrator in the Prologues to Gavin Douglas's *Eneados*." *Chaucer Review* 14.4 (1980): 353–65.

Eco, Umberto. *Art and Beauty in the Middle Ages*. New Haven: Yale University Press, 1986.

_____. *The Name of the Rose*. Trans. William Weaver. New York: Harcourt Brace, 1983.

_____. *The Role of the Reader: Explorations in the Semiotics of Texts*. Bloomington: Indiana University Press, 1979.

Ellis, Roger. *Patterns of Religious Narrative in the Canterbury Tales*. Totowa, NJ: Barnes & Noble Books, 1986.

Emmerson, Richard K., and Ronald B. Herzman, eds. *The Apocalyptic Imagination in Medieval Literature*. Philadelphia: University of Pennsylvania Press, 1992.

Faulkes, Anthony, ed. *Snorri Sturluson's Edda: Prologue and Gylfaginning*. London: Oxford University Press, 1982/1988; reprinted Exeter: Short Run Press Limited, 2000.

Field, P.J. *The Life and Times of Sir Thomas Malory*. Arthurian Studies Vol. 29. London: D.S. Brewer, 1993.

Frese, Dolores. "*Wulf and Eadwacer*: The Adulterous Woman Reconsidered." *Notre Dame English Journal* 15.1 (1983): 1–22.

Friedman, Susan Stanford. "Spatialization: A Strategy for Reading Narrative." *Narrative* 1 (1993).

Frye, Northrop. *Anatomy of Criticism: Four Essays*. Princeton: Princeton University Press, 1957.

_____. *The Return of Eden: Five Essays on Milton's Epic*. Toronto: University of Toronto Press, 1965.

Genette, Gérard. *Narrative Discourse: An Essay in Method*. Trans. Jane E.

Bibliography

Lewin. Ithaca: Cornell University Press, 1980.

Goddard, Harold. *The Meaning of Shakespeare*. Vol. 2. Chicago: University of Chicago Press, 1951.

Goldberg, Jonathan. *Endlesse Work: Spenser and the Structures of Discourse*. Baltimore: Johns Hopkins University Press, 1981.

Goodrich, Peter. "Ritual Sacrifice and the Pre-Christian Subtext of Gawain's Green Girdle." *Sir Gawain and the Classical Tradition*. Ed. E.L. Risden. Jefferson, NC: McFarland, 2006. 65–81.

Greenblatt, Stephen. *Renaissance Self-Fashioning: From More to Shakespeare*. Chicago: University of Chicago Press, 1980.

Gurevich, A.J. *Categories in Medieval Culture*. Trans. G.L. Campbell. London: Routledge & Kegan Paul, 1985.

Halldórsson, Óskar. "Snorri og Edda." *Snorri: Átta alda minning*. Reykjavík: Sögufélag, 1979. 89–111.

Hanks, D. Thomas, Jr. "Malory's *Book of Sir Tristram*: Focusing *Le Morte D'Arthur*." *Quondam et Fururus* 3.1 (1993): 14–31.

Hardyment, Christina. *Malory: The Knight Who Became King Arthur's Chronicler*. New York: Harper, 2006.

Harmon, William, and C. Hugh Holman, eds. *A Handbook to Literature*. 8th edition. Upper Saddle River, NJ: Prentice Hall, 2000.

Haydock, Nickolas A. *Situational Poetics in Robert Henryson's The Testament of Cresseid*. Amherst, NY: Cambria Press, 2010.

Henryson, Robert. *The Poems of Robert Henryson*. Ed. Robert Kindrick. Kalamazoo: Medieval Institute Publications, 1997.

Hill, John. *The Narrative Pulse of Beowulf: Arrivals and Departures*. Toronto: University of Toronto Press, 2008.

Hollander, Lee M. *The Poetic Edda*. 2nd ed. Austin: University of Texas Press, 1962.

Holtsmark, Anne. *Studier i Snorres Mytologi*. Oslo: Universitetsforlaget, 1964.

Hoover, David L. *A New Theory of Old English Meter*. New York: Peter Lang, 1985.

Horton, Ronald Arthur. *The Unity of the Faerie Queene*. Athens: University of Georgia Press, 1978.

Howard, Donald R. *The Idea of the Canterbury Tales*. Berkeley: University of California Press, 1976.

Ihle, Sandra Ness. *Malory's Grail Quest: Invention and Adaptation in Medieval Prose Romance*. Madison: University of Wisconsin Press, 1983.

James, Heather. *Shakespeare's Troy: Drama, Politics, and the Translation of Empire*. Cambridge: Cambridge University Press, 1997.

Jónsson, Guðni, ed. *Fornaldar sögur*. 4 vols. Akureyri: Íslendingasagnaútgáfan, 1954.

_____, ed. *Íslendinga sögur*. 2nd ed. 13 volumes. Akureyri: Íslendingasagnaútgáfan, 1953.

Kendal, Gordon M. *Translation as Creative Retelling: Constituents, Patterning and Shift in Gavin Douglas' Eneados*. PhD thesis, University of St. Andrews, 2008.

Ker, W.P. *Epic and Romance: Essays on Medieval Literature*. 1896. New York: Dover, 1957.

Kermode, Frank. *The Genesis of Secrecy: On the Interpretation of Narrative*. Cambridge: Harvard University Press, 1979.

_____. *The Sense of an Ending: Studies in the Theory of Fiction*. New York: Oxford University Press, 1966.

Kittredge, George Lyman. "Chaucer's Discussion of Marriage." *Modern Philology* IX (1911–12): 435–67.

Knight, G. Wilson. *The Wheel of Fire:*

Bibliography

Interpretation of Shakespeare's Tragedy. Cleveland: Meridian, 1957.

Krapp, George Philip, and Elliott van Kirk Dobbie. *The Anglo-Saxon Poetic Records.* 6 vols. New York: Columbia University Press, 1931–53.

Kuhn, Hans. "Das Nordgermanische Heidentum in den ersten Christlichen Jarhhunderten." *Zeitschrift für deutsches Altertum* 79 (1942): 133–66.

———. *Edda: Die Lieder des Codex Regius Nebst Verwandten Denkmälern.* Heidelberg: Carl Winter Univeritätsverlag, 1983.

Langland, William. *Piers the Plowman.* Trans. with introduction by J.F. Goodridge. Harmondsworth: Penguin, 1959.

Lawrence, William Witherle. *Shakespeare's Problem Comedies.* New York: Macmillan, 1931.

Le Goff, Jacques. *The Birth of Purgatory.* Trans. Arthur Goldhammer. Chicago: University of Chicago Press, 1984.

Leyerle, John. "The Interlace Structure of Beowulf." *University of Toronto Quarterly* 37 (1967): 1–17.

Malory, Thomas. *Works.* Ed. Eugène Vinaver. Oxford: Oxford University Press, 1971.

Mandelbaum, Allen, trans. *The Divine Comedy of Dante: Inferno.* New York: Bantam, 1982.

Martin, John Stanley. *Ragnarök: An Investigation into Old Norse Concepts of the Fate of the Gods.* Melbourne Monographs in Germanic Studies 3. Assen: Van Gorcum, 1972.

Martos, Joseph. *Doors to the Sacred: A Historical Introduction to Sacraments in the Catholic Church* (1981). Expanded edition. Liguori, MO: Triumph Books, 1991.

Matarasso, P.M., trans. *The Quest of the Holy Grail.* Baltimore: Penguin, 1969.

Matthews, William. *The Ill-Framed Knight: A Skeptical Inquiry into the Identity of Sir Thomas Malory.* Berkeley: University of California Press, 1966.

Mazzota, Giuseppe. *Cosmopoiesis: The Renaissance Experiment.* Toronto: University of Toronto Press, 2001.

McNeill, John T., and Helena M. Gamer. *Medieval Handbooks of Penance: A Translation of the Principal Libri Poenitentiales.* (1938). New York: Columbia University Press, 1990.

Miller, Dean A. *The Epic Hero.* Baltimore: Johns Hopkins University Press, 2000.

Miller, J. Hillis. "Line." In Onega and Landa. 286–295. Reprinted from *Ariadne's Thread: Story Lines.* New Haven: Yale University Press, 1992.

———. *Reading Narrative.* Norman: University of Oklahoma Press, 1998.

Murray, Stephen. "Narrative the Gothic: The Cathedral Plot." *Gothic Art and Thought in the Later Medieval Period: Essays in Honor of Willibald Sauerländer.* Ed. Colum Hourihane. Princeton: Princeton University Press, and University Park: Pennsylvania State University Press, 2011. 55–63.

Mustard, Helen M., and Charles E. Passage. "Introduction." *Parzival*, by Wolfram von Eschenbach. New York: Vintage, 1961. vii–lv.

New Catholic Encyclopedia. 2nd ed. Eds. Bernard L. Marthaler, et al. Detroit: Thomson Gale, 2003, Volume 11.

New Dictionary of Theology. Ed. Joseph Komonchak, Mary Collins, and Dermot Lane. Wilmington, DE: Michael Glazier, 1987.

Nist, J. "The Structure of *Beowulf.*" *PMASAL* 43 (1958): 307–14.

Nordal, Sigurður. *Snorri Sturluson.* Reykjavík: [n.p.], 1920.

_____. "Three Essays on *Völuspá*, trans. B.S. Benedikz and J.S. McKinnell." *Saga-Book of the Viking Society* 18 [1971]: 79–135.

O'Donoghue, Heather. *Old Norse Literature: A Short Introduction*. Oxford: Blackwell, 2004.

Old Norse-Icelandic Literature: A Critical Guide. Ed. Carol Clover and John Lindow. Islendica XLV. Ithaca: Cornell University Press, 1985.

Onega, Susanna, and José Angel Garcia Landa. *Narratology: An Introduction*. London: Longman, 1996.

Orton, Peter. "An Approach to *Wulf and Eadwacer*." *Proceedings of the Royal Irish Academy* 85C (1985): 223–58.

Paasche, Frederik. *Snorre Sturlason og Sturlungerne*. Oslo: H. Aschehoug, 1922.

Pater, Walter. *The Renaissance: Studies in Art and Poetry*. London: Macmillan, 1873.

Patterson, Lee W. "Christian and Pagan in *The Testament of Cressid*." *Philological Quarterly* 52 (1973): 696–714.

Pauphilet, Albert, ed. *La Queste del Saint Graal*. Paris: Champion, 1949.

Pearsall, Derek. *The Canterbury Tales*. London: George Allen & Unwin, 1985.

Piers Plowman by William Langland: An Edition of the C-text. Ed. Derek Pearsall. Berkeley: University of California Press, 1978.

Pritchard, Elenore Cole. "The *Völuspá*: A Commentary." PhD dissertation, University of Pennsylvania, 1972 (AAI 33.4, 1694-A).

A Revelation of Purgatory by an Unknown, Fifteenth-Century Woman Visionary: Introduction, Critical Text, and Translation. Ed. Marta Powell Harley. Lewiston, NY: Edwin Mellen, 1985.

Ricoeur, Paul. "Narrative Hermeneutics." *Essays on Aesthetics: Perspectives on the Word of Monroe C. Beardsley*. Ed. John Fisher. Philadelphia: Temple University Press, 1983. 149–60.

Risden, E.L. *Shakespeare and the Problem Play: Complex Forms, Crossed Genres, and Moral Quandaries*. Jefferson, NC: McFarland, 2012.

_____. "The World's Greatest Knight: Malory, Theme and Form." *Publications of the Medieval Association of the Midwest* 7 (2000): 126–38.

Robertson, D.W., Jr. *Preface to Chaucer: Studies in Medieval Perspectives*. Princeton: Princeton University Press, 1962.

Ruggiers, Paul G. *The Art of the Canterbury Tales*. Madison: University of Wisconsin Press, 1965.

Russell, Frank D. *Picasso's Guernica: The Labyrinth of Narrative and Vision*. Montclair, NJ: Allanheld & Schram, 1980.

Schach, Paul. *Icelandic Sagas*. Boston: Twayne, 1984.

_____. "Some Thoughts on Völuspá." *Edda: A Collection of Essays*. Ed. R.J. Glendinning and Haraldur Bessason. University of Manitoba Icelandic Studies 4. Winnipeg: University of Manitoba Press, 1983. 86–116.

Scholes, Robert, James Phelan, and Robert Kellogg. *The Nature of Narrative*. 1966. 40th Anniversary Edition. New York: Oxford University Press, 2006.

Scott, Mary Jane. "James Thomson and Gavin Douglas: Some Continuities in Scottish Augustan Verse." www2.unca.edu/postscript/postscript/ps.1.15.pdf. 106–14.

Shakespeare, William. *The Riverside Shakespeare*. Ed. G. Blakemore Evans et al. Boston: Houghton Mifflin, 1974.

Sir Gawain and the Green Knight. Ed.

Bibliography

J.R.R. Tolkien and E.V. Gordon, rev. Norman Davis. Oxford: Oxford University Press, 1968.

Sir Perceval of Galles. Ed. Mary Flowers Braswell. Kalamazoo: Medieval Institute Publications, 1995. www.lib.rochester.edu/camelot/teams/perc.htm.

Steiner, T.R. *English Translation Theory 1650–1800*. Assen: Van Gorcum, 1975.

Sweeney, Michelle. *Magic in Medieval Romance from Chrétien de Troyes to Geoffrey Chaucer*. Dublin: Four Courts, 2000.

Taylor, A.B. *An Introduction to Medieval Romance*. 1930. Bungay, Suffolk: Folcroft Library Editions, 1971.

Tolkien, J.R.R. "*Beowulf*: The Monsters and the Critics." *An Anthology of Beowulf Criticism*. Ed. Lewis E. Nicholson. Notre Dame: University of Notre Dame Press, 1963. 51–103.

Turner, Victor. *The Ritual Process: Structure and Anti-Structure*. Chicago: University of Chicago Press, 1969.

Turville-Petre, E.O.G. *Myth and Religion of the North*. London: Weidenfeld and Nicolson, 1964.

Vinaver, Eugène, ed. *The Works of Thomas Malory*. 2nd ed. Oxford: Oxford University Press, 1968.

Völuspá. Trans. B.S. Benedikz and John McKinnell. Durham and St. Andrews Medieval Texts 1. Durham: Dept. of English Language and Medieval Literature, 1978.

Weales, Gerald. "Afterword: Tristram Shandy's Anti-Book." 1960. Lawrence Sterne. *The Life and Opinions of Tristram Shandy, Gentleman*. 1762, 1765. New York: NAL, 1980. 527–44.

Werblowsky, R.J. Zwi. "Introduction" to *In Praise of the New Knighthood* in *Treatises III*, from the *Works of St. Bernard*. Volume Seven. Kalamazoo: Cistercian Publications, 1977.

Windeatt, Barry. *Literary Structures in Chaucer*. *The Cambridge Companion to Chaucer*. Ed. Piero Boitani and Jill Mann. Cambridge: Cambridge University Press, 2003. 214–32.

Wolfram von Eschenbach. *Parzival*. With modern German trans. by Peter Knecht. Berlin: De Gruyter, 2003.

Wright, Louis B., and Virginia A. LaMar. *The Folger Guide to Shakespeare*. New York: Pocket Books, 1969.

Young, Jean I., trans. *The Prose Edda of Snorri Sturluson: Tales from Norse Mythology*. Berkeley: University of California Press, 1965.

Zeldin, Theodore. *An Intimate History of Humanity*. New York: HarperCollins, 1994.

Index

absolution 104–106
Aeneas 131, 148, 158–161, 163–164
Aeneid 158, 160, 163, 174, 176
Albus, Anita 20, 175
allegory 4–5, 8–9, 12, 16, 18, 33, 35, 62, 70–71, 74, 157
Aristotle 17, 40, 56, 171
Arthur, King 6, 30, 32, 47, 88–90, 94–100, 113–115, 117–122, 169, 173, 177
Auerbach, Erich 171, 175
Auden, W.H. 21

Bailly, Harry 11
Bakhtin, M.M. 168, 175
Bal, Mieke 2, 17, 167, 175
Bardar Saga 83
Barnstone, Willis 159, 174, 175
Baroque 2, 5, 7, 31, 49
Barth, John 19, 26, 37, 175
Barthes, Roland 8–9, 168, 175
Barton, Anne 9, 175
Benoît de Sainte-Maure 128, 138
Benson, C. David 10, 175
Benson, Larry 119, 121
Beowulf 18, 26–29, 31, 36, 49–57, 59–61, 73, 81, 159, 164, 169–170, 175–176, 178, 180
Bevington, David 125–126, 175
Bishop, Morris 105, 172, 175
Boccaccio, Giovanni 10, 128–129, 138, 140–141, 146
Bonjour, Adrien 52, 175
Bremond, Claude 9
Brennu-Njáls Saga 84
Breughel, Pieter 21

Campbell, Joseph 24
The Canterbury Tales 10, 111–112, 140, 167, 175–177, 179

Casablanca 40
Chaucer, Geoffrey 10–12, 31–32, 88, 105, 111–112, 125, 127–130, 134–135, 137–143, 145–148, 151, 158, 164–165, 173–177, 179–180
Chrétien de Troyes 89–90, 95, 180
Christ (Jesus) 20–22, 29–35
Christ-types 69–71 152–153
Clover, Carol 171, 175, 179
Coleridge, Samuel Taylor 26, 102
Commedia 107–108, 144
contemptus mundi 102, 121
contrapasso 107
Cooper, Helen 10, 176
cosmopoiesis 52, 178
courtly love 138, 146
Culler, Jonathan 9, 168, 176

Dalí, Salvador 23
Dante Alighieri 34, 104, 107–108, 112, 144, 168, 172, 178
Deleuze, Gilles 2, 176
"Deor" 62, 67–70, 73
Derrida, Jacques 3, 13, 124, 167, 176
"Descent into Hell" 30–31
Desmond, Marilynn 160, 174, 176
digression 7, 25, 27–29, 49–52, 54, 59, 175
Doctor Faustus 25
Don Quixote 37
Douglas, Gavin 157–165, 174, 176, 179
Dryden, John 127, 157–159
dryht 62–63, 65–67, 69, 72, 74
Duchamp, Marcel 20
Dumézil, Georges 170, 176
Duns Scotus 105

Ebin, Lois 160, 174, 176
Eco, Umberto 2, 32, 49–50, 61, 167, 176

183

Index

Egils Saga 82
Eliot, T.S. 74
Ellis, Roger 10, 176
Eneados 157–160, 162–164, 174, 176–177
Exeter Book 66, 69
exile 26, 62–66, 69–74, 165
fable 18, 27, 33, 49, 53, 60, 74, 158
fabula 5, 15, 17, 43, 167
The Faerie Queene 5, 7, 9–10, 130, 173, 177
Faust 22–23, 25, 26
"The Fortunes of Men" 62, 66–67
Fox, Denton 142, 174
Frese, Dolores 73, 176
Friedman, Susan Stanford 169, 176
Frye, Northrop 114, 171, 176

Galahad 29–30, 36, 89–90, 93–94, 97–102, 115–122, 172
Genette, Gérard 167–168, 176
Goddard, Harold 135, 177
Goethe, Johann Wolfgang von 23, 25–26
Goldberg, Jonathan 7, 177
Goodrich, Peter 169, 177
Goodridge, J.F. 103, 172, 178
Gosforth Cross 21–22
Great Chain of Being 26
Greenblatt, Stephen 169, 177
Grettis Saga 83
Guernica 19, 179
Gurevich, A.J. 167, 177
"Gylfaginning" 77, 170, 176

hamartia 40
Hamlet 26, 42–44, 47, 133, 168–169
Haydock, Nickolas 129, 134, 158, 173, 177
Henryson, Robert 124, 127–130, 132, 134–135, 137, 140–142, 145–147, 151, 158, 173–174, 177
Hill, John 53–54, 177
Hitchcock, Alfred 23
Holy Grail 18, 29, 88–101, 116, 118, 120–121, 171, 178
Homer 157, 161
Hoover, David 56, 177
Horace 39, 127

Horton, Ronald Arthur 9, 177
Howard, Donald 167, 177
hubris 40–41, 47
"The Husband's Lament" 62

Ihle, Sandra 171–172, 177
irony 2, 21, 41, 131, 139

James, Heather 142, 174, 177

Kelly, Gene 23
Kempe, Margery 108, 172, 175
Kendall, Gordon 160, 174, 176–177
Ker, W.P. 171, 177
Kermode, Frank 8, 177
King Lear 26, 148
Kittredge, George Lyman 10, 177
Knight, G. Wilson 125
koan 15, 17
kolbítr 51

Lancelot 29–30, 93, 95, 97–102, 115–122, 173
Landa, José 2, 17, 178–179
Langland, William 34, 103–104, 172, 178–179
Lawrence, W.W. 125, 178
Le Goff, Jacques 173, 178
Levi-Strauss, Claude 9
El Libro de Buen Amor 37
Liszt, Franz 22

Malory, Thomas 29, 89–98, 101–102, 1130117, 119–123, 171–173, 176–180
Mandelbaum, Allen 107, 172, 178
Mandeville, John 106
Marlowe, Christopher 23, 25–26
marriage group 10
Martos, Joseph 172, 178
Matthews, William 173, 178
Mazzota, Giuseppe 52–53, 178
medievalism 5, 124
miasma 40, 47
Miller, Dean 170, 178
Miller, J. Hillis 2, 18, 178
More, Thomas 106, 177
Morrison, Toni 25
Le Morte D'Arthur 29, 88–89, 91–92, 94, 98, 101, 113–123

Index

Mrs. Dalloway 25
Murray, Stephen 60, 178
mystery 2, 17, 32, 167, 171
mythopoiesis 52, 76

The Name of the Rose 2, 167, 176
narratology 1, 17, 43, 175, 179
narreme 9, 18, 20
nostalgia 54, 59, 65–66

objective correlative 74
Oðin 22, 77–79
Oedipus 40–44, 47
Onega, Susan 2, 17, 178–179
Orton, Peter 73, 179

Parzival 90–92, 96, 171, 178, 180
Pater, Walter 53–54, 179
Pearsall, Derek 11, 103, 179
Penance 34, 94, 101–109, 111, 165, 172, 178
picaresque 37
Picasso, Pablo 19, 179
Piero della Francesca 21
Piers Plowman 13, 18, 33–34, 36, 103, 172, 179
The Princess Bride 87
prophecy 42
Propp, Vladimir 9
Prose Lancelot 29, 89
purgatory 42, 104, 106–112, 144, 173, 179

The Quest of the Holy Grail 18, 29, 171, 178
Queste del Saint Graal 89, 98, 179

Ragnarök 22, 77–79, 81, 170–171, 178
Raskin, Victor 12
Reader Response 8
A Revelation of Purgatory 109, 111–112, 173, 179
Ricoeur, Paul 38, 52, 179
Riemann sum 20
Rococo 7
romance 2, 5, 7–8, 12, 30, 37, 44, 88–102, 124, 126, 129, 132, 134–136, 138–140, 143, 145, 147, 171–172, 174, 177, 180

Romeo and Juliet 74
Ruggiers, Paul 167, 179
Ruiz, Juan 37
Russell, Frank 19, 179

Schach, Paul 81, 170, 179
Schlegel, Friedrich 2
Scholes, Robert 4, 167, 179
Scott, Mary Jane 160, 174, 179
"The Seafarer" 62, 64–67, 70
Shakespeare, William 16, 26, 37, 114, 123–131, 134–138, 140–149, 151–152, 154–155, 173–175, 177–179
simony 34
Sir Gawain and the Green Knight 18, 30, 36, 44, 88, 98, 157, 179
Sir Orfeo 2
Sir Perceval of Galles 89, 91, 93–94, 96, 180
sjuzhet 5, 167
Sliding Doors 24
Snorra Edda 81
Snorri Sturluson 77–80, 170, 176–178, 180
Spenser, Edmund 5, 7–9, 130, 173, 177
Star Wars 24
Statius 108
Steiner, T.R. 159, 174, 180
Sterne, Lawrence 1, 25, 35, 180
stream of consciousness 25

Tolkien, J.R.R. 51–54, 57, 61, 180
trawþe 30, 31, 46, 137
Tristram, Sir 101, 114–116, 120–122, 173, 177
Tristram Shandy 1, 25, 180
Troilus and Cressida 124–155, 173–175
Troilus and Crisseyde 88
Turner, Victor 169, 180

ubi sunt 57, 59, 64

van Eyck, Jan 20
Vegio, Maffeo 160
Vergil 107–108, 157–165
Veselovsky, R.N. 9
Viðar 22, 79

185

Index

Vinaver, Eugène 113–114, 171, 178, 180
Völuspá 76–81, 170, 176, 179–180

"The Wanderer" 62, 64–67, 70
Weales, Gerald 25, 180
Werblowsky, R.J. 105, 172, 180
"Widsið" 62, 71–72
"The Wife's Message" 62
Windeatt, Barry 10, 172, 175, 180
Wolfram von Eschenbach 89, 90–92, 95, 98, 171, 178, 180

Woolf, Virginia 25
"Wulf and Eadwacer" 62, 72, 176, 179
Wulfstan 50

xenia 41

Young, Jean 170, 180

Zeldin, Theodore 168, 180
Zen 15

www.ingramcontent.com/pod-product-compliance
Ingram Content Group UK Ltd.
Pitfield, Milton Keynes, MK11 3LW, UK
UKHW042013140426
5217IPUK00015B/1152